THE MARK OF THE
BEAST;
COMING SOON
TO A
CHURCH
NEAR YOU

How your pastor,
like the serpent in Eden,
will entice you to get
what God forbids

MARTIN MIRANDA

www.trafford.com
North America & international
toll-free: 1 888 232 4444 (USA & Canada)
fax: 812 355 4082

CONTENTS

"Those who guide these people lead them astray. Those who are guided by them will be destroyed" Isaiah 9:16

INTRODUCTION

Since the book of Revelation was written, millions of sincere Christians have shown great interest in knowing the true interpretation of the passage registered in verses 16 to 18 of the 13th chapter of Revelation. It is said in that passage that a mark will be placed on the right hand or forehead of the inhabitants of the world. Due to erroneous interpretations, there are millions of people today that are very worried because they would not be able, according to the Scripture, to buy or sell unless they submit themselves to the authority inspired and directed by Satan.

We will abide by the principle of Scripture study that is outlined in the Bible itself: *"For precept must be upon precept,... line upon line,.... here a little, and there a little."* (Isaiah 28:10,13). That means that we should compare one verse with others that discuss the same subject in order to reach the right conclusions. In this way, we will see how the Bible explains itself and that we don't need any human being to teach us the truth. Let the Author of it, the Holy Spirit, illuminate your mind. Please, compare what you read here with your Bible. We should never accept teachings from anyone unless we come to the same conclusions by our own personal study of the Holy Scriptures. It doesn't matter how much we love and trust our religious leaders. Do not believe anything that is not solidly based on the Bible. They could be as wrong as Saul of Tarsus before he met Jesus, rejecting the truth. On this, we need to learn from the Bereans: *"And the brethren immediately sent away Paul and Silas by night to Berea: whom coming thither went into the synagogue of the Jews. These were more noble than those in Thessalonica, in that they received the word with all readiness of mind, and searched the scriptures daily, whether those things were so"* (Acts 17:10,11). Who were the people preaching to them? Not less than the great apostle Paul and his friend Silas. Regardless of the source of their information, they still felt the need to compare it with the Scriptures to verify if they were being told the truth. Please, do the same with this writing (remove the dust from your Bible if you have to, but for the sake of your soul, check to see if these things are true).

It is the author's purpose to analyze objectively these passages, allowing the Bible to clarify its meaning. It is not the purpose at all to offend, or to hurt anybody's feelings. Rather, I want to teach the truth, in the hope that I can help some people grow in the knowledge of our compassionate God. I am not prejudiced against any religion, since I was raised Catholic, some of my friends are from different religions, and I preach to churches of different denominations. Please, read this study without prejudice.

It will be very wise to follow this counsel also: "Do not read the Word in the light of former opinions; but, with a mind free from prejudice, search it carefully and prayerfully. If, as you read conviction comes, and you see that your cherished opinions are not in harmony with the Word, do not try to make the Word fit these opinions. Make your opinions fit the Word. Do not allow what you have believed or practiced in the past to control your understanding." *Messages to Young People*, p. 260.

Several years have been dedicated to the study of this subject, innumerable prayers have been sent to the throne of grace (I asked several people to pray for me, so the truths presented here would have enough honey), and hundreds of hours were spent in deep study of the Scripture, to ensure that only the truth is presented. Truth is not always pleasant, but remember that if you love Jesus, you will accept what He teaches and requires of his friends, because He only wants the best for you, as any loving parent would.

Referring to people that turned from truth to fables, the book *Last Day Events* says in page 237: "If, after the Holy Spirit has brought conviction to their hearts, they resist the truth and use their influence to block the way so that others will not receive it, they will never be convinced. They did not seek for transformation of character in the time given them, and Christ will not give them opportunity to pass over the ground again. The decision is a final one."

My fear is that some reading this study will reject it for fear of what others may say. Don't give peer pressure a chance where your salvation is concerned. In Jesus' times there were spiritual bullies called the Pharisees (the ones that plotted to kill Jesus). Don't forget that your friends did not buy your salvation. They did not go to the cross for you. Worldly prestige and false security provided by a salary can not equal the price He paid to redeem your soul. Trust Jesus, be faithful to Him no matter what, and He will take great and loving care of you (including your income and a better reputation in the kingdom of heaven for all eternity). May God give you light and love for it.

Why was this study written? It was written in obedience to the words found in James 5:19 and 20: "My brothers, if one of you should wander from the truth and someone should bring him back, remember this: Whoever turns a sinner from the error of his way will save him from death and cover over a multitude of sins." This is my wish: that people in error will come to the light and rejoice in it.

The preferred Bible version used here is the KJV. Others are also used. However, some verses are freely translated by the author to modern English for better understanding, on behalf of foreigners that are now learning this language. For those of you that believe that it has to be only the King James Version or none at all, I must remind you that the KJV is a translation and as such it is not perfect. I know this as a professional translator. No translation of any book is perfect and no Bible translation is either. In case that you did not know it, English was not a language yet when the Bible was first written. The original languages in which it was written are considered dead languages because they have evolved so much through the millennia. If you speak to a Greek or Jewish person today using the words from those days, he/she will not understand what you say at all, unless he/she studied the archaic Biblical languages. Some Bible terminology was not clearly understood until the 20th century when archaeologists unearthed documents and clay tablets that shed light on the meaning and usage of such words in their historic context.

When FBI employees are being trained to spot false currency, they spend a few days studying the real paper money. Some of them get a little impatient because they want to see the false $50.00 and $100.00 bills right away, but the trainers consider that they must get to carefully study the real money first and know it well. I find convenient then, to present the truth of how are we saved first and then we will discuss the teachings of the Beast.

HOW ARE WE SAVED?
- A CONVERSATION WITH GOD

Q: Lord, I am very happy with all the doctrines that I know. What do you think, haven't I made great progress?

A: "For when for the time ye ought to be teachers, ye have need that one teach you again which be the first principles of the oracles of God; and are become such as have need of milk, and not of strong meat" (Hebrews 5:12).

Q: Lord, How much should I pay you for the salvation of my soul?

A: "They that trust in their wealth, and boast themselves in the multitude of their riches; none of them can by any means redeem his brother, nor give to God a ransom for him: (For the redemption of their soul is precious, and it ceaseth for ever:) That he should still live for ever, and not see corruption" (Psalm 49:6-9).

Q: How many good works shall I do to be saved?

A: "For by grace are ye saved through faith; and that not of yourselves: it is the gift of God: <u>Not of works</u>, lest any man should boast" (Ephesians 2:8,9).

Q: I always heard that you approve good works for salvation. What are the good works that you accept?

A: "Jesus answered and said to them, this is the work of God, <u>that ye believe</u> on Him whom He hath sent" (John 6:29).

Q: I have a heavy burden "For mine iniquities are gone over mine head: as an heavy burden they are too heavy for me." (Psalm 38:4).

A: "Come to me, all you that labor and are heavy laden, and I will give you rest" (Matthew 11:28).

Q: Do I have to confess my sins to a priest in order to be forgiven?

A: "I acknowledged my sin to thee, and mine iniquity have I not hid. I said, <u>I will confess my transgressions</u> **to the LORD**; and you forgave the iniquity of my sin. Selah" (Psalm 32:5).

Q: Can I go directly to you, or there is a bureaucracy in heaven that makes it necessary to go to your mother first, or the apostles, so I can just obtain salvation from you?

A: "Let us therefore come boldly to the throne of grace, that we may obtain mercy, and find grace to help in time of need." (Hebrews 4:16). There is no indication in any part of the Bible that says that we need somebody other than Jesus Himself to obtain forgiveness. Thanks God for that.

Q: I feel dirty because of my sins, would you receive me if I come home to you?

A: "There is joy in the presence of the angels of God over one sinner that repents" (Luke.15:10).

In the Gospel of Luke, we find a passage that describes the reaction of the Father when we ask to be forgiven. "A certain man had two sons: And the younger of them said to his father, Father, give me the portion of goods that belongs to me. And he divided to them his living. And not many days after, the younger son gathered all together, and took his journey into a far country, and there wasted his substance with riotous living. And when he had spent all, there arose a mighty famine in that land; and he began to be in need. And he went and joined himself to a citizen of that country; and he sent him into his fields to feed swine. And he would gladly have filled his belly with the husks that the swine ate: and no man gave to him. And when he came to himself, he said, How many hired servants of my father's have bread enough and to spare, and I perish with hunger! I will arise and go to my father, and will say to him, Father, I have sinned against heaven, and before you, and am no more worthy to be called thy son: make me as one of your hired servants. And he arose, and came to his father. But <u>when he was yet a great way off,</u> <u>his father saw him, and had compassion, and ran, and fell on his neck, and kissed him.</u> And the son said to him, Father, I have sinned against heaven, and in your sight, and am no more worthy to be called your son. But the Father said to his servants, '<u>Bring forth the best robe, and put it on him;</u> and put a ring on his hand, and shoes on his feet: And bring here the fatted calf, and kill it; and let us eat, and be merry: For this <u>my son was dead, and is alive again; he was lost, and is found</u>. <u>And they began to be merry [festive]</u>.'" (Luke 15:11-24). Notice how the Father does not wait for the prodigal son to come back home all the way before even considering forgiving him. He ran and came up to the ungrateful son. While this young man was taking care of the pigs, he probably fell more than once in the mud. After he wasted all his money, he was homeless. I am sure that he did not even take a shower in the way back home. He came back with a terrible smell, all sweaty, very filthy, but his wealthy father kissed him. Dirty or not, that was his beloved son and he was coming home. No wonder Paul calls Him "<u>the Father of mercies</u>, and the God of all comfort" (1 Corinthians 1:3).The son was planning to ask for a servant position after his confession, but the Father did not let him humiliate himself. He was too joyful to see him back at home, at last. Notice that it is not the son who gets dressed, which would indicate that he can obtain salvation through his own efforts. Rather, he is dressed at the orders of the Father (like in the case of Joshua, the high priest- see the section An Unfair Judge).

"<u>We have access to God through the merits of the name of Christ</u>, and <u>God invites us to bring to Him our trials and temptations; for He understands them all</u>. He would not have us pour out our woes to human ears. <u>Through the blood of Christ we may come to the throne of grace and find grace to help in time of need. We may come with assurance, saying, 'My acceptance is in the Beloved</u>.' 'For through him we both **have access** by one Spirit to the Father.' 'In whom we have boldness and access with confidence by the faith of him' (Eph. 2:18; 3:12).

"As an earthly parent encourages his child to come to him at all times, so the Lord encourages us to lay before Him our wants and perplexities, our gratitude and love. Every promise is sure. Jesus is our Surety and Mediator, and has placed at our command every resource, that we may have a perfect character" *In Heavenly Places*, page 18.

THE REAL CHARACTER OF OUR GOD

Jesus indicated that the Father is not a being to be feared, but to be loved. "Fear not, little flock; for it is your Father's good pleasure to give you the kingdom" (Luke 12:32). Our Savior never said "if you <u>fear</u> me, keep my commandments," but rather His words were "If ye <u>love</u> me, keep my commandments" (John 14:15). God is anxious to receive us and to save us. God relates to us in a close, personal way: "But thou, Israel, art my servant, Jacob whom I have chosen, the seed of <u>Abraham my friend</u>" (Isaiah 41:8).

First Corinthians 1:15 says that Jesus is "the image of the invisible God," of whom the Bible says that is love (1 John 4:8). When he was being arrested, he addressed Judas calling him <u>friend</u> (Matthew 26:50). It was prophesied in the Old Testament that when some people will see Jesus for the first time, they will ask Him: "What are these wounds in thine hands? Then he shall answer, those with which <u>I was wounded in the house of my friends</u>" (Zechariah 13:6). That is the same Savior that pronounced the most wonderful prayer for forgiveness: "Father, forgive them; for they know not what they do" (Luke 23:34). "Greater love hath no man than this, that a man <u>lay down his life for his friends</u>" (John 15:13). Can you understand that love that makes Jesus call friends those that betrayed and crucified Him? I urge you to come to this merciful Savior while there is still time. Please, don't delay your decision. Delaying it will be fatal. He will come soon looking for you, so don't hurt the heart of the only real Friend that you have.

AN UNFAIR JUDGE

The Bible teaches that Jesus will come soon to judge both the dead and the living. The reason why this section was included   is   to help people understand that there is nothing to fear from the Judge of all souls, if He is our friend, if He is supreme in our hearts.

Receiving a court citation and being accused of a crime is not precisely what we could call good news. We never look forward to get one of those even if we have the assurance that we will be acquitted. It can happen that the judge that gets assigned to our case has a price and can be bought by our enemies. Then we can have our victory overturned in favor of our adversaries. Thousands of people have even been sent to prison for crimes that they have never committed. Many don't survive the time assigned to serve, or don't have the resources to appeal and get a second trial to prove their innocence.

The Bible says that all of us "will stand before God's judgment seat" (Romans 14:10). In Hebrews 10:30 & 31 says that "God will judge his people" (see also 1Pet. 4:17), and adds "It is a dreadful thing to fall into the hands of the living God". Probably we share Job's feelings when we read in chapter 9:20, 30 & 31:

"Even if I were innocent, my mouth would condemn me; if I were blameless, it would pronounce me guilty.... Even if I wash myself with soap and my hands with washing soda, you would plunge me into a slime pit so that even my clothes would detest me".

And David adds:

"Do not bring your servant into judgment, for no one living is righteous before you" (Psalm 143:2).

The New Testament declares that Jesus is the judge (John 5:22). Would it be possible that his sufferings on the cross had quenched his love for us and he can turn into a terrible adversary in the judgment against us? Let's consider some Bible passages that will expose a different angle:

Psalm 34:22: "...No one will be condemned who takes refuge in Him"

Psalm 76:9: "When you, o God rose up to judge, to save all the afflicted of the land" (notice that the judgment is an act to save His people, not to condemn them, for only the wicked have to fear from God). In the Hebrew text, the words judge and save appear as synonyms.

Job 22:21-30: "He will deliver even one who is not innocent..." (who among us is innocent anyway?).

But the Bible goes on with the good news:

Job 17:3- He places bond in our favor.

Job 16:19-The Almighty will be the believer's witness

1 John 2:1- Jesus is our Lawyer- Did anybody ever heard that he lost a case yet? He never did and never will lose the case of a soul entrusted to his care.

John 5:22 with Hebrews 4:16- Jesus is our judge and He encourages us to trust him, to approach his "throne of grace with confidence".

Revelation 12:1- There is no prosecutor (accuser). He was driven away. In the past he was allowed to go to the portals of heaven and accuse the chosen ones (Zac.3: 1-5). Let's read that passage: "And he showed me Joshua the high priest standing before the angel of the LORD, and Satan standing at his right hand to resist him. And the LORD said to Satan, the LORD rebuke thee, O Satan; even the LORD that hath chosen Jerusalem rebuke thee: is not this a brand plucked out of the fire? Now Joshua was clothed with filthy garments, and stood before the angel. And he answered and spoke to those that stood before him, saying, Take away the filthy garments from him. And to him he said, Behold, I have caused thine iniquity to pass from thee, and I will clothe thee with change of raiment. And I said, Let them set a fair mitre upon his head. So they set a fair mitre upon his head, and clothed him with garments. And the angel of the LORD stood by."

The filthy garments are a symbol of the iniquity, the sin in Joshua's life. When the prodigal son came back home, the father ordered his servants to dress him with the "best robe" (Luke 15:22). That robe represents the character of Jesus, His righteousness (His perfect life) imputed (credited) to us. The people of God are presented in the Bible as dressed in white clothes, like fine linen. Talking to John the revelator, the angel explained: "the fine linen is the righteousness of the saints." The life of Jesus is the one examined in the judgment. His righteousness takes the place of our failures. My sins are removed from the records and instead, the Father sees the perfect life of Jesus (33 ½ years of spotless obedience to the will of God). When you accept Jesus' services as your lawyer, it is not you who are judged; it is Jesus Himself, because his life takes the place of yours. This makes it possible for you to earn the right to the kingdom of heaven through the life of your Savior. This happens only by faith: "For by grace are ye saved through faith; and that not of yourselves: it is the gift of God" (Ephesians 2:8).

Romans 8:33, 34 presents a challenge to whosoever dares to even think about accusing one of God's servants: "Who shall lay any thing to the charge of God's elect? It is God that justifies. Who is he that condemns? It is Christ that died, yea rather, that is risen again, who is even at the right hand of God, who also makes intercession for us."

Illustration: Martin Luther had dream. Satan was accusing him. "HE is mine," he said to God, but Luther noticed that Satan was covering a part of Luther's life record with his hand. Luther tried to read the part of the record that was being covered, but he couldn't see it, so he demanded in the name of Jesus to let him see what was there. It read: "Washed in the blood of the Lamb." When Satan shows you the sins of your past, just remind him of his future. We had been great sinners, but <u>we have a greater Savior</u>: "Where sin abounded, grace abounded much more" (Romans 5:20).

Let us read Col. 1:21,22 "And you, that were sometime alienated and enemies in your mind by wicked works, yet now hath He reconciled in the body of his flesh through death, <u>to present</u> you <u>holy and unblameable and unreproveable</u> in his sight:" The part that reads "to present," means to "bring to court". Now, lets compare that with Hebrews 7:26 about Jesus: "For such a High Priest was suitable for us, who is <u>holy, harmless, undefiled</u>, separate from sinners, and made higher than the heavens." What the Bible says about Jesus is applied to us in the judgment. When we are judged, the father sees Jesus in us. When our case is presented in the heavenly courts, we are considered as <u>holy, harmless, undefiled</u>, just as Jesus is.

We could conclude this section saying that in order to reap these blessings, we need to persevere in Jesus. "<u>**If**</u> ye continue in the faith grounded and settled, and be not moved away from the hope of the gospel" (Col. 1:23), Jesus will side with us. Since Jesus is our Judge, Lawyer, Witness, the one who posts our bond for us, and the prosecutor has been taken away (he says that the Judge is not fair), we have nothing to fear, but a glorious expectation of judgment, for God is on our side. See Job 23:10.

THE APOSTATE CHURCH ("THE ONE THAT JESUS LEFT ON EARTH")

It was the year 31 AD and the young church was having great success in all Jerusalem, Samaria and to the very end of their known world, and "the Lord added to the church, every day those that were being saved" (Acts 2:47). The gospel had been preached with such divine power starting on Pentecost and later on, that by the year 65 AD, Paul was able to say that it was preached in all "the creation that is under the heavens" (Col. 1:23). Before such growth, Satan used both Jews and Gentiles to unleash bloody persecutions that fortunately, made the church grow even more. Someone wrote that the blood of the martyrs was like seed. As persecutions did not give good results, Satan started to infiltrate heretic doctrines in an underhanded way, but God never leaves his children without orientation.

It had been prophesied that the <u>apostolic</u>, pure church that Jesus left on earth, <u>would apostatize</u>. Acts 20: 29 & 30 says: "because I know that after my departure <u>will come among you</u> savage wolves that will not spare the flock. And <u>from among yourselves</u>, men will rise that will speak wicked things to draw away the disciples after themselves." 2 Thes. 2:3,4 & 7 refers to this also when it says: "Let no one <u>deceive</u> you by any means; for [Jesus] will not come unless the <u>apostasy</u> comes first, and the man of sin is revealed, the son of perdition, who opposes and exalt himself above anything that is called God or that is worshiped, so that he <u>sits in the temple of God, posing as God</u>...Because the mystery of lawlessness is already at work; only that there is whom at the present stops him, until he is taken out of the way." The "whom" here mentioned was either Paul or John, the last two disciples alive. The word apostasy implies the abandonment of the previous set of beliefs. The doctrine that once was handed down pure, uncontaminated from Jesus to His disciples, was going to be mixed with human teachings (commandments of men).

According to these passages, the antichrist started to be active in the bosom of the primitive church. This point is important because the majority of Christianity believes that the antichrist will be a Jew and will come in the future, ignoring what was so clearly stated by John in the first of his epistles. He said that "**the antichrist is now already in the world**" (1John 4:3). Eminent Christians of the very first century had the same understanding that John had. It is also worthwhile mentioning that the Bible presents indistinctly the antichrist both as a man and as a power, which indicates that it is a dynasty.

Another generalized mistake is to think that the antichrist will exert tyrannical dominion for 7 years over the Jews. This error is caused by the belief that the enemy of the people of God is only, simply, a man, when the Bible shows that in reality it is a power or religious institution that <u>fakes</u> faithfulness to God (we will expound in the paragraph that follows the analysis of the word teitan).

In order to come to this erratic conclusion about the seven years of the dominion of the antichrist, some people (most of them well intentioned) take out of context a passage from the 9th chapter of Daniel, where it mentions the seventy weeks (490 years, according to the principle of one prophetic day = to a 360 days Hebrew year- see Numbers 14:34, Ezekiel 4:6) that were determined (separated) or cut off for the Jews. Daniel 9:24 says that during that time period, God would work "to **finish the transgression, and to make an end of sins, and to make reconciliation for iniquity, and to bring in everlasting righteousness**, and to seal up the vision and prophecy, and to anoint the most Holy." The beauty of this verse is that it prophesied that during the time set apart for the Jews, Jesus would die in order to reconcile humanity to God. Verse 25 points to the beginning of this period of time: "Know therefore and understand that from the time that the order is given to restore and build Jerusalem until the Messiah [=anointed] the Prince, shall be seven weeks and sixty-two weeks." The order was given by Artaxerxes Longimanus through a decree that went into effect in the autumn of the year 457 BC (see Ezra 6:14 & 7:1,2) From this time, 483 years extend to the autumn of the year 27 AD. In that year Jesus received the anointing (Acts 10:38) of the Holy Spirit and began his ministry. Then the message was proclaimed, "The time is fulfilled" (Mark 1:15), referring to the first 69 weeks, which indicates that Jesus was aware of the fulfillment of the prophecy of Daniel.

Verse 27 states that <u>in the middle of the last prophetic week</u> of the period separated for the Jews (3½ years after His baptism), "**He shall bring an end to the sacrifice and offering**." In the spring of the year 31 AD, Jesus was crucified and the veil of the Temple was torn from top to bottom by an invisible hand (Matthew 27:51), indicating that Christ, the true sacrifice, the only one whose blood can cleanse us from our sins, had been offered. There was no more need to sacrifice animals because "the Lamb of God that taketh away the sin of the world" (John 1:29) had laid down His life for us. The seventy weeks ended in AD 34 when Stephen was stoned to death. In that moment, the Jews (as a nation) rejected God. Now, according to Paul, whoever believes in Jesus is counted as a Jew. The book of Acts, chapter 8 says that the believers were scattered away by persecution and started to preach to the gentiles. The following chart will help to understand this important prophecy in its true context:

Order given	Restoration finished		Baptism	Crucifixion	Gospel to Gentiles
B.C 457 BC	408		27 AD	31AD	34AD

The reason why the period of 49 years (457 to 408) is separated from the rest of the 70 weeks (490 years), is because that was the time that it took to reconstruct the wall & government houses in Jerusalem.

Regarding the death of Jesus at the middle of the last of the seventy weeks, the Bible says that Jesus, when He started his ministry, was 30 years old (Luke 3:21,23). It also says that John (six months older) started his ministry in the 15th year of Tiberius, which was in the autumn of the year 27 AD. That was when Jesus was baptized. The Bible registers that Jesus attended 4 Passovers (John 2:13;5:1;6:4 & 13:1) and was crucified during the last one, in the spring of the year 31 AD, precisely in the middle of the last of the seventy weeks. The prophecy declares: "and after the 62 weeks [after the year 27 AD] the Messiah shall be cut off," and adds: "but at the middle of the [remaining] week He shall bring an end to the sacrifice and offering" (Dan. 9:26,27). That means that when Jesus died (in the middle of the last week of the 70), it was no longer necessary to offer sacrifices. The 70 weeks were fulfilled in its totality in the year 34 AD when by the stoning of Stephen, the Jews gave their final rejection to the gospel. There is no reason to separate the last week of this period of 70 weeks and applying it to future events, depriving it in this way of its glorious meaning. This prophecy points to the sublime sacrifice of Jesus on our behalf, indicating when He was baptized and when He was crucified. Since this prophecy pointed so clearly to the specific time when Jesus was baptized and crucified we can only think that Satan would be interested in ruining its glorious meaning with a doctrine like the secret rapture in which this passage is erroneously applied instead to the antichrist by the dispensationalists.

R.H. Blodgett wrote a great book on the subject entitled What is the Secret Rapture? I recommend it.

THE MYSTERY OF INIQUITY

The Scriptures mention the duration of the dominion of the mystery of iniquity: 1,260 days or years (according to Ez. 4:6- "I have appointed thee each day for a year;" see also Num. 14:34). The passages where his hegemony (dominion) is mentioned are Dan 7:25; 12:7; Revelation 11:2,3; 12:6,14 & 13:5. It is presented in three different but equivalent ways:

A) 42 months   B) 1,260 days   C) 3 Times & half a time (a time is a year)

Note: The Hebrew year had only 360 days, with each month having 30 days each. The Hebrews knew that the earth revolves around the sun in a circular motion (orbit) so they divided that circle in 360 degrees- one degree per day.

According to the verses in Ezekiel 4 and Numbers 14, the 1,260 days are equivalent to 1,260 years. Only one power has had oppressive dominion for all that time. This tyrant power started to twist the Scriptures in apostolic times. Peter points this out, when he wrote that the letters of Paul were being misinterpreted (2 Peter 3:15,16). This epistle also says that false teachers and prophets would introduce destructive heresies deceitfully, which will have many followers (2 Peter 2:1-3). This would be a religion of majority and exert a catholic (= universal) dominion. Revelation 17:1,2 says that the inhabitants of "the earth have been made drunk with the wine of her fornication. Wine is a symbol for doctrines. Revelation 17:15 & 18 shows that this power has dominion over the multitudes and over the kings of the earth. Also, Paul wrote to the Colossians that they should be careful so they would not be seduced with enticing words, <u>philosophy</u> and vain deceit, after the <u>tradition</u> of men, and not after Christ (Col. 2:8). From what we have studied to this point, we can conclude that the antichrist is a religious majority power that exerts world tyrannical power and that <u>philosophy</u> and <u>tradition</u> are essential part of its teaching.

The Bible calls the enemy of God's people: antichrist, man of sin, son of perdition, <u>mystery</u> of iniquity (2 Thessalonians 2:3), Babylon (Revelation 14,17,18), beast (Revelation chapters 13-16 & 19), little horn (Dan. 7:24), and compares it with a corrupted woman (Revelation 17). The woman of Revelation 17 represents the apostate church, (which is why it is represented as a whore) the direct opposite of the true church represented by the woman of Revelation 12.

Note: Isaiah 55:1-3 compares buying wine with obtaining salvation. "Every one that is thirsty, come to the waters, and he that has no money; come, buy, and eat; yes, come, **buy wine** and milk without money and without price. Why do you spend money for that which is not bread? And your labor for that which does not satisfies? <u>Lend an ear diligently to me</u>, and eat that which is good, and let your soul delight itself in fatness. Incline your ear, and come to me: **<u>hear, and your soul shall live</u>**; and I will make an everlasting covenant with you, even the sure mercies of David." So, buying wine is to hear the good news about salvation (=the Gospel). In Revelation 14, we find 3 angels flying in the midst of heaven with the everlasting Gospel (which would be the good wine). Later in the same chapter, we read about the wine of Babylon. This would be the false doctrines. The passage says: "she <u>made all nations drink of the wine</u> of the wrath of her fornication." In other words, she forced the inhabitants of the earth, to drink of the wine of her false doctrines.

Now we will analyze some Bible passages that identify the antichrist.

HOW TO IDENTIFY
THE ANTICHRIST

Prophecy	Fulfillment
1) The woman (a symbol of a church, see Ez. 23:2-21;Hosea 2:5;3:1; Revelation 14:4) is adorned with gold and precious stones. Revelation 17:4	1) The popular church has always enjoyed pomp. "Thus is represented the papal power, which with all deceivableness of unrighteousness, **by outside attraction and gorgeous display**, deceives all nations; promising them, as did Satan our first parents, all good to those who receive its mark, and all harm to those who oppose its fallacies. The power which has the deepest inward corruption will make the greatest display, and will clothe itself with the most elaborate signs of power. The Bible plainly declares that this covers a corrupt and deceiving wickedness. 'Upon her forehead was a name written, Mystery, Babylon the Great, The Mother of Harlots and Abominations of the Earth' "S.D.A. Bible Commentary Vol. 7, page 983

2) Its headquarters are established over 7 hills (Revelation17:9,18)	2) Rome is known as the city of the 7 hills. The Vatican (from the Latin vaticanus = center of divination) is an additional mount located in Rome but counted as part of the city. Another opinion on the meaning of Vaticanus is that "vaticanus collis means "the prophetic hill", which can be rephrased as *the hill or mountain of prophecy...* Interestingly, the word *anus* in Latin also means "old woman", so Vaticanus is a combination of two words that also result in *The Old Woman of Prophecy,* this woman being symbolic of the Catholic Church" (text from aloha.net/~mikesch/vatican.htm). The *American Heritage Dictionary* defines divination as: "The art or act of foretelling future events or revealing **occult** knowledge by means of augury or alleged supernatural agency." We know about the apparitions of the Virgin foretelling terrible things.
3) Will prohibit marriage (1 Timothy4:3).	3) Rome demands from priests and nuns to remain celibate.
4) It has characteristics of a: a) lion, b) bear, c) leopard and the d) terrible beast (Revelation 13). See Daniel 7.	4) The Catholic Church inherited from the a) lion (Babylon) the taste for majesty (pomp, splendor), and paganism, standing out the veneration of the intercessory mother, that the Catholic Church applied to Mary (called the queen of heaven), the use of the rosary, and other pagan ideas, in order to entice pagans into joining the church. b) From the bear (Medo-Persia) got the cruelty (remember the inquisition?

Read the secret Oath of the Knights of Columbus included in this material), the cult to the sun (this is why they keep **_Sunday_** as day of rest, and the feast of Mitra's birthday on December 25ᵗʰ, which, in order to make it acceptable, it was said that it was to honor Jesus' birthday, (He was not born in winter- remember that there were shepherds in the field and that Mary wrapped Jesus only in swaddling clothes? See Luke 2:7 & 12). c) From the leopard (Greece) it inherited the doctrine of the immortality of the soul and the philosophy of Plato and Aristotle. d) From the terrible beast (Rome) it inherited the intolerance, ferrous discipline and the throne of Caesar.

5) It would rise after the Greeks and come from the Roman empire (Dan. 8:23).

5) The Catholic power arose in the Christian era of the Roman empire (Daniel 8:21-23).

6) Once strengthened, it would caused the fall of three other powers (Daniel 8:24).

6) The Catholic power caused the fall of the Heruli (493 BC), the Vandals (534 DC) and the Ostrogoths (538 BC), three Arian powers (they taught that Jesus was created).

7) It would be strong, but not with its own strength (Dan. 8:24).

7) Roman Catholicism used the power of the state to affirm and sustain its authority.

8) Would cast the truth down to the ground (Dan.8:12).	8) Romanism prefers the <u>traditions</u> of men, rather than the Bible (which its leader never carries). The Catholics admit that they teach things that are not biblical and that such doctrines are based only on the authority of the church and on tradition (see the analysis of the Greek word paradosis). "In the interval between the days of the apostles and the conversion of Constantine… rites and ceremonies, of which neither Paul nor Peter ever heard, crept silently into use, and then claimed the ranks of divine institutions." Ancient Church Preface, pp.vi, vii.
9) Would have a mouth speaking great things (Dan. 7:8; Revelation 13:5).	9) Doctrines such as the purgatory, eternal hell, the natural immortality of the soul, the intercession of Mary and the saints, papal infallibility, the indulgences, the rosary, infant baptism, etc are not biblical.
10) Would speak arrogant words (Revelation 13:15).	10) The Pope used to choose and depose kings as he pleased because he affirms to have received authority from Jesus to rule the world. He also says that he has the power to forgive sins, which is a divine prerogative.
11) Would command to abstain from foods (1 Timothy 4:6).	11) On Good Friday and other sacred days, which is a pagan practice. For Catholics, eating meat on Fridays is forbidden.
12) Would dominate during 1260 years (Daniel 7:25).	12) The papacy reigned from 538 AD until 1798 A.D., equaling 1260 years, jut as the Bible foretold!

13) Would change the Ten Commandments (Dan. 7:25), also known as the Law.	13) The papacy eliminated the second commandment that prohibits to honor or worship images and changed the fourth one that requires the observance of the Sabbath, transferring the solemnity of the holy day of the Lord to **Sun**day (which some people call the day of the Lord, but they don't say of which lord it is). They also divided the tenth into two in order to have ten commandments. Please read the original 10 Commandments in the Catholic Bible. They are found in Exodus chapter 20. Then, compare them with any catechism. See section **The Law of God**.
14) Has a golden cup (Revelation 17:4).	14) The cup of the mass. See pictures in the comments about the mass.
15) It is identified as a woman covered in purple and scarlet (Revelation 17:3).	15) The colors of the royalty were used by the popes and cardinals who pretended to be the representatives of the One that did not have where to lay His head on. They live like royalty.
16) Performs miracles (2 Thessalonians 2:9)	16) The "miracles" of the Virgin & the saints are very well known. Shrines are built all over the world where peregrines go by thousands looking for healing or to see a miracle, such as a bleeding statue or an image that appears at some time of the day.
17) Would suffer a deadly wound (Revelation 13:3). The leader would be taken captive (Revelation 13:10).	17) Pope Pius VI was kidnapped in 1798 by the French general Berthier, obeying orders from Napoleon Bonaparte, and was brought to France, where he died the following year. This marked the end of the 1260 years (538-1798 AD prophecy of Daniel 7:25.

18) His mortal wound was healed and all the earth marveled and followed the beast (Revelation 13:3)

18) The papacy recuperated thanks to astute agreements (in 1929 the Italian government recognized the Vatican city as an independent state-right now, most of the countries of the world have an ambassador or some kind of relationship with the Vatican) and you should see how the multitudes follow the leader of the system that the Bible calls the beast! Talking about the influence of the pope on politics and human rights, the spokesman for pope John Paul II said that his legacy on human rights gives him powerful leverage on these issues and illustrates how much things have changed over the last 100 years.

19) Would persecute the children of God (Dan. 7:25; 8:24; Revelation 12:17; 17:6).

19) Before, during and after the inquisition, Rome killed the Christians that sustained the biblical truth. It is estimated that Rome has killed over 60 million people. In 1997, the Catholic Church said that it was sorry for collaborating with the Nazis during World War II in killing the Jews. Even Pope Pius XII named Hitler protector of the church when he was committing genocide. This apology is just a new strategy to accomplish her goal of world dominion. She wants to look like she is sorry, but it's not to be trusted. It is still a wolf on sheep's clothes.

20) Would destroy many by surprise (Dan.8:25).

20) The Massacre of St. Bartholomew in France stands as the most horrible mass killing of the dark ages. Seventy thousand people, from the babies in their mothers' arms to the people of gray hair were killed, trusting in the promises of their king and the church leaders. Historians tell us that Pope Gregory XIII went to the church of St. Louis to celebrate when he heard the news and a medal was struck to commemorate the massacre. See *The Triumph of God's Love*, chapter 15.

21) Shows himself that he is God (2 Thessalonians 2:4; Dan.11:36).

21) The leader of this system shows himself as God, by adopting attributes of the Trinity:

a) God the Father- when he affirms that he is the king of heaven, earth, and lower places (that's why he has a triple crown). He is called holy father, a title that Jesus applied to God the Father (John 17:11). Pope Leo XIII said: "We occupy on this earth, the place of God Almighty." This is in direct opposition to what the Bible specifies: "And **call no man your father upon the earth**: for one is your Father, which is in heaven"(Matthew 23:9).

b) The Son- When he is called high priest, a title that belongs to Jesus (Hebrews 8:1), when pretending to forgive sins, and when he proclaims that he is the head of the church, since the Head is Christ (Ephesians 5:23).

c) The Holy Spirit- When he claims that he is the vicar (or representative) of Jesus on earth (see John 16:6, 13 & 14).

When the pope visited Puerto Rico in the late 80's, posters were placed all over that had a picture of John Paul II with a Bible verse that is very familiar to us, applied to the pope: "Blessed is He who comes in the name of the Lord." (Matthew 21:9). It was blasphemous to apply this verse to a man, when it only can be applied to Jesus.

In 1993, at the World Youth Day in Denver, USA, where thousands of young people from several nations and from all the continents were congregated, a young person read some verses referring to the pope, who was sited on a throne- like chair. The passage was from the book of Revelation: "Behold a great multitude which no man could number, from every nation, from all tribes and peoples and tongues, standing before the throne and before the Lamb, clothed in white robes, with palm branches in their hands, and crying out with a loud voice, Salvation belongs to our God who sits upon the throne, and to the Lamb" (Revelation 7:9,10). Can you find in modern times a bigger blasphemy than this one? The pope, a spiritual leader, in both occasions accepted the honor, being treated like God and did not correct the people that applied the Scriptures that refers to Jesus, to him, a mere mortal.

22) It is a mother (Revelation 17:5)	22) The popular church enjoys being called holy mother. The Scriptures reveal that in fact, it is a mother, but of harlots, this is, the apostate Protestant churches that had departed from the truth that cost the blood of so many of their founders, like Huss, Jerome, Hamilton and Wishart (these 2 in Scotland), Louis de Berquin in France, Tyndale (translated the Bible to English) and so many others. Oh, if those martyrs would come back to life now, how bitterly they would weep seeing the apostasy of those churches that stop protesting against the heresies of Rome!
23) Has world dominion- (Revelation 13:3,7,8;17:18).	23) The multitudes in the world, even the non-Christians are looking up to the pope of Rome. He is gaining more influence and was recognized as "primus inter pares" (=first among equals) by the oriental Catholic leader a few years ago.
24. Rides a beast (Revelation 17:3)	24) This represents the combination of the ecclesiastical power of the church (the woman) and the political power of the state (the beast). A woman in prophecy is a symbol of a church (both the faithful and the apostate). Passages like Jeremiah 6:2 ("I have likened the daughter of Zion to a comely and delicate woman") and Revelation 12:1 ("And there appeared a great wonder in heaven; a woman clothed with the sun, and the moon under her feet, and upon her head a crown of twelve stars") represent the true church, both in the Old and New Testaments.

Revelation 17:3-6 represents the false church that pretends to be the one founded by Jesus ("I saw a woman sit upon a scarlet colored beast, full of names of blasphemy, having seven heads and ten horns. And **the woman was arrayed in purple and scarlet color**, and **decked with gold and precious stones and pearls**, **having a golden cup in her hand** full of abominations and filthiness of her fornication: And upon her forehead was a name written, **MYSTERY**, BABYLON THE GREAT, THE **MOTHER OF HARLOTS** AND ABOMINATIONS OF THE EARTH. And **I saw the woman drunken with the blood of the saints**, **and with the blood of the martyrs of Jesus**: and when I saw her, I wondered with great admiration."). Regarding the beast as a power or the state, see Daniel 7:23 ("The fourth beast shall be the fourth kingdom upon earth,") & 8:20,21.

Now consider the following quote:

"After warning against the worship of the beast and its image, the prophecy declares: 'here is the patience of the saints; here they are, those which keep the commandments of God, and the faith of Jesus' (Revelation 14:12). In light of the fact that those which keep the commandments of God are put thus in contrast with those which adore the beast and its image and receive its mark, it is deduced that the observance of the law of God on one hand, and its violation, on the other, establish the distinction between those which adore God and those which adore the beast.

"The most characteristic feature of the beast... it is the breaking of God's commandments. Daniel says of the little horn that he will *think* to change the times and the law (Dan.7:25). And Saint Paul calls the same power the man of sin that was to exalt himself above

God. One prophecy is complement of the other." There has been only one power that has claimed the right to make a change thus, being exalted above God: the papacy. He attempted to change the law of God. The second commandment, that prohibits the cult to the images, it has been erased from the law, and the fourth commandment has been adulterated in such a way that authorizes the observance of the first day in place of the seventh, as day of rest. How is that change explained or justified? "<u>The pope has power to change times, to abrogate laws, and to dispense with all things, even the precepts of Christ</u>" *Decretal, de Tranlatic Episcop.*

"The change introduced in the fourth commandment exactly fulfils the prophecy. For the only authority claimed is that of the church. Here the papal power openly sets itself above God. What is, since, the change of the day of rest, but the sign or mark of the authority of the Roman church, the mark of the beast? It is since, to accept **Sun**day as day of rest, what constitutes receiving the mark in the forehead, and to observe it, what constitutes to receive the mark in the right hand." *The Triumph of God's Love* chapter entitled *God's Law Immutable.* The word Sunday is named that way because it was dedicated to worship the sun.

The word mark is translated from the Greek χάραγμα (*charagma*). The Strong's Concordance has this description for this word translated as mark in Revelation 13:16:

1) A stamp, an imprinted mark
   a) Of the mark stamped on the forehead or the right hand as the badge of the followers of the Antichrist
   b) The mark branded upon horses
2) Thing **carved**, sculpture, **graven** work
   a) Of idolatrous images

Paul used exactly the same word *charagma,* translated as "graven" in Acts 17:29: *"Forasmuch then as we are the offspring of God, we ought not to think that the Godhead is like unto gold, or silver, or stone, graven by art and man's device."* It is interesting that this word is linked to idolatry since the Catholic Church has so many graven images in the churches.

The Bible presents a contrast between the mark of the beast and the mark of God. Revelation 7 mentions that the faithful of God will receive the seal of God in their forehead. Romans 4:11 shows that seal is synonym with mark or sign. The Sabbath of the fourth Commandment is presented as a sign or mark between God and His people. "Verily My Sabbaths ye shall keep: for it is a sign between Me and you throughout your generations; that ye may know that I am the LORD that doth sanctify you.... It is a sign between Me and the children of Israel forever: for in six days the LORD made heaven and earth, and on the seventh day He rested, and was refreshed" (Exodus 31:13,17). Notice that the **Me** appears before the **you**, indicating the sovereignty of God above man.

Revelation mentions the seal of God and the Mark of the Beast. Both are applied similarly. In Greek, it uses the phrase "ἐπί αὐτός μέτωπον" *(epi autos metōpon)* translated as "in their foreheads." The same phrase appears in both Revelation 7:3 & Revelation 13:16, indicating that both marks are received in the same way. The word "epi" appears 896 times in the Bible, of which is translated as "in" 120 times. One example is found in Matthew 18:16: *"But if he will not hear thee, then take with thee one or two more, that in the mouth of two or three witnesses every word may be established."* Here, as in many other passages, it means inside. Although the word can also be translated as "on" or "upon," the distinction the passage makes in referring also to the hand with respect to the mark of the Beast, establishes an important difference: the Beast's mark goes beyond what God requires. We know that salvation is obtained by faith, not by works (Ephesians 2:8). Since God requires only faith, this second element indicates an additional effort from man to assure that salvation: works. In this, the Beast's teachings had been very clear in requesting the believers to do pilgrimages, to offer votive and monetary offerings, etc. in order to gain merits to enter heaven. In their case, their faith is expressed externally (hand) after it is conceived internally in the brain (forehead). The seal of God, however, is something that stays in the inside and it is not exteriorized because it is based on a relationship with God.

Both marks are accepted as a matter of conscience, of principle, and devotion. Both are going to distinguish whom we worship. Neither the mark of the beast nor the seal of God are visible, but the character will reveal who has which mark of authority.

Michael Scheifler presents the following analysis of the meaning of the word Sabbath:

THE WORD SABBATH IN DIFFERENT LANGUAGES

Unlike English, many languages refer to the seventh day of the week as Sabbath rather than Saturday, which means day of Saturn. There is no distinction in Spanish where the word for Saturday is the same for Sabbath. That word is sábado (Sabbath). In Russian it is Subbota (суббота = Sabbath). In Polish it is Sobota (Sabbath). In French it is Samedi (Sabbath). In Portuguese it is sábado (Sabbath). In Italian it is Sabato (Sabbath). In Hungarian it is Szombat (Sabbath). In Turkish it is yom-es-sabt (day the Sabbath). In Arabic it is as-sabt (تبسلا = the Sabbath). In Malayan it is hari-sabtu (the Sabbath). In Malagassy spoken in Madagascar it is alsabotsy (the Sabbath). In Swahili it is as-sabt (the Sabbath). The Armenian word is *Shabat* (Շաբաթ). ***Present Truth, April 2000- adapted.***

THE MEANING OF THE WORD SABBATH

In the word **Sabbath** there are the following elements:

> **"ab"** means *father* (See Strong's Hebrew Dictionary, word H1)

> **"b"** means *dwelling place,* **or** *of* (i.e. *Tisha B' Av* in Hebrew means the ninth day *of* the month of Av)

> **"ath"** (oth) means *sign or seal* (See Strong's Hebrew Dictionary, word H226)

> So **"S-ab-b-ath"** means the <u>**dwelling place of the** *seal* *of the Father*</u>.

The seal of God is found in the keeping of the Sabbath (Saturday), not on keeping a spurious day (according to the *American Heritage Dictionary*, spurious means: "1. Lacking authenticity or validity; false. 2.Constituting a forgery or interpolation. 3. Illegitimate; bastard. 4. *Bot.* Similar in appearance but unlike in structure or function"). Even the botanical application fits <u>**Sun**</u>day worship very well!

The Real Issue in the Final Conflict.--[Revelation 14:9, 10 quoted.] "It is for the interest of all to understand what the mark of the beast is, and how they may escape the dread threatenings of God. **Why are men not interested to know what constitutes the mark of the beast and his image**? It is in direct contrast with the mark of God." "The Sabbath question will be the issue in the great conflict in which all the world will act a part. [Ex. 31:12-17 quoted.] **What is the**

Mark of the Beast?--John was called to behold a people distinct from those who worship the beast and his image by keeping the first day of the week. The observance of this day is the mark of the beast."

Warning Against receiving the Mark of the Beast.--The third angel's message has been sent forth to the world, warning men against receiving the mark of the beast or of his image in their foreheads or in their hands. To receive this mark means to come to the same decision as the beast has done, and to advocate the same ideas, in direct opposition to the Word of God. Of all who receive this mark, God says, "The same shall drink of the wine of the wrath of God, which is poured out without mixture into the cup of his indignation; and he shall be tormented with fire and brimstone in the presence of the holy angels, and in the presence of the Lamb." S.D.A. Bible Commentary Vol. 7, page 979.

"If the light of truth has been presented to you, revealing the Sabbath of the fourth commandment, and showing that there is no foundation in the Word of God for Sunday observance, and yet you still cling to the false Sabbath, refusing to keep holy the Sabbath which God calls 'My holy day,' you receive the mark of the beast. When does this take place? When you obey the decree that commands you to cease from labor on Sunday and worship God, while you know that there is not a word in the Bible showing Sunday to be other than a common working day, you consent to receive the mark of the beast, and refuse the seal of God. If we receive this mark in our foreheads or in our hands, the judgments pronounced against the disobedient must fall upon us. But the seal of the living God is placed upon those who conscientiously keep the Sabbath of the Lord"

"When the test comes, it will be clearly shown what the mark of the beast is. It is the keeping of **_Sun_**day. Those who, after having heard the truth, continue to regard this day as holy, bear the signature of the man of sin, who thought to change times and laws." Ibid., page 980.

DIES DOMINI

In July, 1998 Pope John Paul II issued an apostolic letter entitled "Dies Domini" (Day of the Lord), in which he proposed to the world to keep **Sun**day holy. In the very first paragraph the pope wrote that it is on **Sun**day that we celebrate the victory of Christ over sin and death. The second part is right, but not the first, because it was on Friday, when Jesus died on the cross, that we were redeemed.

From the beginning of the document and all the way to the end, he applies passages in the Scriptures that either have nothing to do with a day of rest, or he applies the declarations that refer to the real Sabbath (Saturday, the Seventh day of the week) to **Sun**day (the first day of the week), thus taking the Bible out of context. One example of the latter is when in sections 12-14 he goes to the book of Genesis and reads about the week of creation. That was when God rested on the 7th day. He wrote: "In the first place, therefore, **Sun**day is the day of rest because it is the day "blessed" by God and "made holy" by him, set apart from the other days to be, among all of them, "the Lord's Day." Here the person in charge of translating the pope's letter dares to twist the Bible in order to prove something that can not be proven with the Holy Writings. The original text of the pope's writing in Latin says in article 14 "day of rest," not Sunday as we read in the English version. The passage that the translator is referring to is Genesis 2:1-3, and applies ONLY to Saturday, the 7th day of the week.

It is not coincidence that in the second paragraph he refers to **Sun**day as the "day after the Sabbath," admitting implicitly that **Sun**day is not the Sabbath, but just, merely, only the day after the Sabbath. It is a day that the Bible does not even mention by name.

In section **18**, the pope wrote that the commandment to keep the Sabbath is the 3rd in the Decalogue. He is not quoting the Bible, where it is the 4th Commandment. At the end of that same section, he implies that the Sabbath was not perfect, which is a contradiction of what God's word says in Genesis 2:1-3: "And God <u>blessed</u> the seventh day, and <u>sanctified</u> it: because that in it he had rested from all his work which God created and made." If God blesses and sanctifies something, is it imperfect? So God didn't know how to do it right and the pope had to fix it, by proclaiming **Sun**day holy, a day that God never sanctified or blessed? These are the pope's words: "In the light of this mystery, the meaning of the Old Testament precept concerning the Lord's Day is recovered, <u>perfected</u> and fully revealed in the glory which shines on the face of the Risen Christ (cf. 2 Cor 4:6). We move from the 'Sabbath' to the 'first day after the Sabbath', from the seventh day to the first day: the dies Domini become the dies Christi (= day of Christ)!"

He mentions the move from Sabbath to the day after, but he does not present even one verse of the Bible to authorize such a change.

***In section **19**, he wrote: "every **Sun**day is the anastàsimos hemèra, the day of Resurrection, and this is why <u>it stands at the heart of all worship</u>." Do you notice that the heart of all worship for the pope is <u>a day</u> and <u>not God</u>?

When Jesus died on Calvary, he accomplished our salvation. Let's see Romans 5: 8-10: "But God commendeth his love toward us, in that, while we were yet sinners, <u>Christ died for us</u>. Much more then, <u>being now justified by his blood</u>, <u>we shall be saved from wrath through him</u>. For if, when we were enemies, we were reconciled to God by the death of his Son, much more, being reconciled, we shall be saved by his life." On Friday we were set free. On **Sun**day, we got the assurance of our own future resurrection. But John Paul II wrote: "This is what the Christian **Sun**day does, leading the faithful each week to ponder and live **the event of Easter, true source of the world's salvation**." In an effort to justify the observance of Sunday, it receives qualities that it doesn't have. The source of the world's salvation was the death of Jesus on Calvary.

Several times he mentions that **Sun**day is a day to commemorate the resurrection of Jesus. Really? Not according to Romans 6, where Paul teaches that baptism is the way to commemorate that glorious event: "Know ye not, that so many of us as were baptized into Jesus Christ were baptized into his death? Therefore we are buried with him by baptism into death: that like as Christ was raised up from the dead by the glory of the Father, even so we also should walk in newness of life. For if we have been planted together in the likeness of his death, we shall be also in the likeness of his resurrection: Knowing this, that our old man is crucified with him, that the body of sin might be destroyed, that henceforth we should not serve sin" Rom 6:4-6.

Quoting John 20:26, the pope says that Jesus appeared to the disciples on **Sun**day, but he missed the count, because 8 days after He appeared to them for the first time, was a Monday. There is no way that from **Sun**day, if you count 8 days it will fall on Sunday again.

In section **23** he calls Saturday "the Jewish Sabbath." For me, that was news, because the Bible always refers to it as "the Sabbath of the Lord your God." Never in the Scriptures it is called the Jewish Sabbath. At least in this section he wrote: "Some communities observed the Sabbath while also celebrating **Sun**day... Moreover, there have always been groups within Christianity which observe both the Sabbath and **Sun**day as "two brother days," which would imply that there was confusion in the church. This is important to notice because that is an evidence that Sunday observance did not come from the authority of the Bible, but from the pagan influences and crept slowly into the church and it took a while to make the transition from one day to the other. This he admits in section 63: "Christians, called as they are to proclaim the liberation won by the blood of Christ, felt that they had the authority to transfer the meaning of the Sabbath to the day of the Resurrection."

Regarding the real origin of **Sun**day, he wrote in section 27: "Wise pastoral intuition suggested to the Church the Christianization of the notion of Sunday as "the day of the **sun**," which was the Roman name for the day and which is retained in some modern languages (in English **Sun**day and in German **Sonn**tag- see next paragraph). This was in order to draw the faithful away from the seduction of cults which worshipped the sun, and to direct the celebration of the day to Christ, humanity's true "sun". Writing to the pagans, Saint Justin uses the language of the time to note that Christians gather together "on the day named after the sun." What an excuse! A pagan day was Christianized in order to attract pagans to the church and keep "the faithful" in.

Before I continue, I just want to mention that in two ancient languages, the word for Sunday means literally "day of the sun": Dies Solis (Latin) and hemera heliu (Greek). Also, in India, Sunday is Ravivar. It is based on Ravi-Vedic the god of the sun. In Dutch, the word is zondag, which also means day of the sun (*Encyclopedia Mythica*). The Japanese word for Sunday is nichiyoobi and means also day of the sun.

Now lets go back to the pope's letter. Without a doubt, the pope is preparing the soil for the persecution of those that will object to the enactment of **Sun**day laws. In section 47 he wrote: "the Church had to make explicit the <u>duty</u> to attend Sunday Mass: more often than not, this was done in the form of exhortation, but at times the Church had to resort to specific canonical precepts. This was the case in a number of local Councils from the fourth century onwards (as at the Council of Elvira of 300, which <u>speaks not of an obligation but of penalties</u> after three absences) and most especially from the sixth century onwards (as at the Council of Agde in 506). These decrees of local Councils led to a universal practice, the obligatory character of which was taken as something quite norMalachi"

"The Code of Canon Law of 1917 for the first time gathered this tradition into a universal law. The present Code reiterates this, saying that 'on Sundays and other holy days of obligation the faithful are bound to attend Mass.' This legislation has normally been understood as entailing a <u>grave obligation</u>: this is the teaching of the Catechism of the Catholic Church, and it is easy to understand why if we keep in mind how vital Sunday is for the Christian life."

In section 64 the pope wrote on the first government law to observe the first day of the week: "Only <u>in the fourth century</u> did <u>the civil law of the Roman Empire recognize the weekly recurrence, determining that on 'the day of the **sun**' the judges, the people of the cities and the various trade corporations would not work.</u>" In Section 66, he adds: "In this matter, my predecessor Pope Leo XIII in his Encyclical Rerum Novarum spoke of **Sun**day rest as a worker's right which **the State must guarantee**." "In our own historical context there remains the obligation to ensure that everyone can enjoy the freedom, rest and relaxation which human dignity requires, together with the associated religious, family, cultural and interpersonal needs which are difficult to meet if there is no guarantee of at least one day of the week on which people can both rest and celebrate." In section 67 he claims the help of the state: "Therefore, also in the particular circumstances of our own time, Christians will naturally <u>strive to ensure</u> that <u>civil legislation</u> <u>respects their **duty** to keep **Sun**day holy</u>. In any case, they are obliged in conscience to arrange their <u>**Sun**</u>day rest in a way which allows them to take part in the Eucharist, refraining from work and activities which are incompatible with the sanctification of the Lord's Day, with its characteristic joy and necessary rest for spirit and body." Legislation?

That is not Jesus' style at all. It sounds just like what the Bible says in Revelation 13, that the beast "<u>causeth</u> all, both small and great, rich and poor, free and bond, to receive a mark in their right hand, or in their foreheads." The word "causeth" indicates a forced action. People have to accept the mark (like a cow's brand) or else. That brand indicates ownership. It is going to be difficult, but you have to make a choice. "<u>Choose you this day whom ye will serve</u>" (Joshua 24:15). "<u>Harden not your hearts</u>," says Paul 3 times to the Hebrews 3:8,15 & 4:7). Listen to the voice of the Lord and learn to live by faith. God is going to provide for all of our needs. He provided for Elijah, when He sent a bird with food for the prophet, He multiplied the food for the widow, her son, and the prophet. Centuries before that, <u>He provided</u> for the Israelites in the desert. "Behold, the LORD'S hand is not shortened, that it cannot save; neither his ear heavy, that it cannot hear" Isaiah 59:1. <u>God will provide and will protect you from any evil because He loves you dearly and you are precious to His eyes.</u>

It comes to my mind the story of Jacob and his older twin brother Esau. In ancient Middle Eastern culture, when a father died, the oldest son received a double portion of the inheritance. One day Esau went hunting and returned tired and very hungry. His brother was cooking lentils. Oh, they smelled so good! Esau asked for a plateful of them and was asked to give up his birthright in exchange, to which he agreed. He sold his birth right for a meal. Likewise, many will accept the mark of the beast over a loaf of bread instead of trusting God to supply for them in their time of need. Our faith in God will be put to the test an we must be found faithful to the end.

The late Dr. Samuel Bacchiocchi, who obtained his doctorate degree at the Catholic Gregorian University in Rome, wrote to several people: "While in Rome I contacted La Sala Stampa - the Press Office of the Vatican as well as the office of the official Vatican paper *L'OSSERVATORE ROMANO.* "I specifically asked if Pope John Paul II has been discussing further plans for implementing **Sun**day observance. Both offices has told me that for the past three months since the release of the Pastoral Letter Dies Domini, practically every **Sun**day, after reciting the 'angelus (a devotional prayer made 3 times daily to commemorate the Annunciation),' the Pope has consistently urged the faithful to rediscover the importance of **Sun**day." Why not invite people to discover the sweet character of Jesus our Savior instead?

According to Bacchiocchi, the reason given by the Catholic hierarchy for such **Sun**day legislation, is "the need to strengthen the family and the need for people to think beyond the material values for at least one day a week." Commendable excuse, but if it's not what the Bible requires from us, why keep the wrong day? Why talk about doing legislation to force its observance?

SUNDAY IN THE BIBLE

Sunday is mentioned only 9 times in the Bible, and it is simply called the first day of the week. It is mentioned for the first time in Genesis 1:5, when God created the light. We see the others 8 occasions:

1) Mathew 28:1- says that the women went to the sepulcher.
2) Mark 16:2- says that the women went to the sepulcher.
3) Mark 16:9- says that Jesus appeared to Mary Magdalene
4) Luke 24:1- it says that the women went to the sepulcher. If you read this verse with the last of the previous chapter, it says that the followers of Jesus <u>kept Saturday according to the commandment</u> after His death.
5) John 20:1- says that Mary Magdalene went to the sepulcher.
6) Acts 20:6,7 & 8- is mentioned only in verse 7, but the context is very important to understand the situation. In verse 6 it says that Paul and his companions spent 7 days in that city. Verse 7 says that they had to depart the following day (morning). Verse 8 says that they had torches lit, something that indicates that the meeting was at night. According to the Bible, the day starts with the obscure part or the sun set (Gen. 1:5; Lev. 23:32). The custom of Paul was keeping Saturday (Acts 17:2,4; 18:1-4,11 - in Corinth he kept 78 Saturdays, since he stayed one and a half years). What happened was that Paul kept Saturday with them and, as he had so much to teach them, extended his meeting until after the sunset, until the first hours of the **Sun**day (in what we now call Saturday night). With respect to parting the bread, Acts says that the believers were parting the bread in the houses (2:42), something which seems to indicate that it was a form of sharing a food, more than the service of

36

the communion of the Lord. It was in this case, as in others, probably a Christian fellowship meeting. If parting the bread makes a day holy, I could propose to keep Thursday, for it was on that day that Jesus established the communion service.

7) 1 Corinthians 16:1,2- Simply speaks in putting apart a quantity of money for the poor in Jerusalem. After giving the tithes and offerings during Saturday, the believers could calculate how much they could give for support to their impoverished brothers. Don't forget the 78 Saturdays that are mentioned in chapter 18 that the Corinthians kept with Paul.

8) John 20:26 - This verse indicates the reason why the disciples were gathered when Jesus was resurrected: ***FOR FEAR*** of the Jews; not to adore or to worship Jesus.

If the fact that Jesus appeared to His followers on **Sun**day indicates that that day is holy, we should also observe Monday, since Jesus appeared also that day to His disciples (John 20:26- eight days after Sunday is Monday).

The above-cited passages are concentrated, not in worshipping Jesus, but in what his followers were doing that day. They did not even believe that Jesus was risen from the dead.

All sincere Christian must apply the following questions to these passages:

1) Does the passage says that Jesus changed the day of rest? **NO!** He did not change the law (Mat. 5:17-19).

2) Does the passage say that **Sun**day is sacred? **NO!**

3) Does the passage say that Jesus sanctified **Sun**day? **NO!**

4) Does the passage say that the disciples changed the day of rest? **NO!** The disciples were mere men and could not do away with a commandment from God himself!

5) Does the passage order Me to keep **Sun**day? **NO!**

6) Does the passage say that Jesus went to the church or synagogue on **Sun**day? **NO!** The Scripture says that the custom of Jesus was to go to the synagogue on Saturday (Luke 4:16).

NAMES SUM

Before considering the following section, it is good to mention that in ancient times, some nations had the custom of assigning numerical value to the letters of the names and then to analyze the result. That usage is alluded to in Revelation 13:18: "Here is wisdom. Who has since, intelligence, <u>calculate</u> the number of the beast, that <u>its number is the one which form the letters of the name of a man</u>, and the number of the beast is six hundred sixty and six" (Spanish Catholic version of Torres- Amat). The Living Bible translates the passage this way: "Here is a puzzle that calls for careful thought to solve it. Let those who are able, interpret this code: <u>the numerical values of the letters in his name add to 666</u>." The Scriptures also present cases in which the name of a person is actually a title (as the case of Rabshakeh in Isaiah 36). Soon, we will analyze a series of titles, all related (coincidence?) with a large power on the earth, but first, we need to see what it means with: "the one, which has intelligence". Job says that wise is he that fears God (Job 28:28). Solomon says that the fear of God must induce us to keep His commandments (Eccles. 12:13). Daniel 12 speaks of the wise that teach justice as the only ones that understand. According to Roman 5:18,19: justice = obedience. From this we can deduct that only those who keep the Ten Commandments can understand the prophecies clearly. If you are sincere and want to understand all the prophecies from the Bible, keep ALL the Commandments first (you can only accomplish this if you are united with Jesus. (see John 15:1-5). Without Him you can do nothing.

TITLES THAT ADD TO 666

Before we analyze the titles or names, I want to mention that if we add the first 6 letters in the Latin alphabet that have a numerical value, the sum will be 666 (six is number of imperfection, represents man, in contrast with 7, which is the number that represents perfection and represents God). The letters are I=1, V=5, X=10, L=50, C=100, D=500. In ancient times the numeral 1,000 was written "CIO," with the "O" being shaped by two opposite "C's." The use of the M for 1,000 is from more recent use. The U and the V have the same value.

1) Teitan= Satan (ancient Greek).

τ	300
ε	5
ι	10
τ	300
α	1
ν	50
=	666

> Satan is the originator of the revolt against God, and the invisible head of the mystery of iniquity. In the same way as Christ dwells with his people and is their king, thus also Satan's dwelling is in Babylon.

Note: Daniel 7:25 mentions a power that is going against God, persecutes His people and changes His law. The meaning of the word "against" in Hebrew, describes one that appears to be on the side of God, but in reality is a constant traitor. Revelation 17:4 describes that same power having in its hand wine of fornication, that is nothing else than the mix of the truth of God with the error of paganism. What is that wine?-her false doctrines. She has given to the world a false Sabbath instead of the Sabbath of the fourth commandment, and has repeated the falsehood that Satan first told Eve in Eden--the natural immortality of the soul. Many errors she has spread far and wide, "But in vain they do worship me, **teaching for doctrines the commandments of men**" (Matthew 15:9).

Now we will expose that power that pretends to be a Christian church:

2) Romiit= Roman kingdom (Hebrew).

r	200	It is undeniable the fact that the Catholic Church is a great kingdom, and above all, calls itself holy mother, Catholic, apostolic and <u>Roman</u>.
o	6	
m	40	
i	10	"For the first seventeen hundred years of the papacy, then, and in a very real sense, it could fairly be said that the Pope was Rome, and Rome was the Pope." Malachi Martin *The Keys of this* Blood, page 118
i	10	
t	400	
=	666	

Romiti, or the Roman Man is:

R	200
o	6
m	40
i	10
t	400
i	<u>10</u>
=	666

3) Latin basileia = Latin kingdom (Greek).

λ	30	Both the Roman empire and the Catholic church, are Latin kingdoms and Latin is the official language of romanism.
α	1	
τ	300	
ι	10	
ν	50	

β	2
α	1
σ	200
ι	10
λ	30
ε	5
ι	10
α	1
=	666

4) Italika ekklesia-- Italian church (Greek).

ι	10
τ	300
α	1
λ	30
ι	10
κ	20
α	1
ε	5
κ	20
κ	20
λ	30
η	8
σ	200
ι	10
α	1
=	666

The Catholic Church has its headquarters in Italy, from where it masters the world, as says in Rev. 17:18. Therefore, it is clear that the Italian church is not what pretends to be, but it fulfils the prophecy regarding the antichrist.

Note: the ETA, transliterated as an e with accent, has a value of 8, without it, it is transliteration of the epsilon and it is worth 5. This is only applied to the titles in Greek.

5) Lateinos = Latin speaking man (Greek).

λ	30
α	1
τ	300
ε	5
ι	10
ν	50
ο	70
ς	200
=	666

It is a very old custom that the pope speaks in Latin in the meetings and councils before the cardinals. The papal bulls are also written in Latin.

Below will be analyzed some titles of the "Latin speaking man."

6) Dux cleri -captain of the clergy (Latin).

D	500
u	5
x	10
C	100
l	50
e	0
r	0
i	1
=	666

This is one of the tittles with which the pope is known, as leader of the clergy (priestly Catholic class).

7) Vicarius Filii Dei = Vicar of the Son of God (Latin).

V	5
i	1
c	100
a	0
r	0
i	1
u	5
s	0
F	0
i	1
l	50
i	1
i	1
D	500
e	0
i	1
=	666

The only Vicarius or representative that Jesus left on the earth was the Holy Spirit, the one who is God (Jn.14:26; Acts 5:3,5). When the papacy is applied this title, it is fulfilling the prophecy that indicated that the antichrist will make itself God (2Tes.2:3,4). Pope Leo XIII declared "we occupy on this earth the place of God Almighty" (The Great Encyclical Letters of Leo XIII, Page 164). "The title of the Pope of Rome is Vicarius Filii Dei and if you take the letters of his title which represent Latin numerals and add them together they come to 666." *Our Sunday Visitor*, Nov. 15, 1914. The word "Anti" in Greek means one that takes the place of another or that is a substitute. Vicarius is, likewise, according to the *American Heritage Dictionary*, a substitute, thus antichrist is a substitute of Christ and when the pope claims to be the vicar of Christ is just admitting to be the antichrist. Antichrist = Vicarius Filli Dei.). Pope John Paul II wrote in *Crossing the threshold of Hope.* "The Pope is considered the man on earth who **represents the Son of God**, who 'takes the place' of the Second Person of the omnipotent God of the Trinity." The title Vicarius Filii Dei applied to the pope is found in Lucius Ferraris, *Prompta Bibliotheca* on the entry Papa (pope).

Modern Catholics deny the use of the triple crown with the title Vicarius Filii Dei, but there are many witnesses' accounts of the existence of such title of authority.

Let's read what a Catholic publication has to say about this: *"What are the letters supposed to be in the Pope's crown, and what do they signify, if anything?*

"The letters inscribed in the Pope's mitre are these: *Vicarius Filii Dei*, which is the Latin for the Vicar of the Son of God. Catholics hold that the church, which is a visible society, must have a visible head. Christ, before His ascension into heaven, appointed St. Peter to act as His representative. Upon the death of Peter the man who succeeded to the office of Peter as Bishop of Rome, was recognized as the head of the Church. Hence to the Bishop of Rome, as head of the Church, was given the title 'Vicar of Christ.'

"Enemies of the Papacy denounce this title as a malicious assumption. But the Bible informs us that Christ did not only give His Church authority to teach, but also to rule. Laying claim to the authority to rule in Christ's spiritual kingdom, in Christ's stead, is not a whit more malicious than laying claim to the authority to teach in Christ's name. And this every Christian minister does." April 18th, 1915 edition of *Our Sunday Visitor*.

The above comments are wrong because: a) Jesus left the Holy Spirit to be in his place (John 16:7), B) Jesus is the head (1 Corinthians 11:3; Ephesians 1:22; 4:15;5:23; Colossians 1:18;2:10), c) Peter is not the Rock; is Jesus (1 Corinthians 10:4).

8) Ludovicus= vicarious chief of the court of Rome (Latin).

L	50
u	5
d	500
o	0
v	5
i	1
c	100
u	5
s	0
=	666

9) Paulo V Vice Deo- Paulo V vicar of God (Latin). The pope that adopted this title governed between the years 1605-1621.

P	0
a	0
u	5
l	50
o	0
V	5
V	5
i	1
c	100
e	0

D 500
e 0
o 0
= 666

10) **IOANES PAVLVS SECVNDO**=John Paul II

I 1
o 0
a 0
n 0
e 0
s 0

P 0
a 0
u 5
l 50
u 5
s 0

S 0
e 0
c 100
u 5
n 0
d 500
o 0
= 666

11) Vicarius generali Dei in terris= general vicar of God on earth
(Latin).

V= 5
i= 1
c= 100
a= 0
r= 0
i= 1
u= 5
s= 0

G= 0
e= 0
n= 0
e= 0
r= 0
a= 0
l= 50
i= 1

D= 500
e= 0
i= 1

i= 1
n= 0

T= 0
e= 0
r= 0
r= 0
i= 1
s= 0
666

The following two titles have a great relationship to the untruthful rest day and the origin of its observance:

12) Stur - was the secret God of the mystery-religion of Babylon. This word is Aramaic and it should be pronounced satur.

S = 200
t = 60
u = 400
r = + 6
666

The Bible calls Catholicism Babylon and it was precisely this group which imposed the observance of the day of the sun as rest day in the council of Laodicea. Catholicism is nothing else than the religion - mystery of Stur or Nimrod (=rebel) resuscitated. From Stur was derived Saturn, called son of the sun by the Romans. By Persian influence, the Romans were worshipping the sun on **Sun**days.

Archeological evidence has been found that shows that the adoration to the sun - god was important part of the religion - mystery of Babylon. The untruthful church of chapter 17 of Revelation, presented as an impure woman, is called <u>mystery</u>, Babylon the great - and those which have heard the rosary (the author grew up with it)- have heard several times the word mystery. We know about these mysteries among many proclaimed by the Catholic Church:

- The mystery of the Church
- The mystery of faith

From the rosary, we find mysteries from beginning to end:

The 5 Joyful Mysteries

- The *Mystery* of the Annunciation
- The *Mystery* of the Visitation
- The *Mystery* of the Birth of the Lord
- The *Mystery* of the Presentation in the Temple
- The *Mystery* of Finding Jesus in the Temple

The 5 Sorrowful Mysteries

- The *Mystery* of the Agony in the Garden
- The *Mystery* of the Scourging at the Pillar
- The *Mystery* of the Crowning with Thorns
- The *Mystery* of Jesus carrying his cross
- The *Mystery* of the Crucifixion

The 5 Glorious Mysteries

- The *Mystery* of the Resurrection
- The *Mystery* of the Ascension of Our Lord
- The *Mystery* of the Descent of the Holy Spirit
- The *Mystery* of the Assumption of the Blessed Virgin
- The *Mystery* of the Coronation of the Blessed Virgin as Queen of Heaven

13) The tables that follow were on the back of some amulets used by priest worshipers of the sun. Any line of these vertical tables added vertically or horizontally, gives as a result 111. If this number is multiplied by the quantity of vertical or horizontal lines (6), gives as product 666. If all the numbers from 1 to 36 are added, this also gives 666. Here are the tables:

6	32	3	34	35	1
7	11	27	28	8	30
19	14	16	15	23	24
18	20	22	21	17	13
25	29	10	9	26	12
36	5	33	4	2	31

1	32	34	3	35	6
30	8	27	28	11	7
20	24	15	16	13	23
19	17	21	22	18	14
10	26	12	9	29	25
31	4	2	33	5	36

Stur was the secret name of Nimrod, founder of Babylon and its first king (Gen.10:8-12). After his death he was venerated as a god.

"She (the church) took the pagan **Sun**day and converted it to the Christian **Sun**day... And thus, pagan **Sun**day, devoted to balder [other name for the sun-god] became the Christian **Sun**day devoted to Jesus" (Catholic World, March of 1894, Page 809).

The book Unfolding the Revelation, by R.A. Anderson, contains photos and more information about these amulets in page 126.

Though the minds are affected by a supernatural somnolence such as the one that engulfed the disciples the night of the arrest of Jesus, it is possible to find evidence of the worship of the sun-god in modern liturgy:

1) Head shaved in round that is used by the Roman leaders and that it was specifically forbidden by God in Leviticus 19:27 ("You shall not round the corners of your heads,"), because it was a practice of the followers of Nimrod.
2) The round form of the communion bread (when Jesus parted the bread, it did not remain round. Try it at home, please) it is a copy of the communion bread that the Egyptian priests were using to adore their sun-god Amon - ra.
3) The black priestly clothes are only an imitation of the clothes that the priests of Baal were using, in whose service, the sun was largely honorable. The priestly clothes that are used while offering the mass, were the same ones used by the Roman priests in their idolatrous service.
4) Nowhere in the Bible is presented Jesus or any of His disciples with a halo on their heads. This usage had its origin in the halo that Circe, the Roman goddess daughter of the sun, had over her head.

As we have seen, the 666 has to do with the observance of **Sun**day as well as with the power that changed it for the real day of rest. Now we will analyze the language in which the New Testament was written originally. There are only two words in the Biblical Greek whose sum is 666. They have been related to Catholicism during all its history, since by thus to say it, describe two of its principal characteristics.

14) Paradosis = tradition (Greek).

π= 80	"You break the commandment of God [Saturday] for your <u>tradition</u> [**Sun**day]" (Mathew 15:2,3). "We Catholics...have precisely the authority for keeping **Sun**day holy instead of Saturday... we followed the <u>tradition</u> in this matter" (Clifton Tracts, volume 4, Page 15). In his Dies Domini letter, pope John Paul II wrote: "The spiritual and pastoral riches of Sunday, as it has been handed on to us by <u>tradition</u>, are truly great."
α= 1	
ρ= 100	
α= 1	
δ= 4	
o= 70	

σ=   200
ι=   10
ς=   +200
      666

15) euporia=wealth (Greek)- according to how it appears in
    Acts 19:25. In Revelation 18 it is used the word emporoi
    (vers.3,11,15 and 23) that is translated merchants and comes
    from the same root as euporia.

ε=   5
υ=   400
π=   80
ο=   70
ρ=   100
ι=   10
α =   1
      666

As Ralph Woodrow wrote in his excellent book, *Babylon
Religious Mystery Ancient and Modern* (page 160), "The wealth, that
characterized the Babylon of Revelation 17, corrupted the honesty
(there were occasions in which the ecclesiastic charges were sold) and
the tradition corrupted the doctrine, making it wine of fornication."

16) Benediktos, the name of Pope Benedict adds up to 666:

β= 2
ε = 5
ν = 50
ε = 5
δ= 4
ι= 10
κ= 20
τ= 300
o= 70
ς= 200
666

Catholics have tried to fabricate ways to come up with other names' sum, but it had resulted in falsehoods, since they force the sum, in order to distract the attention from Vicarius Filii Dei totaling 666. The following 3 paragraphs are an example:

"Some will suggest that the book of Revelation was written only for those living at the time, and that 666 most probably applies to Caesar Nero, who ruled Rome from 54 to 68 AD, rather than someone from latter centuries. This point of view, which suggests Revelation was historic rather than prophetic, is known as *preterism*, and is commonly held by the Catholic Church. So, just how is Nero linked to 666?

"The preterist takes a relatively uncommon form of Nero's name, Nero Caesar or Caesar Nero, and adds an "n", resulting in Neron Caesar. Next the Latin is transliterated into Aramaic, resulting in *nrwn qsr*, which when using the numeric equivalent of the letters, then adds up to 666 as follows:

Nun	=	50
Resh	=	200
Waw	=	6
Nun	=	50
Qoph	=	100
Samech	=	60
Resh	=	200
		666

"There is a problem though with the above calculation. According to the rules of Jewish numerology, known as *gematria*, when the letter Nun appears a second time in a word, it is known as a "Final", and takes the value of 700.* So to be precise, NRWN QSR actually adds up to 1316 and not 666."

*Source: Behind Numerology, by Shirley Blackwell Lawrence, copyright 1989, published by Newcastle Publishing Co., Inc., North Hollywood, California, ISBN 0-87877-145-X, page 41. As quoted on the Internet site of Michael Scheifler (http://www.aloha.net/~mikesch).

Some say that the number in Revelation 13 is 616, not 666 based on some ancient Bible manuscripts. However, Irenæus [A.D. 120-202] attributes the 616 to only a copyist error (*Against Heresies: Book V Chapter XXX.*). *Ibid.*

I think that this will be a good place to mention that although a lot of emphasis is placed on the <u>number</u> of the beast, it does not constitute the <u>mark</u> of the beast. In other words, they are not one and the same thing. I often see illustrations of people with the 666 tattooed to their foreheads but this is a misconception.

A NEW WORLD ORDER

Time magazine, in the December 11th, 1989 issue mentioned former President George Bush's (the father) vision of a united world: "We have before us the opportunity to forge a new world order in which a credible United Nations can use its peacekeeping role to fulfill the promise and the vision of the UN founders."

Along that line of thought, President Bill Clinton had expressed his enthusiasm for the idea based on the belief that it will finally bring peace to this world.

Since 1987 the UN budget had increased 1,000%, with the United States Government being its mayor contributor.

Another person who favored world unity, James Warhorg, from the counsel of Foreign Relations said in 1919 "we shall have world government, whether or not we like it. The question is whether world government will be achieved by consent or by conquest." It is said that the personnel named by both presidents, Bush and Clinton are members of that counsel or the Trilateral Commission. In the 1996 elections, all three candidates belonged to that commission. They are very powerful and they want to have the control of all the laws enacted in the nation. They want the leaders of the USA to follow the commission's agenda.

Malachi Martin, a Jesuit and Vatican insider, in his book *Keys of This Blood,* page 492, says that the pope insists that "men have no reliable hope of creating a viable geopolitical system, unless it is on the basis of Roman Catholic Christianity."

This dream of a united world was initiated by Nimrod, not too long after the flood. Nimrod "began to be a mighty one in the earth. He was a mighty hunter before the LORD: wherefore it is said, Even as Nimrod the mighty hunter before the LORD. And the beginning of his kingdom was **Babel**, and Erech, and Accad, and Calneh, in the land of Shinar. Out of that land went forth Asshur, and builded Nineveh, and the city Rehoboth, and Calah, And Resen between Nineveh and Calah: the same is a great city" (Genesis 10:9-11). He built an empire, dreaming to have the whole planet under his control. His ambition was in direct opposition with the order given by God to Adam and Noah to disperse and fill the earth.

There have been 4 great empires in the world: Babylon, Medo-Persia, Greece, and Rome. After that, there are no more world empires prophesied. The prophet Daniel said to king Nebuchednezar that the kingdoms will try to unite "but they shall not cleave one to another, even as iron is not mixed with clay" (Daniel 2:43). Charlemagne, Charles V, Napoleon, Hitler, Mussolini are the names of ambitious men that tried to conquer the world, defying these 8 words, but did not succeed. The new world order will probably exist for a very short time, because during the sixth plague (see Revelation 16), the nations would cease to give support to the beast, in order to prepare the way for the kings of the East (Jesus and his angels, since He will come from that direction), but they shall not cleave one to another, even as iron is not mixed with clay.

ECONOMICAL CHANGES

From Europe, we have people pushing the Common Market as a way to achieve the unity in the continent that mighty armies couldn't keep for long. In May 1998, France started the production of coins that are valid in many European countries. We know the new money as the euro. The first countries that joined, with 350 million people (USA has 313), were: Austria, Belgium, Finland, France, Germany, Ireland, Italy, Luxembourg, Portugal, Spain and The Netherlands. The new currency also circulates within Vatican City, as well as other small European principalities such as Monaco and San Marino and even former members of the former USSR.

Under the terms of the monetary agreement adopted by the nations of the European Union, the new currency is uniform in all states, and does not carry the standard or emblem of any particular country, although some nations are trying to personalize theirs.

This agreement was supposed to ease trade barriers and decrease tax rates. The commercial transactions are faster and businesses save money. It is easier to trade and less complicated for the consumer to make purchases.

In *Business Week*, May 4,1998, there was an article that said that these group of nations "will be the world's second-largest economy and generate nearly 20%" of this planet's "total gross domestic product." The unified Europe is expected to command world power status.

Another big change in the economic world is the mergers and especially the mega-mergers. Big and small companies in different industries are combining their capitals in a desperate effort to survive. There is what is called a "merger Frenzy" that is transcending even countries frontiers. Banks are consolidating, not only merging. Old foes are now in blissful marriage, in an effort to control bigger markets, reduce cost, improve productivity and eliminate the threat presented by smaller firms that are sprouting everywhere. The stock market is seeing a superb growth, but I think that this is just an artificial progress, that could be destined in the end to collapse and bring economical ruin.

All these economical alliances are just a rehearsal to make it easier to accomplish the political union of different countries and create an artificial peace, so the way will be paved for the papacy to take control.

In different parts of the world, there is a big preoccupation for the increase of crimes and illegal activity like: kidnappings, bank robberies, drug addiction, prostitution, etc. There have been hundreds of ideas proposed to finish with all these maladies, but there is one that stands out way over all the others: the elimination of money. A cashless society where people can not rob a bank because they will not get any money from doing so. We all know about the proliferation of cashless electronic transactions that happen all around us every day. ATM and credit cards, wired money transactions, computer shopping and transfer of money over the internet, etc. Every day at least 6 trillion dollars change hands electronically. My check goes to the bank and I have plastic to represent that money. You can use your ATM card at the bank machine to buy among other things (according to *USA Weekend*, Oct. 30-Nov. 1, 1998):

- Stamps
- Airline tickets
- Pre-paid telephone cards
- Coupons for dry cleaners

In the experimental stage:

- Pay your tithe and give offerings at your church
- Will ask if you want to open a money market account, apply for a car loan, etc.

Time Magazine, in April 27,1998 published an article that described the use of cybermoney. It mentioned the most recent banks megamergers, quoting Banc One Chairman as saying that in the future, "the industry would have just five or six major banks." It continued saying that MasterCard has invested millions in the development of an E-cash system that they call Mondex. The users would be issued a smart card, with embedded microchips "that can store not only electronic dollars but also five other types of currency, an abbreviated medical history and even a personalized electronic "key" that can open everything from your apartment to your office." The cards can be personalized, so they would be what they called life-style cards.

What is being proposed is a card that would substitute your cash, credit cards, ATM cards, identification cards, your insurance and vital data. As *Time* Magazine puts it: "one card, or one chip, with your life on it" (*Time*, April 27, 1998, page 51).

This electronic cash, also known as smart cash, <u>will be traceable</u>. This means that you can be able to send money to a member of your family and <u>find out how he spent it</u>. When you send the money, it will be encoded into digits. Again, *Time* Magazine says: "Your daughter can store the money any way she wants- on her laptop, on a debit card, even (in the not too distant future) <u>on a chip implanted under her skin</u>. And, perhaps best of all, you can program the money to be spent only in specific ways. You might instruct some of the digits to go for books, some for food and some for movies. Unless you pass along a few digits that can be cashed at the local pub, she'll have to find someone else to buy the drinks" (Ibid). My question is: how the people in the jungle will use that microchip? Will they use a scanner to trade bananas for skins?

There also have been lots of speculative declarations of Christians that fear that this will bring the mark of the beast, because it had been said that in order to buy or sell under this new system, the person will have to have a mark either on the forehead or on the right hand. Nothing is farther from the truth, since this is just a way to blindfold the Christians so that they would not identify the real mark of the beast, which is the keeping of **Sun**day. I am not saying that this system it is not going to be used. I think that it will be used and that eventually it will be the way how those in power will try to seduce the people to receive (accept in their minds) the mark of the beast. It will be an issue of faith and loyalty. "If you keep Sunday, we give you this mark and you can keep buying groceries for your family. You care about your family, don't you?"

Loss of privacy is an issue that worries many people. Right now, the strip on driver's licenses used on many states is capable of carrying a lot of private information- and not only your address. At the present time the amount of data contained there is limited but a lot more could be added in the future. The government, mostly for fear of what happened on Sept 11th, 2001, is collecting information on phone conversations, internet activities, etc. Nobody knows what is being done with that information.

There are even talks about programming the black boxes (better know as Event Data Recorders because they let police know what happened just before an accident) found in some vehicles (similar to the ones found in airplanes) so they can track where drivers go. Some rental car companies use them to know if the renters had gone out of the state where the vehicle was rented. If your vehicle's owners manual says: "Your vehicle is equipped with a crash sensing and diagnostic module, which records information about the air bag system..." it has a black box. As you can see, the language is meant to conceal the fact that the box is there.

The map websites like Yahoo Maps, Google Maps and others are presenting aerial maps that show with detail your whole property and the neighbors'. You can even see what shape is your neighbors' pool, even though he might have a tall fence to protect their privacy. Well, there is no such thing as privacy any more.

WHO IS THE WINNER IN ALL THIS?

As I said at the beginning of this study, I think that this is only a distraction that Satan and his followers, the popular preachers, mostly the TV and radio evangelists, are using to keep their church members scared and sending them money. When people are scared they are not too attached to their money. These preachers know all the money that the Roman power got from the people in the Middle Ages when the coffers of the churches were full for fear of going to hell or purgatory. The message of Jesus was: "… Repent: for the kingdom of heaven is at hand" (Mat 4:17). According to Jesus, the reason to repent was that God was opening the door of heaven, a second chance to reconcile with God. The message of today's popular preachers is a gospel of fear: "repent or you will go to hell." This other message is asking people to repent because [God] is opening the door of hell.

The majority of these ministries are just bu$ine$$e$, just as Paul described them in 2 Corinthians 2:17: "For we are not like the rest, adulterating the word of God **for gain**…" The Spanish Valera 1977 revision says: "For we are not like the majority, trafficking with the word of God." I heard a TV preacher asking for listeners to send him a thousand dollar donation each. Can you imagine if he gets a thousand people to send him such an offering? You will surely find him either in Cancun, Jamaica, or Hawaii the following Sunday.

These preachers are not at all representing Jesus, who didn't even own a pillow to rest his head. Prestige and money motivate the popular preachers, and they are no better than a wolf shepherding sheep. They are just like the leaders of ancient Israel: "**Her priests have violated my law**, and have profaned mine holy things: they have put no difference between the holy and profane, **neither have they showed difference between the unclean and the clean**, and **have hid their**

59

eyes from my Sabbaths, and I am profaned among them. Her princes in the midst thereof are like wolves ravening the prey, to shed blood, and to destroy souls, <u>to get dishonest gain</u>." Ezekiel 22:26,27. Does this sound familiar? Today's preachers profane Saturday, their church members suffer health problems because they eat all kinds of unclean meats (they ignore Leviticus 11, and Psalm 89:34 where it says that God does not change his mind and Job 14:4 where says that nobody can get a clean thing out of an unclean and preachers take out of context the verse that says that everything is sanctified through prayer), and all those pastors and evangelists care about is to expand their business. These people don't realize that God will make them accountable for the loss of those souls that they are deceiving and keeping in darkness (see Ezekiel 33:6).

Unfortunately, the majority of these preachers will not recognize the truth, even though so many of them have recognized that there is not such a thing as *eternal* hell (as they teach it) or authority to keep holy other day than Saturday.

CHURCH AND STATE

Remember Nimrod? He was the head of both the church and state. Remember Nebuchadnezzar? In Daniel chapter 3 we can read that this king of Babylon made a statue and ordered everybody to worship it. He made an image of his nation, which in Daniel 7 was represented by a beast. So he made an image of the beast in those times. It resulted in <u>intolerance</u> of those that did not submit to the request of recognizing the authority of the absolute leader.

In the times of Jesus, when the state and religion were united, Jesus was crucified. During the dark ages, the church and the state were united also. This resulted in the killing of over 50 million Christians. That was <u>bigotry</u> to the extreme.

> "That the Church of Rome has shed more innocent blood than any other institution that has ever existed among mankind, will be questioned by no Protestant who has a competent knowledge of history." — W. E. H. Lecky, *History of the Rise and Influence of the Spirit of Rationalism in Europe*, (reprint: New York: Braziller, 1955), Vol. 2, pages. 40-45.

The Bible prophesies that in the time of the end, there will be another image of the beast being made. Like in the times of Daniel, it will be <u>also the result of the union of the church and the state</u>. It will be <u>the church using the power of the law to achieve its ecclesiastical plans and to bring about its agenda</u>.

Did you read the story about the student from a Catholic school that grew up to be a world leader? I am sure you have heard his name: Adolf Hitler. Frans Von Papen, a Jesuit, Hitler's mentor, wrote in his book: *My Conversations with Hitler*: "Hitler has put into practice the high ideals of the papacy". This statement was making reference to the death camps where the Jews were sent by the millions to be slaughtered.

This brings to mind the protest of the Jews over the sainthood cause of Eugenio Pacelli (Pope Pius XII) for his World War II policies. He blessed Hitler for his efforts in defending the interest of the church. Elected pope on the eve of WW II, he reigned from 1939-58. The ambassador of Israel to the Vatican, Aharon Lopez, wanted the sainthood process to be delayed at least 50 years. Jesuit Father Peter Gumpel, who has being working in the sainthood cause, called the request of the ambassador foolishness, and that by giving his opinion on this case, he went completely outside the competence of an ambassador. Father Peter Gumpel said that a beatification is strictly an internal affair of the Catholic Church. In other words, "we run the show, your job is to sit, watch, accept whatever we decide, so shut your mouth, we don't welcome opinions or inquiries." Here spoke the dragon with its characteristic arrogance.

There are comments that Pope Pius XII even went as far as naming Hitler protector of the church when he was exterminating the Jews. The pope, not wanting to stain his "Christian" reputation, pretended to be a humanitarian and worked in front of the journalists relieving the suffering caused by the war. After the Allied victory, however, many international groups and leaders criticized him for not doing enough to prevent the persecution and killing of the Jews. By not condemning the slaughter, he sided with the leaders of the genocide. Due to the pope's careless attitude, some Jewish groups have requested to put a moratorium in the above mentioned sainthood cause, arguing that more investigations are needed from the wartime period, but Rome is not willing to let the Jews check the records. Jewish groups have demanded a complete opening of the Vatican archives. The Vatican, which has published 12 lengthy volumes of documents from World War II, considers the matter closed. The reason presented is that the Vatican doesn't simply throw open the doors to its archives, because of the "sensitive nature of the contents." Could the nature of the contents be more sensitive than the suffering of the poor Jewish victims of the infamous killing of 6 million men, women and children of the race of Jesus? Could the problem be that those documents may uncover the involvement of the church leaders in the killing of Jews, money given to Hitler and then the disappearing of the war criminals?

What was the real motivation of Hitler and Mussolini? Both were Catholic soldiers, obeying orders from their superior. Europe saw for centuries the efforts of the crusaders going to Jerusalem to set that territory free from the Muslims. Wrong. The real and primary purpose was to exterminate the Jews. To expel the Muslims was secondary and I would say just a screen to cover the truth. Why wasn't the same effort put into setting other Catholic territories free from the followers of Mohammed (founder of the Islam)? Word War II was just another crusade to rid Europe from the Jews. That is why they were targeted in the first place. That is why there was such a genocide of six million people. There was a second motivation: to unify Europe to turn it over to the papacy, creating an empire where the Catholic Church would be supreme in authority, to please the pope. One thing that bothers me is that after years of reading Catholic books and documents, I have never found that either Hitler, or Mussolini was ever ex-communicated for their crimes in WW II.

Concerning the Vatican-German investments, Loftus and Aarons are quite clear in their book *The Secret War Against the Jews*:

"That the Vatican encouraged such investments and even donated money to Hitler himself cannot be denied. A German nun, Sister Pascalina, was present at its creation. In the early 1920s she was the housekeeper for Archbishop of the Vatican-Nazi connection . . . Eugenio Pacelli, then the papal nuncio in Munich. Sister Pascalina vividly recalls receiving Adolf Hitler late one night and watching the archbishop give Hitler a large amount of Church money."

For those that take their time to study history, they will find that the Catholic Church hierarchy, especially Eugenio Pacelli, before and after he became Pope Pius XII, aided the Nazis in many ways. Indeed, Pacelli and the Church played a central and active role in making Hitler the dictator of Germany. There was an intense campaign in churches reading a pastoral letter written by the German bishops urging Catholics to vote for Hitler (as in the USA most churches ask the members to vote Democrat).

In July 20, 1933 the Catholic Church, represented by Msgr. Eugenio Pacelli (the future Pope Pius XII) and the ultra-conservative Roman Catholic Von Papen, Hitler's Vice-Chancellor on behalf of

Nazi Germany, negotiated a concordat that granted rights to the church and simultaneously guaranteed the church's endorsement of the Nazi party. Article 16 contains the oath of allegiance of the bishops: *"I swear and vow to honor the constitutional government and to make my clergy honor it."* This concordat served to give legitimacy to the Nazi government, increasing Hitler's influence, destroying democracy- which made Pacelli and pope Pius XI very happy- and wide-opening the doors for the Holocaust. The Church and the State were in bed together.

After Germany's defeat in WWII, the allies started a hunt for war criminals. How could be possible for them to escape justice now? Here came into play what is known as the Ratline. It was the clandestine way how the Nazi criminals were smuggled out of Europe and given refuge in Argentina and other South American countries. The usual way to take them out from Germany and other European countries was to smuggle them as priests and monks. One of the supervisors of this reprehensible operation was Monsignor Giovanni Montini, who later became Pope Paul VI. The most common route was to go first to Italy, hide in monasteries and churches and then, with false passports provided by a self appointed Red Cross leader (Father Vilim Cecelja), they were shipped to South America. In Argentina, they established a colony with so many Germans, that became like a second Germany.

The Argentinean dictator Juan Domingo Perón, a faithful Catholic, received them with gladness, especially a man that had been accused of masterminding the torture and killing of thousands of innocent people during World War II in Bosnia. Over a million people were killed, deported to concentration camps and enslaved, for the sole crime of not being a Catholic (you probably have heard of the Croats, who are Catholics, and the Serbs, who are Orthodox).

This man's name was Ante Pavelic, leader of the Ustashi, described as a sadist mass murderer, who enjoyed torturing his victims. His followers delighted in destroying entire villages, torturing, raping, killing every man, woman and child that weren't Catholics. They always looked for every opportunity to have their pictures taken next to their victims with an opened abdomen, or carrying their heads down the streets of Zagreb, while showing a smile, or holding buckets full of eyes or other organs which they showed as trophies.

Ante used to brag before Hitler that he had finished with the problem of the Jews in his territory. He either killed them or sent them to the concentration camps. Some of the people that he persecuted were not Jews, but Orthodox Serbs and gypsies. They were butchered mercilessly. Now people see how the Serbs are fighting, and don't realize that they are taking revenge for their families that were killed for refusing to become Roman Catholics by force.

The Catholic leader of that territory was Archbishop Stepinac (later rewarded with a promotion to Cardinal), a person whose name has been on the Internet lately, because the Vatican wanted to make him a saint. The Vatican says that he has been *"maliciously defamed."* After the war was over, the government from Yugoslavia arrested and sentenced him to prison, but a worldwide campaign well orchestrated by the Vatican, got his early release, claiming that he was a "victim" of the communist party persecution.

These leaders were so cruel that it is said that even the Gestapo protected some Jews from falling into the hands of the Catholic Ustashi. Historians describe this particular war "an act of 'ethnic cleansing' before that hideous term came into vogue, it was an attempt to create a 'pure' Catholic Croatia by enforced conversions, deportations, and mass exterminations. So dreadful were the acts of torture and murder that even hardened German troops registered their horror. Even by comparison with the recent bloodshed in Yugoslavia at the time of writing, Pavelic's onslaught against the Orthodox Serbs remains one of the most appalling civilian massacres known to history" (John Cornwell, **Hitler's Pope: The Secret History of Pius XII** *page 249).* The Ustashi were always received as heroes in Rome, usually by Pope Pius XII (pope 1939-1958) himself and Assistant Secretary of State, Montini (1897-1978), who latter became Pope Paul VI (1963-1978). Of course the latter came to cover the tracks of the former. The aforementioned book adds in page 254: "Priests, invariably Franciscans, took a leading part in the massacres. Many, went around routinely armed and performed their murderous acts with zeal. A Father Bozidar Bralow, known for the machine gun that was his constant companion, was accused of performing a dance around the bodies of 180 massacred Serbs at Alipasin-Most. Individual Franciscans killed, set fire to homes, sacked villages, and laid waste the Bosnian countryside at the head of Ustashe bands. In September of

1941, an Italian reporter wrote of a Franciscan he had witnessed south of Banja Luka urging on a band of Ustashe with his crucifix." Priest, who were expected to represent Christ, manifested satanic intolerance and joined in the commission of crimes against humanity without showing even the slightest sign of remorse. I cannot find this behavior in the book of Acts. True, there were killings in the Old Testament, but those were of nations that sacrificed their own children. That approach was necessary because the cruel, loveless custom was spreading from nation to nation and was a cancer that needed to be extirpated. It even spread to the nation of Israel. In Yugoslavia neither the Serbs, nor the Jews, nor the Roma (gypsies) did such a thing; they loved their children. Their only crime was not being Catholic. That is what is coming to America and to the rest of the world once the imposition of Sunday as the day of rest becomes universal law.

Mussolini, the Italian leader during World War Two, was very well aware of the fact that what was going on was not as much a war to conquer more territory and make an empire, but a "holy war." In such an enterprise, Germany and Italy would try to cede the dominion to the pope. It was a 20th century resurrection of the Dark Ages persecution of anybody who did not conform to the state's chosen religion.

As mentioned previously, Perón, founder of Argentina's dominant party, encouraged several prominent Nazis to settle in his country. He was just answering the call from the Vatican to provide for them a safe haven, where they could escape from the tribunals in Europe. Among those prominent Nazis that found refuge in Argentina where "Adolf Eichmann, Franz Stangl (the commandant of Treblinka), Walter Rauff (the inventor of the 'mobile' gas chambers), Klaus Barbie (the 'Butcher of Lyons') and Ante Pavelic (the bloody dictator of Croatia)." From the cover of *UNHOLY TRINITY.* All of those names were in the papers in recent years particularly on the 50th anniversary of the trial of Eichmann, who was kidnapped by a Jewish spy in Argentina, brought to Israel for trial, and executed for his war crimes in 1962.

In 1999, to calm the claims for justice from the Jews, the then president of Argentina, Carlos Menem (a Catholic convert from Islam), named a commission to investigate the activities of the Nazis in his country. Initially, the investigation was supposed to last one year, but now it's going to be extended indefinitely, which will just provide more time to make people forget about the matter and ignore the past. What they are doing is waiting for the survivors from the concentration camps to die, because the younger generations will not pursue the matter with the same passion.

"Catholic countries were duty bound to do their part in furthering the Vatican interest. Part of that duty included providing safe haven for those sons of Mother Church whom she wished to protect in the pursuit of her great mission to create God's world on earth. Those in far-off Latin America were strategically located to best perform that service, and they did so." Dave Hunt, *A Woman Rides the Beast*, page 316. Non Catholics were persecuted, sent to jail, and executed in Columbia and other South American countries. God miraculously intervened to save many of his children so they could preserve and preach the truth. I met and developed friendships with some of these people that were sent to prison for preserving the truth of the Sabbath.

The church still tries to defend their leaders that cooperated with dictators, specially the communists. Pope Benedict XVI said in May 2006 that "We must guard against the arrogant claim of setting ourselves up to judge earlier generations who lived in different times and in different circumstances." In other words, he justifies cooperating with oppressing regimes if they put strain on the church leader.

CHURCH AND STATE IN USA AFTER WORLD WAR II

After the Second World War, the churches in America got very involved in political campaigns and demonstrations. Their pulpits were used by political candidates, union leaders, civil rights speakers, etc. They covered a wide range of subjects like desegregation, abortion, and others. There were Sundays when the preachers, instead of feeding the flock, sat to listen to a politician make a speech to gain votes from the congregation. In recent decades, the politicians have learned not to ignore the power of the clergy and the importance of courting the church members.

Describing the union of church and state, John declares that the second beast of Revelation 13, which represents United States (it is represented as a beast with horns as a lamb, indicating young age at the time when the other beast suffered its mortal wound in 1798 AD), will deceive "them that dwell on the <u>earth</u> by the means of those miracles which he had power to do in the sight of the beast; saying to them that dwell on the earth, that they should make an image to the beast, which had the wound by a sword, and did live. And <u>he had power to give life to the image of the beast</u>, that the image of the beast should both speak, and cause that as many as would not worship the image of the beast should be killed. And <u>he causeth all</u>, both small and great, rich and poor, free and bond, <u>to receive a mark</u> in their right hand, or in their foreheads: And that no man might buy or sell, save he that had the mark, or the name of the beast, or the number of his name" (Rev 13:14-17).

The imposition of the mark will have three aspects:

- Economical -The person can not buy or sell
- Religious -The person must have the mark
- Political – Whoever refuses the mark will be threatened with death

This power imposes the submission to the first beast of Revelation 13. It is going to be through legislation that the United States will force the people to accept the mark of the beast, and the rest of the nations will follow. There is no doubt that the nations of the world observe everything that happens in America with great interest. Although some nations are bitter enemies of the USA, many nations either envy or even imitate everything American.

The leaders of some countries are alarmed with the "Americanization" of their youth (rock music, dress, lifestyle, etc), and the trend indicates that people around the world are willing to imitate everything that is American. Business transactions are usually made in English, and the American dollar is the favorite currency in the World. American politicians are acting like "the police of the planet." A great number of nations have a constitution that is almost a copy of the American. In recent years, I have seen in the newspapers pictures of demonstrations in which the marchers upheld (not burned) American flags. A few years ago there was a demonstration in China where the young protesters clearly said that they wanted their country to change to copy America. The nations of this planet have the same problems that America has. They are looking up to the USA to see what the older brother is going to do so that they can also implement it.

Blue laws

In almost all the States of the Union, there are some enactments known as Blue Laws. This term was first used in 1781 to describe laws of the Puritan colony at New Haven, which were printed on blue paper (whether or not this is true, it's irrelevant), and is usually applied to laws in the US that regulate the opening of businesses and recreational activities on **Sun**day.

The dignitaries of church and state will unite to bribe, persuade, or compel all classes to honor the <u>Sun</u>day. The lack of divine authority will be supplied by oppressive enactments. Political corruption is destroying love of justice and regard for truth; and even in free America, rulers and legislators, in order to secure public favor, will yield to the popular demand for a law enforcing Sunday observance. Liberty of conscience, which has cost so great a sacrifice, will no longer be respected. Pope Pius IX, in his Encyclical letter from August 15, 1854 wrote: "The absurd and erroneous doctrines or ravings in defense of <u>liberty of conscience are a most pestilential error</u> — a pest, of all others, most to be dreaded in a state." In the soon-coming conflict we shall see exemplified the prophet's words: "**<u>The dragon was wroth with the woman, and went to make war with the remnant of her seed, which keep the commandments of God</u>**, and have the testimony of Jesus Christ." Revelation 12:17

ECUMENISM

Several books and articles have been written regarding the new world order and also about the one world church. Inter-religious and ecumenical relations is one of the favorite topics of the pope. The Second Vatican Council (1962-65), marked a new era in the church's relationship with non-Christian religions, since the popes of that time (John XXIII and Paul VI) encourage dialogue with them. The Second Vatican Council was the 21st ecumenical council of the Catholic Church. It was convened on October 11, 1962 at the Vatican by Pope John XXIII and at his death, Pope Paul VI continued it. The council issued a total of 16 documents through which it intended to promote a spiritual renewal within the Catholic Church. It was important for the ecumenical movement (a movement that seeks the unity of all world religions) because it invited representatives from both Protestant and Eastern Orthodox churches to observe the proceedings. Its principal accomplishments included modification of the liturgy of the Mass, which was allowed to be translated into the vernacular of the nations, support for the spirit of ecumenism, and condemnation of anti-Semitism (this is nothing more than a screen).

It is said that the wide-ranging reforms approved at the Council have had a major impact on the church. The ecumenical movement is growing in sympathizers all around the world, even among those religions that are not Christians, and that even had been traditional enemies of the followers of Jesus. Among those religions involved in "peace" conversations are: Moslem, Buddhist, Shintoist, Confucionist, Jewish, Jainist, Sikh, Zorastrian and American Indians. The leaders of these religions had several meetings with either the pope himself or with any of his representatives. All these religions are preparing to recognize the supremacy of the pope. In 1998 a treaty was negotiated

71

in Ireland, where Catholics and Protestants had been fighting for so many years. That peace seemed like an impossible dream.

The Ecumenical movement had its origins in the 19th century among Protestant churches. The Evangelical Alliance was founded in 1846. One element that helped to inspire the unity, to provide the cohesion among the churches involved in ecumenism, was the interest in the baptism in the Spirit, which spread like fire among Pentecostals. The ecumenical movement became international in the 20th century with the establishment of the World Missionary Conference in 1910.

Not long before he died, John Paul II indicated that the growth of dialogue and mutual respect among members of the Catholic Church with other Christian communities and with the world's great religions has a great future. For him, unity and ecumenical concerns should have priority. The pope has indicated that **all religions are opening themselves to dialogue with trust**.

Pope John Paul II had said that the Eastern Rite churches can serve as bridges between the Catholic and the Orthodox churches. He mentions that the Catholic arms are stretched out offering full communion. That reminds me how some people trap unsuspecting birds. They put a track of seeds that leads to a box, upheld by a stick, to which a long string has been attached. Under the box is an abundant quantity of seed, and when the bird gets under the box, the string is pulled and the bird is trapped. It is not going to be full communion; rather it will be full *dominion* from the pope over the unsuspected victims that accept the offer from Rome.

We need to read between the lines to discover what is behind, what is really meant in the papal offers and declarations. God will not allow us to be trapped if we pray and depend on Him. The Vatican recently asked for cooperation with the pope. What is meant is submission. John Paul II also talked about the obligation of Eastern-rite Catholics to work toward the full unity of all the Christians, even if in their memories the hunting wounds of the past are still vivid. He is telling them "forget the past, trust me again," without any evidence of change.

In June 1998, John Paul II asked the Orthodox Church to work towards unity. He met on June 28 with a small delegation representing the ecumenical Orthodox Patriarch Bartholomew of Constantinople.

The pope said that both Christians and Jews share ethical, some common beliefs (like worshipping the same God) and moral obligations, which include working together for a world of true respect for the life and dignity of every human being, without discrimination of any kind. Can you believe that, coming from the biggest anti-Semite institution in the world? The pope's efforts were rewarded when <u>Jewish and Catholic leaders pledged to work together</u>.

The Judeo-Catholic statement was approved May 5, 1998 in Baltimore, Maryland, USA during a two-day Catholic-Jewish consultation on the millennium. Pope John Paul II hoped to make peace with the Jews before the celebration of the jubilee in Jerusalem in the year 2000. Although this experienced some delay and the Pope died, I do not doubt that the negotiations continue. There have been other joint statements by the group that dealt with moral values in public education (1990), pornography (1993) and condemnation of Holocaust denial (1994). Yes you read right. The Catholic Church was at the head of those that were denying that the holocaust ever happened. They forgot that cameras had been invented and used to document the findings at the concentration camps, and that many of the survivors and witnesses were still alive with their camp numbers tattooed on their forearms. The concentration camps' survivors launched a campaign of their own to prove that such a terrible chapter of human history was indeed real. Rome had been confronted and condemned for their roll and for not defending the Jews from the slaughter. Now in that joint statement, the Catholics vowed to work against bigotry, exploitation and violence (as if a piece of paper will change Rome from a wolf into a lamb).

In August 1998, Pope John Paul II told a Catholic-Anglican dialogue commission, that the church's teaching authority must be firmly enunciated (made clear, sharp, distinct) in order to confront a crisis of truth (of course, the Catholic version of truth that is by no means Biblical truth) in modern society. Whose teaching authority? Of course, Rome is going to be the winner. Papal authority (<u>not Bible authority</u>) has become a very important topic in the dialogue between these two churches.

The pope says that "seeds of truth," are present in every religion, even non- Christians, even though they do not claim Jesus as humanity's savior. Truth in Buddhism? No way. He further states that collaboration takes place when it is opportune. So now we get to the heart of Rome: a religion of convenience. It is a great contradiction when he talks about respecting the beliefs of other religions and at the same time he talks about evangelizing the whole world. Evangelism for the Catholic Church is a one way street in which only them have the right to do it and the rest of the world just have the option to reply in the affirmative. This proselytizing by the Catholic Church is contrary to the respect and collaboration that they are requesting from other churches. Rome called for intense inter-religious dialogue in the year 2000, and wanted peace and fraternity with the faithful of all the world's religions. The problem is that the peace they propose is obtained through submission to the pope.

"A development that has captured the attention of Seventh-day Adventists in North America is the growing influence of the Religious Right, of which the Christian Coalition is the most obvious expression. The increasing popularity of conservative talk- radio programs such as that of Rush Limbaugh, goes hand-in-hand with the growth in power of the Religious Right. And on a worldwide basis we see the Roman Catholic Church emerging as the world's moral policeman. On certain moral issues even fundamentalist Muslims are joining hands with them!" Marvin Moore in *The Coming Great Calamity.*

Now in the new millennium, both Evangelical and Catholic groups see a golden age of political cooperation ahead. They want to secure the blind submission of all the inhabitants of this world. One of the leading groups promoting church unity is the World Council of Churches. "The WCC brings together more than 340 churches, denominations and church fellowships in over 100 countries and territories throughout the world, representing some 550 million Christians and including most of the world's Orthodox churches, scores of denominations from such historic traditions of the Protestant Reformation as Anglican, Baptist, Lutheran, Methodist and Reformed, as well as many united and independent churches." (from http://wcc-coe.org/wcc/who/index-e.html). The WCC held its first assembly in 1948 and in 1961 merged with the International Missionary Council (IMC). The United Church of Christ is the result of the merger of a number of Protestant groups, members of the WCC.

An example of how the ecumenical movement is seeking to achieve worldwide Christian unity occurred on Dec. 30, 1971, when an international commission of Roman Catholic and Anglican theologians reported an agreement on basic teachings concerning the Eucharist (communion). What is significant about this is the fact that for centuries, both sides considered each other's teaching on the subject as blasphemous.

The United Religions Initiative is another group promoting ecumenism. In their Declaration of Vision and Purpose, written in June, 1996 at their first global gathering, they declared that as people of faith, they "wish to create permanent centers where the world's religions and spiritual movements will gather daily to engage in prayerful dialogue to make peace among religions, leading to cooperative action for the sake of all… We believe that the wisdom of our religious and spiritual **traditions** must be shared for the sake of all." They add: "We unite in cooperative action to bring the wisdom of our religious **traditions** to bear on the economic, environmental and social crises that confront us at the dawn of the new millennium.

"We unite to be a voice of shared values in the international arenas of politics, economics, and the media, and to serve as a forum for research and excellence on values in action." Their motives are commendable, but the only wisdom that matters is biblical wisdom. They are uniting, with no respect for the truth, which is not even mentioned. The churches are getting involved in politics, forgetting or ignoring that Jesus said clearly that His "kingdom is not of this world."

Another influential group that is making lots of noise is the Christian Coalition, which was founded in 1989 by TV preacher Pat Robertson to give Christians a voice in government. They say that they represent a growing group of nearly 2 million members and supporters. It has been said that the Christian Coalition is the largest and most effective political movement of Christian activists in the history of our nation.

They worked hard to recruit 100,000 volunteers to serve as liaisons between the churches and the local Christian Coalition groups, in an effort to mobilize hundreds of thousands of pro-family activists by November 2000, on time for the presidential elections. They wanted a Christian Coalition puppet to be the next president. In the 2016 presidential race, that candidate was Ted Cruz. They forgot that it is God who "changes the times and the seasons: <u>he removes kings, and sets up kings</u>: he gives wisdom to the wise, and knowledge to them that know understanding" (Dan 2:21). Instead of being activists, God would rather see them on their knees asking Him to impress the voters' hearts. The best we can do is pray that God will impress upon our minds and show us whom He wants us to vote for. Jesus never ran for president. He never pronounced a command to run for office. He said: "Go ye into all the world, and <u>preach the gospel</u> to every creature" (Mark 16:15). In the way they are doing it, it seems that it is the power of the Christian Coalition who is putting the mayors, representatives, senators, governors, and even the president in their positions. God does not need any help to do His job.

On May 28, 1982 Pope John Paul II visited Great Britain, where he held meetings with Anglican leaders, an action which marked a significant step in efforts to reestablish ties between the English church and Rome. The Church of England split from the Roman Catholic Church in 1534 amidst a power struggle between the King of England and the pope.

A month later, on June 1998, the Pope declared that Catholics and Orthodox must seek unity. Since 1977, with the exception of 1997, both groups have held ecumenical exchange of a delegation on their church's respective patron feast days, as a way to prepare for open dialogue.

In October 1998, the pope encouraged new efforts in the dialogue with non-Christians. He expressed the desire to see more cooperation between religions. The pope was speaking to the Pontifical Council for Interreligious Dialogue, which was preparing a major interfaith encounter in 1999 to welcome the new millennium. He said that Christians have to "acknowledge, preserve and encourage the spiritual and moral truths found among non-Christians." "He said the church needs particularly to deepen its dialogue with Muslims, and with the religions of Asia - Hinduism, Buddhism, Shintoism and others." (Catholic News Service- 10-30-98). Let's see some of the beliefs of these religions.

Buddhism? The Detroit Free Press from Sunday, November 8, 1998 had an article on the Dalai Lama, where it says that all creatures are sentient beings (conscious and alive), and are equal and that all of them have the Buddha nature. The article goes on to say that according to Buddhism, there is no creator. "Each individual, not only human beings, but other sentient beings, like animals or insects, they in a deep sense are the same sentient beings.... The Buddhist believe the mind is the creator. Everything depends on oneself. So that's why Buddha stated [that] you are your own master." They also believe in reincarnation, thus not relying on a Savior, but in self- realization.

Shintoism is the aboriginal religion of Japan, and is characterized by the <u>veneration</u> of nature spirits and <u>of ancestors</u>. "The sovereignty of the emperor was exercised by divine right through his reputed <u>descent from the sun</u> goddess Amaterasu Omikami, who is considered the founder of the Japanese nation. Related beliefs included the doctrines that the Japanese were superior to other peoples because of their descent from the gods, and that the emperor was destined to rule over the entire world. Until the defeat of Japan in World War II, these beliefs were of the utmost importance in assuring popular support for the military expansion of the Japanese Empire." *Infopedia*

Hinduism is syncretist (this is the attempt to unite or reconcile different religious beliefs), and they worship hundreds of gods (they have deities peculiar to a particular village or even to a particular family). Most Hindus sing the gayatri <u>hymn to the sun</u> at dawn, although very few practices or beliefs are shared by all. Also, after death, they think that the soul leaves the body and is reborn (reincarnation) in the body of another person, animal, vegetable, or mineral, where they have the opportunity to progress to a higher level (transmigration).

How can Buddhism, Shintoism and Hinduism be united with Christianity? They don't even believe in God. Can you see God working in that ecumenical movement? I can't, not at all, because He wants those people to repent and come out of those ways. "**Forasmuch then as we are the offspring of God, we ought not to think that the Godhead is like unto gold, or silver, or stone, graven by art and man's device. And the times of this ignorance God winked at; but now commands all men every where to repent**" (Acts 17:29,30).

The World Council of Churches is composed of Protestant churches only. "The Roman Catholic Church is not a member of the World Council, though it sends observers to its meetings. But the Roman church has done a great deal to promote ecumenism through the work of the Second Vatican Council, held from 1962 to 1965, that was convened by Pope John XXIII. His successors Paul VI and John Paul II have continued to support the movement toward unity. The efforts by the Roman church are carried out through the Secretariat for the Promotion of Christian Unity, which accepts the idea of unity within diversity and works for dialogue to bring churches closer together." *Compton's Encyclopedia on line*

Now, before the Catholics and Protestants unite, we see the trend of merging among the Protestant churches themselves:

"The Evangelical Lutheran Church in America, the largest Lutheran church in North America; formed in 1988 by the merger of two major Lutheran denominations, the American Lutheran Church and the Lutheran Church in America, along with the Association of Evangelical Lutheran Churches; cut across ethnic lines and was designed to give Lutherans a more coherent voice in ecumenical discussions with other Christian churches in the U.S.; at its founding the church had more than 5,000,000 members and comprised about two-thirds of the Lutherans in the U.S.; headquarters in Chicago." *Compton's Encyclopedia on line.*

Those mergers will make it easier for the unification dialogues with Rome. It will just make it easier for the wolf to eat the sheep.

According to the Detroit News from Saturday, November 21, 1998 a group known as the Consultation on Church Union called to celebrate a meeting on January 20, 1999. Nine denominations with 23 million members, were said to respond to a pro-ecumenical document approved in 1988. These denominations were: "African Methodist Episcopal Church, African Methodist Episcopal Zion Church, Christian Church (Disciples of Christ), Christian Methodist Episcopal Church, Episcopal Church, International Council of Community Churches, Presbyterian Church (USA), United Church of Christ and United Methodist Church." –The Detroit News.

My impression on the meeting held on St. Louis, MO, is that those churches wanted to approve their union as a gift for the pope, who was to be in that same city 7 days later. This is no coincidence. The carefully planned purpose behind this is to stimulate other denominations and organizations to follow with similar agreements.

"Methodists have always been open to relationships with other denominations and have therefore taken a lead in the 20th-century ecumenical movement." *Compton's Encyclopedia on line.*

"During the latter part of the 20th century, the Lutheran churches became involved in the ecumenical movement, an attempt--particularly through the World Council of Churches--to bring all the Christian denominations into closer working harmony. Interdenominational cooperation has also been encouraged at the local level, in worship services and in social mission efforts." *Compton's Encyclopedia on line*

The plans for the year 2000, known as the jubilee year, released on Nov. 29, 1998 included a bull from the pope, in which he described the dates and procedures for holy years. The document had a five-page appendix on <u>indulgences</u>. The dates for the Holy Year were chosen from Dec. 24, 1999, to Jan. 6, 2001.

Catholicism gained great momentum with the pope's frequents visits to countries around the world and with his audiences. After he celebrated 20 years of pontificate in October 1998, the Vatican press office said that the general audiences held by Pope John Paul added up to 877 in all, to which some 14 million followers have attended.

The Detroit Free press on Saturday, October 17, 1998 presented some data about the pontificate of John Paul II:

- Traveled 694,700 miles, nearly 28 times the circumference of the earth.
- Made 134 trips in Italy and visited 117 countries.
- Spent 839 days outside the Vatican-about 11.5 percent of his papacy.
- Held about 877 public audiences at the Vatican, attended by some 14 million people.
- Granted more than 1,000 private audiences.
- Issued 89 major documents, including 13 encyclicals and 37 apostolic letters.
- Beautified 805 people.
- Canonized 280 people.
- **Met 766 times with <u>heads of state</u> or government.**

Revelation 17 and 18 talk about the woman fornicating <u>with the kings of the earth through "holy alliances" (remember the cover of Time magazine portraying President Ronald Reagan and Pope John</u>

Paul II on occasion of the fall of communism in Poland?). The Bible compares Catholicism with a woman "with whom the kings of the earth have committed fornication, and the inhabitants of the earth have been made drunk with the wine of her fornication" (Rev 17:2).

Ecumenisn – the movement to unify all the faiths

Ecumenism? This term is not biblical at all. The sympathizers of this movement claim that the Holy Spirit drives them, but what does the Bible say (remember that we need to ask the Book) Jesus said that the Spirit would have a special work to do: "Howbeit when He, the Spirit of truth, is come, **He will guide you into all truth**: for He shall not speak of himself; but whatsoever He shall hear, that shall He speak: and He will show you things to come" (John 16:13). How can all those churches that are ecumenical say that the Spirit is guiding them to be united in one body? How do you explain that they have so many different theological ideas, some of them diametrical opposed, and still claim to be led by the Spirit that guides to ALL the truth. Not to a partial truth, but to <u>the whole truth</u>.

God is not a God of confusion, but of order. He emphasizes that He cares about the truth (Bible evidence presented later in section **Is truth important?**). He can not have so many contradictions being preached on His Name as if they were important truths, without sending the Holy Spirit to guide them to <u>the</u> truth.

We can not sacrifice the truth on behalf of achieving unity. We can not accept the union of the Bible with paganism (this union is called syncretism). When God took His people out of Egypt, He specified to the Israelites not to unite with the pagans (see Exodus 23:32).

In times of Nehemiah and Ezra, the Samaritans wanted to help in the rebuilding of the city, but their offer was rejected. "Now when the adversaries of Judah and Benjamin heard that the children of the captivity were building the temple to the LORD God of Israel; Then they came to Zerubbabel, and to the chief of the fathers, and said to them, <u>Let us build with you: for **we seek your God, as you do**</u>; and we do sacrifice to him since the days of Esarhaddon king of Assur, which brought us up here. But Zerubbabel, and Jeshua, and the rest of the chief of the fathers of Israel, said to them, You have nothing to do with us to build a house to our God; but we ourselves together will build to the LORD God of Israel, as king Cyrus the king of Persia has commanded us" (Ezra 4:1-3). They believed in the same God but they also had pagan ideas. Their truth was corrupted. Centuries later, Jesus told them the truth, which they accepted, and eventually, after having accepted the truth, became part of the church. We can not afford to allow the one with impure faith and contaminated truth to **build beside us**. What communion has the darkness with the truth?

Let's listen to Paul's opinion on this subject. An opinion that can be applied freely to every relationship that we can establish, be it partnerships in business, in marriage, or in the spiritual world. "Be not you unequally yoked together with unbelievers: for what fellowship has righteousness with unrighteousness? and **what communion has light with darkness**? And what concord has Christ with Belial? or what part has he that believes with an infidel? And what agreement has the temple of God with **idols**? for you are the temple of the living God; as God had said, I will dwell in them, and walk in them; and I will be their God, and they shall be my people. Wherefore come out from among them, and be ye separate, says the Lord, and do not touch the unclean thing; and I will receive you, and will be a Father to you, and you shall be my sons and daughters, says the Lord Almighty" (2 Corinthians 6:14-18). Compromising the truth puts us in the same level with unbelievers.

How paganism crept into the church? "We are told by Eusebius that Constantine, in order to recommend the new religion to the heathen, transferred into it all the outward ornaments to which they had been accustomed in their own religion.... The use of temples, those dedicated to particular saints, candles, holy water, processions, the ring in marriage, turning to the east, images at a later date, all are of pagan origin and sanctified by their adoption into the church." Cardinal John Henry Newman, *Development of Christian Doctrine*, page 372.

And what is the modern church doing to attract pagans into the church? The leaders of this trend are removing the very symbol that has stood for centuries as the banner of the Christian faith: the cross. This is a public relations move to facilitate the union with non-Christians because they consider the cross an offensive symbol. The cross has become again a scandal (Galatians 5:11).

THE WINE (DOCTRINES)
OF BABYLON:

The soul is immortal
The State of the Dead- What the Bible really teaches

For centuries, people have been talking about the soul of a man going out of their bodies and being moved to heaven or somewhere else after death. The funny thing is that *not even in one verse of the Bible does it say that we have a soul.* The truth is that WE DON'T HAVE A SOUL; *WE ARE A SOUL*. Bible proof needed? Of course I will give it. Let's begin. Genesis 2:7 says that God shaped man from *"the dust of the ground, and breathed into his nostrils the breath of life; and man became a living soul."* It does not say that man has a soul, but instead that *man became a soul.* To help understand this concept, we can do some math:

Dust
+Breath of life
= Soul

That is a simple formula. Now, if we remove either one of the components, we have no soul. So, again, according to the Bible, **we don't have a soul, we are a soul**. There has been big misunderstandings about the real nature of man. Pagan concepts have prevailed and are accepted as Biblical truth. The majority of Christendom believes in the immortality of the soul, while the Bible says in Isaiah 51:12 that man is mortal. By contrast, in 1 Timothy 6:16, Paul declares that **only God is immortal**. The biggest problem that church goers have is that they listen to their preachers and accept whatever teaching is told to them, without going to the Bible and compare man's teachings with the word of God. Just remember that the Bereans did not accept what Paul said until they found it by themselves in the Bible (Acts 17:11). I think that Paul was closer to God than any preacher that we know. We need to consult with the Book, and not with men.

Now, what is the most widely known Bible verse? It is John 3:16 (I will refer to this verse later on in the study). What does it say? That God so loved the world that he gave his only begotten Son, that <u>whosoever believes</u> *"in Him should not perish, but have everlasting life."* This passage teaches clearly that it is necessary that a man believes in Jesus first, and <u>then</u> he will have eternal life. Man is not naturally immortal. So, if you don't have Jesus, you don't have eternal life. Only the Creator is immortal.

Life is a gift (Romans 6:23) that will be given to the righteous at the last day (John 6:54). A gift is something that you do not deserve. No one can take away the eternal life that God bestows. (See also Luke 12:4, 5.)

Now, let's see some more Biblical evidence:

"<u>The dead do not praise the Lord</u>, nor any who go down to silence" Psalm 115:17.

"For in death there is <u>no remembrance of You</u>; In the grave who will give you thanks?" Psalm 6:5

*"Will You work wonders for the dead? <u>Shall the dead arise and praise You</u>? Shall Your lovingkindness be declared in the grave? Or Your faithfulness in the place of destruction? Shall Your wonders be known in the dark? And Your righteousness in the **<u>land of forgetfulness</u>**?"* Psalm 88:10-12.

"For Sheol cannot thank You, death cannot praise you; <u>those who go down to the pit cannot hope for Your truth</u>" Isaiah 38:18.

*"For the living know that they will die; but **<u>the dead Know nothing</u>**, and **<u>they have no reward</u>**, for <u>the memory of them is forgotten</u>. Also their love, their hatred, and their envy have now perished; <u>nevermore will they have a share in anything done under the sun</u>.... Whatever your hands finds to do, do it with all your might; for there is no work or device or knowledge or wisdom **<u>in the grave where you are going</u>**"* Ecclesiastes 9:5,6,10. It is clear that we *go to the grave, not to heaven or hell*, and that we don't remember anything.

"As the cloud disappears and vanishes away, so he who goes down to the grave does not come up" Job 7:9.

"But man dies and lies prostrate; indeed he breathes his last and where is he? As waters disappears from the sea, and a river becomes parched and dries up, so man lies down and does not rise. Till the heavens are no more, they will not awake nor be roused from their sleep" Job 14:10-12. It is when Jesus comes that the dead will be resurrected: *"Marvel not at this: for the hour is coming, in the which all that are in the graves shall hear his voice, And shall come forth; they that have done good, unto the resurrection of life; and they that have done evil, unto the resurrection of damnation"* (John 5:28,29)

"Then shall the dust return to the earth as it was; and the spirit shall return to God who gave it." Ecclesiastes 12:7.

Now, let's consider some statements from **amazingfacts.org** (adapted):

What is the "spirit" that returns to God at death?

"The body without the spirit [breath, see Bible margin] *is dead."* James 2:26. *"The spirit of God* [the breath, Hebrew roo'-akh (=wind, air), which God gave him] *is in my nostrils."* Job 27:3.

Do souls die?

"The soul that sins, it shall die." Ezekiel 18:4,20. *"Every living soul died in the sea."* Revelation 16:3.

Do good people go to heaven when they die?

"All that are in the graves shall hear His voice, and shall come forth." John 5:28, 29. *"David . . . is both dead and buried, and his sepulcher is with us to this day." "For David is not ascended into the heavens."* Acts 2:29, 34. Just remember that *David was a man "after God's own Heart."* Still, he is not enjoying the bliss of heaven yet. He is still waiting for that day in his grave.

"If I wait, the grave is mine house." Job 17:13.

Jesus called the unconscious state of the dead "sleep" in John 11:11-14. How long will they sleep?

"So man lies down, and rises not; till the heavens be no more." Job 14:12.

Answer: The dead will sleep until the great day of the Lord at the end of the world. In death, humans are totally unconscious with no activity or knowledge of any kind.

What happens to the righteous dead at the second coming of Christ?

"Behold, I come quickly; and My reward is with Me, to give every man according as his work shall be." Revelation 22:12. *"The Lord Himself shall descend from heaven with a shout, . . . and the dead in Christ shall rise . . . and so shall we ever be with the Lord."* 1 Thessalonians 4:16, 17. *"We shall all be changed, in a moment, in the twinkling of an eye, . . . and the dead shall be raised incorruptible. . . . For this corruptible must put on incorruption, and this mortal must put on immortality."* 1 Corinthians 15:51-53.

Answer: They will be rewarded. They will be raised, given immortal bodies, and caught up to meet the Lord in the air. There would be no purpose in a resurrection if people were taken to heaven at death. Peter indicates clearly that the punishment of the wicked is held back until the day of judgment: *"The Lord knoweth how to deliver the godly out of temptations, and to reserve the unjust <u>unto the day of judgment to be punished</u>"* (2 Peter 2:9). No one is being burned as popular preachers teach.

How did the teaching of immortality of the soul originated?

"And the serpent said to the woman, Ye shall not surely die." Genesis 3:4. It was a lie from *"That old serpent, called the Devil, and Satan."* Revelation 12:9.

Answer: Satan told Eve that sin would not bring death as God had clearly indicated.

The Bible Says that after death, a person: returns to dust (Psalm 104:29), knows nothing (Ecclesiastes 9:5), possesses no mental powers (Psalm 146:4), has nothing to do with anything on earth (Ecclesiastes 9:6), does not live (2 Kings 20:1), waits in the grave (Job 17:13), and continues not (Job 14:1, 2).

Satan invented the teaching that the dead are alive. Reincarnation, channeling, communication with spirits, spirit worship, and the "undying soul" are all inventions of Satan, with one aim—to convince people that when you die you are not really dead.

When people believe that the dead are alive, *"spirits of devils, working miracles"* (Revelation 16:14) and posing as spirits of the dead, Satan will be able to deceive and lead them astray virtually 100 percent of the time (Matthew 24:24). Those who insist on Scripture proof for all doctrines will not be led astray by Satan.

Evangelist Mark Finley stated that:

* <u>The Bible mentions 1,600 times the word soul, and never once does it say "immortal soul."</u>
* 53 times the Bible compares death with a sleep.

YOUR QUESTIONS ANSWERED (adapted from Amazing Facts)

1. Didn't the thief on the cross go to paradise with Christ the day He died?
    Answer: No. In fact, on **Sun**day morning, Jesus said to Mary, "I am not yet ascended to My Father." John 20:17. This shows that Christ did not go to heaven immediately after his death. Also note that the punctuation of the Bible is not inspired, but was added by men. The comma in Luke 23:43 should be placed after the words "today" rather than before, so the passage should read, "Verily I say to thee today, shalt thou be with me in paradise." Or, "telling you today—when it seems that I can save no one, when I Myself am being crucified as a criminal—I give you the assurance today that you will be with Me in paradise." Christ's kingdom is set up <u>at His Second Coming</u> – not before (Matthew 25:31), and all the righteous of all ages will enter it at that time (1 Thessalonians 4:15-17) and not at death.

2. Doesn't the Bible speak of the "undying," "immortal" soul?
    Answer: No, the undying, immortal soul is not mentioned in the Bible. The word immortal is found only twice in the Bible, and it is in reference to God (1 Timothy 1:17;6:16) alone. The word immortality appears 5 times in the Bible (more on this below), in one of the cases refers to God (1 Timothy 6:16) in the other 4 cases, indicates that immortality is given to us through the Gospel (Romans 2:7; 1 Corinthians 15:53, 54; & 2 Timothy 1:10). These verses will be presented later on.

3. At death the body returns to dust and the spirit (or breath, air) returns to God. But where does the soul go?
    Answer: It goes nowhere. Instead, it simply ceases to exist. Two things must be combined to make a soul: body and breath. When the breath departs, the soul ceases to exist because it is a combination of two things. When you turn

off a light, where does the light go? It does not go anywhere. It just ceases to exist. Two things must combine to make a light: a bulb and electricity. Without the combination, a light is impossible. So with the soul; unless body and breath are combined, there can be no soul. There is no such thing as a disembodied soul.

4. Does the word soul ever mean anything other than a living being?

   Answer: Yes, it may mean also (1) life itself, or (2) the mind, or intellect. No matter which meaning is intended, the soul is still a combination of two things (body and breath), and it ceases to exist at death.

5. Can you explain John 11:26, which says, *"And whosoever liveth and believeth in Me shall never die"*?

   Answer: This refers not to the first death, which all people die (Hebrews 9:27), but to the second death, which only the wicked die and from which there is no resurrection (Revelation 2:11; 21:8).

6. Matthew 10:28 says, *"Fear not them that kill the body, but are not able to kill the soul."* Doesn't this prove that the soul is undying?

   Answer: No, if we read the last half of the same verse it proves the opposite. It provides evidence that souls do die. It says, *"But rather fear him which is able to destroy both soul and body in hell."* Here we see the importance of considering the context of a passage. Revelation 20 shows that the fire comes down from God and devours the wicked. If they are devoured, then there is no life left.

7. What about the souls crying out from under the altar in Revelation 6:9, 10? Doesn't this prove that souls don't die?

This cry was figurative, as was the cry of Abel's blood (Genesis 4:10). The word soul is a synonym of people or living beings (Genesis 2:7 remember, we don't have a soul, we ARE a soul). Can you imagine if the souls who die literally lie under the altar? What kind of heaven would it be, if you have to be like sardines in a box under the altar? Do you know that Papal Rome alone has killed over 60 million martyrs? Another thing that we should not overlook is the act of the righteous begging God to punish their enemies. Instead, the righteous beg for mercy for their enemies, because they love those that are prisoners of Satan, as Christ did on the cross (Luke 23:34), and Stephen when he was being stoned to death (Acts 7:60).

As previously stated, the word immortality it's mentioned only 5 times in the Bible. It is translated from the Greek aphtharsia [af-thar-see'-ah[that could be translated also as perpetuity. Those verses are:

a) *"To them who by patient continuance in well doing __seek__ for glory and honor and __immortality__, eternal life"* (Romans 2:7). *If you have to look for something it is because you don't have it yet.*

b) *"For this corruptible must put on incorruption, and this mortal must put on __immortality__"* (1 Corinthians 15:53).

c) *"So when this corruptible shall have put on incorruption, and this mortal shall have put on __immortality__, then shall be brought to pass the saying that is written, Death is swallowed up in victory"* (1 Corinthians 15:54). *These two verses indicate that nobody is eternal until Jesus comes back.*

d) *"But is now made manifest by the appearing of our Savior Jesus Christ, who has abolished death, and __has brought life and immortality to light__ through the gospel"* (2 Timothy 1:10). *Immortality is not possible without the cross. It is not natural to man. Remember that Adam and Eve were taken out from the garden of Eden so they would not eat of the fruit of the tree that would perpetuate their existence: "And the LORD God said, Behold, the man is become as one of us, to know good and evil: and now, lest he put forth his hand, and take also of the tree of life, and __eat, and live for ever__: Therefore the LORD God sent him forth from the garden of Eden, to till the ground from whence he was taken. So he drove out the man; and he placed at the east of the garden of Eden Cherubims, and a flaming sword which turned every way, to keep the way of the tree of life." (Genesis 3:22-24).*

e) *"Which in his times he shall show, who is the blessed and only Potentate, the King of kings, and Lord of lords; __Who only has immortality__, dwelling in the light which no man can approach to; whom no man has seen, nor can see: to whom be honor and power everlasting. Amen"* (1 Timothy

6:15). It is very clear now that if **the only one that has immortality is God**, then no other creature has it, unless He grants it when Jesus comes.

8. Why does it mention the souls under the altar? Jesus is in the Holy of Holies, celebrating the judgment. He uses books, which have the names of His followers written on them. Those books are in the Holy of Holies too. The names imply the character of the persons that carry those names. What John saw was the names of the martyrs and not the actual souls, since everybody that dies goes to the grave until Jesus comes.

9. Doesn't 1 Peter 4:6 say the gospel was preached to dead people?

    Answer: No, it says the gospel "was" preached to those who "are" dead. The gospel "was" preached to them while they were yet living.

The Great Controversy, page 549, says:

"But if the dead are already enjoying the bliss of heaven or writhing in the flames of hell, what need of a future judgment? The teachings of God's word on these important points are neither obscure nor contradictory; they may be understood by common minds. But what candid mind can see either wisdom or justice in the current theory? Will the righteous, after the investigation of their cases at the judgment, receive the commendation, *"Well done, thou good and faithful servant: . . . enter thou into the joy of thy Lord,"* when they have been dwelling in His presence, perhaps for long ages? Are the wicked summoned from the place of torment to receive sentence from the Judge of all the earth: *"Depart from Me, ye cursed, into everlasting fire"*? Matthew 25:21, 41. Oh, solemn mockery! shameful impeachment of the wisdom and justice of God!

"The theory of the immortality of the soul was one of those false doctrines that Rome, borrowing from paganism, incorporated into the religion of Christendom. Martin Luther classed it with the 'monstrous fables that form part of the Roman dunghill of decretals.'"--E. Petavel, The Problem of Immortality, page 255. Commenting on the words of Solomon in Ecclesiastes, that the dead don't know anything, the Reformer says: "Another place proving that the dead have no . . . feeling. There is, saith he, no duty, no science, no knowledge, no wisdom there. Solomon judgeth that the dead are asleep, and feel nothing at all. For the dead lie there, accounting neither days nor years, but when they are awaked, they shall seem to have slept scarce one minute."- Martin Luther, *Exposition of Solomon's Book Called Ecclesiastes*, page 152."

In the same book, page 550, says:

"Nowhere in the Sacred Scriptures is found the statement that the righteous go to [enjoy] their reward or the wicked to [suffer] their punishment at death. The patriarchs and prophets have left no such assurance. Christ and His apostles have given no hint of it. The Bible clearly teaches that the dead do not go immediately to heaven [when they die]. They are represented as sleeping until the resurrection. I Thessalonians 4:14; Job 14:10-12. In the very day when the silver cord is loosed and the golden bowl broken (Ecclesiastes 12:6), man's thoughts perish. They that go down to the grave are in silence. They know no more of anything that is done under the sun. Job 14:21. Blessed rest for the weary righteous! Time, be it long or short, is but a moment to them. They sleep; they are awakened by the trump of God to a glorious immortality. *"For the trumpet shall sound, and the dead shall be raised incorruptible. . . . So when this corruptible shall have put on incorruption, and this mortal shall have put on immortality, then shall be brought to pass the saying that is written, Death is swallowed up in victory."* I Corinthians 15:52-54. As they are called forth from their deep slumber they begin to think just where they ceased. The last sensation was the pang of death; the last thought, that they were falling beneath the power of the grave. When they arise from the tomb, their first glad thought will be echoed in the triumphal shout: *"O death, where is thy sting? O grave, where is thy victory?"* Verse 55."

DID JESUS DESCEND TO HELL?

The Catholic creed says that Jesus went to hell, but there is not one single passage in the Bible to prove that. There is one however, where it says that Jesus preached to the Spirits that were prisoners, in the days of Noah (1 Peter 3:18-20). The "spirits in prison" refers to people whose lives were in bondage to Satan. (See Psalm 142:7; Isaiah 42:6, 7; 61:1; and Luke 4:18). That's why He says: *"Therefore if the Son makes you free, you shall be free indeed"* (John 8:36). The preaching was done "by the Spirit" (verse 18) in Noah's day—to people who were then living (verses 19, 20).

There is a lot of confusion because people let paganism permeate the truth. That was prophesied by Paul in Acts 20:28-31 & 1 Timothy 4:1-3. When people die, they do not go to hell or heaven. They go to the grave until Jesus comes to judge the dead and the living (John 5:28,29; 1 Thessalonians 4:15-17; 1 Corinthians 15:51-55). The Bible teaches that dead people have no love, hate, memory and that they go to the grave (Ecclesiastes 9:5,6 & 10). It will make no sense to read Revelation 22:12, where He says: *"I am coming quickly, and My reward is with Me, to give to everyone according to his work,"* if at the same time people would be supposedly enjoying or suffering their reward already. No, it would make no sense at all because there is nobody in "hell" as it is taught by the churches today. The word hell in the Bible is hades in Greek, and sheol in Hebrew. In both cases means grave, but the Catholic Church adopted the pagan teaching to inspire fear in the people, so the churches would always be full. There are a lot of errors that people are teaching and at the same time they twist the Scriptures to make them say what they want, not what God means. This is just done to control people. It is not God's way to bring people to the church.

More truths on the state of the dead:

Many churches teach doctrines that are not Biblical, like the immortality of the soul when, as we mentioned before, 1 Timothy 6:16 says that the <u>only one that is immortal is God</u>. Isaiah 51:12 says that man is mortal, Ezekiel 18:4 says that *"the soul that sinneth **it shall die**."*

Why John 3:16 is not understood properly? It says that the ones that have eternal life are those that <u>believe</u>. We can conclude without fear of being blasphemous, that if somebody does not believe, he or she does not have eternal life. Romans 2:7 talks about those that <u>seek</u> eternal life, immortality. If you have to seek immortality, do you have it? NO! It would make no sense to look for something that you already have (like somebody looking for his glasses, when he has them on). Immortality will be given only to those that accept Jesus as Savior and remain, through His power, faithful to Him to the very end.

What about eternal fire? Jude says that Sodom and other cities were put for example, suffering the punishment of the eternal fire. They are not burning right now. Jeremiah 17:27 says that if the Jews did not stop doing business on the Sabbath, the city of Jerusalem would burn with fire that shall not be quenched. Nehemiah 1:3 says that Jerusalem suffered that punishment already. Is it still burning? NO! In Exodus 21:6 says that a man could be a slave forever. Do you think that we will have slaves in heaven? NO! So the phrases eternal, forever, etc. referring to the wicked indicate only until the judgment is executed, until the being is punished enough for his or her sins; <u>until the fire serves its purpose</u>. Malachi 4:1-3 indicates that only ashes will remain from the wicked. Isaiah 47:14 clearly states that not even the light of a candle will be left. I found out that the doctrine of eternal fire and hell was borrowed from the Greeks, and the meaning of Bible verses was forced, to make us believe that the doctrine is Biblical.

Jesus used a parable (the rich and Lazarus- Luke 16:19-31) that was a common story (some kind of a fable) in His times to teach an important <u>lesson about life decisions</u> and Christians today use it to "prove" the doctrine of hell, without reading the context of the parable or comparing it with the rest of the Bible. The people that see this parable as literal should remember what Solomon wrote: ***"As a thorn goeth up into the hand of a drunkard, so is a parable in the mouth of fools"*** (Prov. 26:9). Also, it will be very wise to listen to Paul: *"Not giving heed to Jewish fables, and commandments of men, that turn from* *the truth"* (Titus 1:14). That parable is not literal because it shows people praying to Abraham. If that is true and acceptable, why not pray to Elijah or Enoch too? Abraham's buxom must be bigger than the territory of Israel to hold all the people that go to him. If when the saved go to heaven and look out their window and see and hear the wicked burning and cursing, I do not think they would consider that a good neighborhood. Better call the realtor to find a better location. Would you enjoy heaven seeing your loved ones out the window of your room, being tortured and begging for your help day and night? If parables are literal, what about the parable found in Judges 9:7-15, where trees talk to a bush and vise versa? We either understand all parables as literal, all of them, or just listen to what they have to teach us, without paying too much attention to the elements present in the stories.

The context of that parable indicates that Jesus was talking to the Pharisees who were *"lovers of money"* (Luke 16:14).

Talking about the other Lazarus, the one that Jesus resurrected, If He was in heaven, why would Jesus called him to suffer some more on this earth? Why was he commanded to *come forward* and not to come down- if he was in heaven?

When King Saul went to the occultist lady, the Bible says that he "understood" that he was seeing Samuel. What the spirit said was true about him dying, but he also said that Saul and his sons would be with Samuel tomorrow. Wait a minute here. Samuel was righteous. So if we accept that the spirit was really Samuel, then the wicked and the righteous go to the same place. Satan can take any form or shape (2 Corinthians 11:14,15). That was not Samuel, it was Satan.

David is called a man after God's own heart. That means that he got God's approval. He was saved. But the bible says that he did not go to heaven (Acts 2:34). We need to read the Bible as if we were lawyers and our clients' life depended on it. Let God bless you with understanding and don't let anybody deceive you. Today, the majority of the churches (daughters of Babylon) teach about eternal hell (there is a hell all right, but not as it is taught by the clergy), just remember that the truth had never been with the majority. Just consider the cases of Noah, Lot, Elijah and even Jesus.

"He has power to bring before men the appearance of their departed friends. The counterfeit is perfect; the familiar look, the words, the tone, are reproduced with marvelous distinctness. Many are comforted with the assurance that their loved ones are enjoying the bliss of heaven, and without suspicion of danger, they give ear *"to seducing spirits, and doctrines of devils." The Great Controversy*, page 552, Chapter Title: "Can Our Dead Speak to Us?" I know about this first hand because for a while, growing up, I ventured into the realm of the darkness and visited mediums. I even saw the dead going through walls in my house. The funny thing is how quickly they disappeared when the name of Jesus was called.

MARY THE INTERCESSOR AND THE TEACHING THAT THE SAINTS LISTEN TO OUR PRAYERS

This section is intended to be an eye opener, and as previously stated in the introduction, the purpose is not to offend anyone, since I believe that the Virgin was a God-fearing woman. That is why she was chosen as the mother of our Lord.

Talking about the Holy Spirit, Paul declared: *"Likewise the Spirit also helps our infirmities: for we know not what we should pray for as we ought: but the Spirit itself makes intercession for us with groanings which cannot be uttered. And he that searches the hearts knows what is the mind of the Spirit, because he makes intercession for the saints according to the will of God"* (Rom 8:26,27). Notice that it is not the saints who make intercession on our behalf. It's the Holy Spirit.

Our Lord and Savior Jesus is portrayed in the Scriptures as our intercessor. *"Neither is there salvation in any other: for there is none other name under heaven given among men, whereby we must be saved"* (Acts 4:12). *"Who is he that condemns? It is Christ that died, yea rather, that is risen again, who is even at the right hand of God, who also maketh intercession for us"* (Rom 8:34). *"Wherefore He is able also to save them to the uttermost that come to God by him, seeing He ever liveth to make intercession for them. For such an high priest became us, who is holy, harmless, undefiled, separate from sinners, and made higher than the heavens"* (Hebrews 7:25,26). *"And to Jesus the mediator of the new covenant, and to the blood of sprinkling, that speaks better things than that of Abel"* (Hebrews 12:24). Moreover, the Bible says that the only mediator is Jesus: *"For there is one God, and **one mediator** between God and men, the man Christ Jesus"* (1 Timothy 2:5). There is no biblical foundation for the idea that there are humans – saints or priests- or even Mary, interceding for us.

Marvin Moore, quoted Omni Magazine in one of his new books: "On March 21, 1994, New York's eleven o'clock Eyewitness News ended with this pious tableau: A solemn, modestly dressed Egyptian immigrant family and their friends crowd an apartment in Bensonhurst, Brooklyn, all of them staring reverently at a glistening copper icon of the Virgin Mary. With detached amusement, the TV anchor announces that this icon, which the Boutros family bought in a church gift shop in Cairo, is weeping oil tears. The camera cuts to an exotic, bearded figure in a long, black cassock, identified as a bishop of the Coptic Orthodox Church, a sect of Christianity hailing from Egypt. He assures the greater New York audience that a miracle has indeed occurred.

"Back in the newsroom, the TV anchor smiles in a who knows kind of way. The story was clearly meant to be a footnote on the richness of life in the Big City" (Omni, October 1994, 54).

"The Omni article goes on to point out that 'Brooklyn's oily miracle is just the latest eruption in a volcanic surge of miraculous events and apparitions involving the Virgin Mary,' indicating that a 'tremendous longing for religious experience--for firsthand contact with the miraculous and the divine . . . is driving people across the country to sites like Bensonhurst.' Omni's article states that many people have been having visions of the Virgin, and mentions some of the better-known alleged appearances across North America and in other parts of the world. Some have occurred in well-to-do neighborhoods, prompting Omni to comment that 'middle-class Americans . . . cannot reconcile the worldly, skeptical, scientific, conscious parts of their minds with their deeply emotional religious longings and fears.'"

"Above all else, you and I must understand that the issue in the story about the weeping icon is not rational proof. It's belief. It's the human need for more than a rational, scientific explanation for everything in life. It's a profound need for the spiritual."

In November 7, 1998 Pope John Paul II awarded the 1998 Pontifical Academy Prize, which carries a cash grant of about $35,000, to Deyanira Flores Gonzales, a Costa Rican scholar for her work in Marian theology. Her work is entitled "The Virgin Mary at the Foot of *the Cross."* Notice that the prize went to somebody that wrote about a human being, not to anybody writing about Jesus.

In one of his new year's prayer, Pope John Paul II called Mary "most holy", while God was referred to just as Father. It is common that Mary receives more glory than God.

While searching some internet sites, I found a title that caught my attention:

"THROUGH MARY TO JESUS."

Meaning that we can not approach Jesus, our friend and Savior, if we don't go first to Mary.

Now, I want to submit some quotes from the book **THE GLORIES OF MARY** by St. Alphonsus Liguori, 1931 edition:

Page 30 "To honor this Queen of Angels is to gain eternal life...." The Bible says *"He that hath the Son hath life..."*(1 John 5:12).

Page 36 "And if Jesus is the King of the universe, Mary is also its Queen." The concept of a queen of heaven had its origins in ancient Babylon, with Semiramis. Jeremiah wrote in chapters 7 & 44 of his book *"**burn incense to the queen of heaven**, ..."*

Page 38 "...the Eternal Father gave the office of judge and avenger to the Son, and that of showing mercy ... to the Mother.'"

Page 75 Abridged edition: But now she restrains her Divine Son, lest He destroy sinners...."

Page 86 Abridged edition: "Many things are asked of God and are not granted; they are asked from Mary and are obtained..."

A passage from the Psalm that the book of Hebrews applies to Jesus, was forcibly applied to Mary: *"God hath anointed thee with the oil of gladness."* Forcing the Scriptures to say what we want is not God's way to interpret them.

Page 43 "the door through which sinners are brought to God'." John 10:7,9 says that Jesus is the door.

Page 80 "Mary is our life." Jesus said: *"I am ...the life."*

Page 83 "Sinners receive pardon by the intercession of Mary alone." *"For there is one God and one Mediator between God and men, the man Christ Jesus"* (1 Timothy 2:5).

Page 93 says the she withholds "the arm of her Son from falling on sinners." *Daniel 4 teaches that <u>nobody</u> can restrain the hand of the Lord.*

Page 137 "Many things- says Nicephorus,- are asked from God, and are not granted: they are asked from Mary, and are obtained." Jesus told His disciples to ask <u>in His name</u> (John 14:13,14;15:7,16;16:23,24 &26). *"Ask and ye shall receive."*

Page 153 "St. Bernard says, 'Let us not imagine that we obscure the glory of the Son by the great praise we lavish on the mother; for the more she is honored, the greater is the glory of her Son.' 'There can be no other doubt,' says the saint, "that whatever we say in praise of the Mother is equally in praise of the Son."

"Saint Bonaventure expressly calls her "Mary, the most faithful <u>mediatress</u> of our salvation" And St. Laurence Justinian asks, "How can she be otherwise than full of grace, who has been made the <u>ladder to paradise</u>, the <u>gate of heaven</u>, the most true <u>mediatress between God and man</u>?" John 1:51 shows that Jesus is the ladder.

Page 155 "We should have <u>all through Mary</u>." See comments about the quote in page 137.

Page 174 "Let us... <u>venerate</u> this divine Mother ...that we should <u>receive every good thing</u> from her hand."- James 1:17: *"Every good gift ...comes down <u>from the Father</u>..."*

Page 181 "<u>At the command of Mary, **all obey, even God**</u>."... "Yes, <u>Mary is omnipotent</u>." What a blasphemy; that God obeys Mary!

Page 238 "To thee, O Lady, are committed the <u>keys</u> and treasures of the kingdom of heaven." Jesus has the keys (Revelation 1:18;3:7).

Page 246 "...'Frequently <u>our petitions are heeded sooner when we address ourselves to Mary the Queen of Mercy ,,, than when we go directly to Jesus</u> who as King of Justice is our Judge' " Is she more powerful than Jesus, or is it that He doesn't love us enough anymore?

Page 256 "...How can the Son refuse to hear his Mother when she shows him ... the breast that gave him suck?" What a sick thought! This quote probably came from a pervert.

Page 256 "...<u>our salvation is in her hands, and depends on her</u>.' "Referring to Jesus, the Bible says: *"Nor is there salvation in any other name under heaven given among men by which we must be saved"* (Acts 4:12).

The preceding quotes showed that this deified woman it is not the same Mary of the Scriptures. This one is the "resurrected" Semiramis. If the real Mary were alive now, she would be horrified seeing people glorifying her, giving her attributes of God. "How could anyone but an infinite God hear simultaneously thousands of prayers offered in hundreds of different languages and know all the intricacies involved in each petition, and be able to give a faithful answer and a true judgment? Think of the circumstances often involved in a single request; the answer of each petition might well involve the petitioner's whole future, and other people will also be affected by the answer. What care needs to be taken with the correct answer to only one solitary request! And how quickly comes the answer!...A moment's consideration will reveal the absurdity, the impossibility, of thinking that anyone but an infinite Savior could actually do the work required to save numbers of people simultaneously and perform that service continuously for thousands of years; it necessitates not only almighty power but also infinite wisdom. Thank God, Jesus our Lord possesses all this power and wisdom which He employs so freely in the salvation of all those who come unto God by Him." Louis F. Were, *The Woman and the Beast in the Book of Revelation*, pages 17,18.

This doctrine presents God as a revengeful being that needs to be appeased by Mary in order to show mercy. That is the way Satan wants us to perceive our loving Creator. Like a being that has to be feared. That is why the demons are so happy when preachers talk about the Catholic doctrine of hell.

Belief in archangels (plural)

WHO IS MICHAEL?

Who is Michael? The term means, "who is like God?" Paul presents Jesus as *"being in the form of God"* (Philippians 2:6), *"the image of the invisible God"* (Colossians 1:15) and *"the express image of His person"* (Hebrews 1:3). He is the only being that is like God. He is not created. He is the Creator Himself: Jesus. One of my favorite books has this quote on the subject:

"Jude (verse 9) declares that Michael is <u>the</u> (indicates that there is only one) Archangel. This word signifies 'head, or chief, angel,' and in our text Gabriel calls Him 'one of (the margin reads, *the first*) the chief princes.' There can be but one archangel, and hence <u>it is manifestly improper to use the word in the plural</u> as some do. The Scriptures never so use it. In 1 Thessalonians 4: 16, Paul states that when the Lord appears the second time to raise the dead, the voice of the archangel is heard. Whose voice is heard when the dead are raised?- The voice of the Son of God. (John 5: 28.) Putting these scriptures together, they prove that the dead are called from their graves by the voice of the Son of God, that the voice which is then heard is the voice of the Archangel [<u>no creature has power over death</u>], proving that the Archangel is the Son of God, and that the Archangel is called Michael, from which it follows that Michael is the Son of God. In the last verse of Daniel 10, He is called "<u>your Prince</u>," and in the first of Daniel 12, "<u>the great Prince</u> which stands [see Acts 7:55] for the children of thy people," expressions which can appropriately be applied to Christ, but to no other being." Uriah Smith in *The Prophecies of Daniel*, page 129.

In Greek, <u>the word archangel appears only **twice**</u> and in both cases is called <u>the</u> archangel, indicating that there is <u>only one</u>.

There are three Hebrew words translated as angel. The First one, mal'âk (pronounced mal-awk') is also the most common. It means messenger and also a prophet, king or angel. The second is elôhîym (pronounced el-o-heem') and means God, great, judge, and mighty. This one is translated for angel only in Psalm 8:5. The third one is 'abbîyr (pronounced ab-beer') and it is translated as angel, mighty one, strong (one). Is it coincidence that Jesus is called prophet, king, God, judge and mighty one also? The word angel, from the Greek angelos (aggelos) means messenger.

In the Old Testament, there were occasions when an angel appeared to some people and was worshipped or treated as Deity. If this were a common angel, he would not have accepted any homage from man. When John was so impressed by an angel, he was not allowed to do worship: *"And I fell at his feet to worship him. And he said unto me, See [thou do it] not: I am thy fellow servant..."* (Revelation 19:10). Let's see Exodus 3:2, 4-6. *"and the Angel of the Lord appeared to him [Moses] in a flame of fire <u>out of the midst of a bush</u>...God called to him <u>out of the midst of a bush</u>...And He said, Draw not nigh hither: <u>put off thy shoes from off thy feet, for the place whereon thou standest is holy ground</u>. Moreover He said, **<u>I am the God of Abraham</u>**..."* at first, we see the Angel of the Lord, but when He speaks, reveals himself as God.

Let's see Joshua 5: 13-15 where Joshua thinks that he sees a soldier, but He identifies Himself as the leader of the angels:

> 13 *"And it came to pass, when Joshua was by Jericho, that he lifted up his eyes and looked, and, behold, there stood a man over against him with his sword drawn in his hand: and Joshua went to him, and said to him, Art thou for us, or for our adversaries?*

> 14 *And he said, Nay; but as <u>captain of the host of the LORD</u> am I now come. And <u>Joshua fell on his face</u> to the earth, and <u>did worship</u>, and said to him, What saith <u>my Lord</u> to his servant?*

> 15 *And the captain of the LORD'S host said to Joshua, Loose thy shoe from off thy foot; for <u>the place whereon thou standest is holy</u>. And Joshua did so."*

Here we can see that Joshua worshipped Him and called Him Lord. Also, the ground was called holy. Only the presence of God himself can make a place holy. The captain of the host is the Archangel, one that can be worshipped and is called Lord, one that makes holy the ground where He appears. We can see that this Archangel is not a creature. He is the Lord, the Creator.

Then, we have Manoah asking the name of the Angel (it was a common pagan belief that knowing the secret name of a deity, gave power over that deity, sort of like a genie).

> "And the angel of the LORD said to him, Why askest thou thus after my name, seeing it is secret? So Manoah took a kid with a meat offering, and offered it upon a rock to the LORD: and the angel did wonderously; and Manoah and his wife looked on. For it came to pass, when the flame went up toward heaven from off the altar, that the angel of the LORD ascended in the flame of the altar. And Manoah and his wife looked on it, and fell on their faces to the ground [an act of worship]. But the angel of the LORD did no more appear to Manoah and to his wife. Then Manoah knew that he was an angel of the LORD." And Manoah said to his wife, We shall surely die, because we have seen God" (Judges 13:18-22).

First, Manoah was told that the name of the angel was "secret." The word for secret in Hebrew is pâlîy' and can be translated also as wonderful. Where else did we see that word? In Isaiah 9:6 where the Messiah is called "wonderful (Hebrew pele')." Both words are from the same root. The angel was saying "I am the one whose name is Wonderful, Admirable." Second, Manoah and his wife worshiped Him and they were not prohibited from doing so. Third, and more important, He was called God.

Genesis 16:7-13 presents the Angel of the Lord talking to Agar. Let's read verses 10-13:

> "And the angel of the LORD said to her, I will multiply thy seed exceedingly, that it shall not be numbered for multitude. [can a simple angel, a creature, make such

a promise?] *And the angel of the LORD said to her, Behold, thou art with child, and shalt bear a son, and shalt call his name Ishmael; because the LORD hath heard thy affliction. And he will be a wild man; his hand will be against every man, and every man's hand against him; and he shall dwell in the presence of all his brethren. And she called <u>the name of the LORD that spoke to her, Thou GOD seest me</u>: for she said, Have I also here looked after him that seeth me?"*

She called the angel God. If this were a mistake, the Bible would have omitted it. God would not allow it to be registered so we could be mislead. That specific angel was Jesus.

Malachi 3:1 says that *"the Lord will come to his temple, even the messenger [angel] of the covenant, whom ye delight in."* The Hebrew word for messenger in this verse is mal'âk, and we already presented that it means angel. In other words, <u>the Angel of the Covenant is called Lord-</u> *whom ye delight in.* Could we delight on a common angel?

When Abraham was asked to sacrifice his son, the angel talked to the father of the faithful in first person and called himself The Lord (Genesis 22:15,16):

"And the <u>angel of the LORD</u> called to Abraham out of heaven the second time, And said, <u>By myself</u> have I sworn, <u>saith the LORD</u>, for because thou hast done this thing, and hast not withheld thy son, thine only son..."

Now, why is Jesus presented as an angel? That's easy to answer. Remember Hebrews 1:1,2?

"God, who at sundry times and in divers manners spoke in time past to the fathers by the prophets, Hath in these last days <u>spoken to us by his Son</u>..."

Jesus is the spokesman of the Trinity. That is why He is presented as an angel. <u>It is a matter of roll playing and not a matter of status.</u> Michael is Jesus, "who is like God." Jesus is not an angel, but the commander of the angels. "The president of the United States is the 'chief' of the armed forces of his country. That does not make him a soldier. The fact that the archangel is the chief of all of the angelic host does not imply that He is a created being." Henry Feyerabend, *Daniel Verse by Verse* page 154.

The Catholic belief in Archangels like Raphael and others is not biblically founded. They are just some more of Rome's distractions. Why are the believers not taught to trust in Jesus alone?

FISH FRIDAY

This practice had its origin in the worship of Freya, a pagan fertility goddess. The week day named Friday comes from the name of that deity. Among the Greeks, Venus was equivalent, being worshiped on Fridays (hence in Spanish, Friday is viernes, in honor of that goddess). The Greeks used fish as an offering consecrated to her. There is no Scripture that commands to eat fish on Fridays. This is just another pagan practice of the church that calls itself keeper of the truth. In the times of Samson, one of the deities worshiped by the Philistines was Dagon, represented with a fish head. That is why the hats of popes and cardinals, when look at from the side, resemble a fish with the mouth opened. Paul wrote that in the end times some people will forbid *"to marry, and commanding to abstain from meats [food], which God hath created to be received with thanksgiving of them which believe and know the truth"* (1 Timothy 4:3).

LENT

Where in the Word of our Lord Jesus does it say that we have to celebrate Lent? This practice has its origin in the times of the Old Testament with the 40 days of fasting in honor of Tammuz, for whom the women of Israel use to weep. *"Then he brought me to the door of the gate of the LORD'S house which was toward the north; and, behold, there sat women weeping for Tammuz"* (Ezek. 8:14). The Israelite women were condemned by God for that practice. According to the superstitious teaching of the Canaanites, Tammuz resurrected every spring, in what we call Easter. Today, paganized "Christian" churches celebrate easter with an egg hunt. Eggs were a pagan symbol of the goddess Ishtar. The day that should remind us of Jesus' victory over death is dedicated to egg hunts. Something is wrong with this picture.

EASTER

This word comes from Ishtar, the name of a pagan goddess worshipped by Assyrians and Babylonians. It is celebrated on the first **Sun**day after the first moon in March. The Phoenicians believed that Astarte (another of Ishtar's names) was in charge of the moon. The Hebrew name was Ashtoreth (Solomon built a temple for her in Jerusalem). When the Greeks took Cyprus from the Phoenicians, they identified their goddesses Aphrodite and Artemis with Astarte. Astarte also has been likened to the Roman goddesses Diana and Juno. Also, with the Egyptians ISIS and Hathor. According to a legend, a huge egg fell from heaven in the Euphrates river, from which the goddess Ishtar was born. That is why the egg was associated with her worship. This festivities with colored eggs are celebrated in different parts of the world (China, Egypt, Greece, Japan, Rome, Northern Europe, etc.) to gods known with diverse names.

This festivity was just one of many that were adopted from paganism to attract people to the church. The motive is apparently worthy of praise, but God had said: *"Take heed to thyself that thou be not snared by following them, after that they be destroyed from before thee; and that thou inquire not after their gods, saying, How did these nations serve their gods? even so will I do likewise"* (Deut. 12:30). It has never been the plan of God that we do like the pagans in order to attract them to worship Jesus. God does not like watered down truth because then, it is no longer the truth. That will be adding to the word of God, our only fountain of truth, and the only reliable source for doctrines. God says: *"What thing soever I command you, observe to do it: thou shalt not add thereto, nor diminish from it"* (Deut. 12:32). Nobody has the right to add any doctrine not biblically based, because they will be only doctrines of men & demons, and will be sinful in nature because will not glorify God.

THE MASS

This is called the sacrifice of the mass. It is believed in Catholic circles, that Jesus' sacrifice on the cross is duplicated every time that a mass is celebrated. That can happen up to 500,000 times a day around the world. Only Satan would like to have Jesus nailed to the cross so many times. He hates to admit that those hands are loose and still have the same power to defeat evil and set your soul free.

Paul says: *"So Christ was <u>once offered</u> to bear the sins of many..."* (Hebrews 9:28). In chapter 7:27 we read: *"Who <u>needeth not daily</u>...to offer up sacrifice...for this He did <u>once</u>, when He offered up Himself."*

The mass is just another heresy inherited from ancient Babylon. To accept this teaching would be equivalent to say that Jesus' sacrifice on the cross was not enough. Don't tell that to the thief that repented and was promised life eternal.

For Catholics, the mass is a re-enactment of the Sacrifice of the Cross, upon the altar. Who would like to have Christ sacrificed time and again everyday? Satan would love to keep Him nailed to the cross forever. The mass is just the continuous **mass**acre of our Savior. But behold He is free and is now our lawyer in the kingdom of heaven. Satan does not want people to know that Jesus is interceding for us before the Father, so he can keep the masses praying to Mary for salvation. Hebrews 9:28 says: *"So **Christ was once offered** to bear the sins of many; and unto them that look for him shall he appear the second time without sin unto salvation."* *"But this man, after He had offered <u>one sacrifice</u> for sins <u>for ever</u>, sat down on the right hand of God... For <u>by one offering</u> He hath perfected <u>for ever</u> them that are sanctified... And their sins and iniquities will I remember no more. Now where remission of these is, **there is NO MORE OFFERING FOR SIN**"* (Hebrews

10:12,14,17,18). It does not say that Jesus is offered every day. His one and only sacrifice was more than enough.

The Bible presents in Revelation 17 that the woman (whore) has a cup in her hand. Just take a look to the reverse of the Vatican money where it clearly shows a woman, symbol of the church, holding the cup (photos by author):

The inscription in front reads: Pius XII- Pontifex Maximus, which was a pagan title for the Roman emperor. The back of the coin reads: City of the Vatican, 100 Lyre, and under the woman, the title Fides that means faith, referring to the Catholic faith, or the Catholic Church. It is not coincidence that the Catholic Church has indeed adopted the symbology of a woman holding a golden cup in fulfillment of the prophecy of Revelation 17. No other Christian denomination but the Catholic Church has represented itself with this symbol.

Notice the wafer of the host. It represents the sun coming up in the horizon. It is that way because the round wafer is just a copy of the one used in the Egyptian rite in honor of Horub, Seb and Isis, hence it has those deities' initials (IHS) in some pictures, like in the one below. Notice that the wafer again is represented as the sun (photo by author).

TRANSUBSTANTIATION

This doctrine teaches that during the mass, the bread and the wine change into the real flesh and real blood of Jesus.

"For Roman Catholics, however, the consecrated bread and wine are more than symbols. In the doctrine of transubstantiation, the Eucharistic elements miraculously become the body and blood of Christ while keeping the appearance of bread and wine." *Compton's Encyclopedia*

St. Augustine, who was the biggest contributor to the acceptance of this doctrine, said: "Marvelous dignity of the priest! In the hands, as in the womb of the blessed Virgin Mary, the Son of god becomes incarnate…Behold the power of the priest! It is more than creating the world. Someone said, Does St. Philomena, then, obey the cure of ARS? Certainly, she may well obey him, since God obeys him. The blessed Virgin cannot make her divine son descend into the host. A priest can, however simple he may be." *The wine of Roman Babylon*, by Mary E. Walsh, page 62.

"But our wonder should be far greater when we find that in obedience to the words of the priests HOC EST CORPUS MEUM (this is my body) God Himself descends on the altar, that He comes wherever they call Him, and places Himself in their hands, even though they should be His enemies. And after having come, He remains, entirely at their disposal; they move Him as they please, from one place to another: they may if they wish, shut Him up in the tabernacle, or expose Him on the altar, or carry Him outside the church: they may, if they choose, eat His flesh, and give Him for food to others." Alphonsus de Liguori, *Dignity and Duties of the Priest*, pages, 26,27 & 32.

When the Lord said "this is My body," He was talking figuratively. In John 6, Jesus was talking about eating His flesh and drinking His blood. He explained that *"the flesh profits nothing: the words that I speak unto you, they are spirit, and they are life."* This service was to be the memorial of His great sacrifice. The Communion service points forward to Christ's second coming. It was designed to keep this blessed hope vivid in the minds of the disciples. *"I will not drink henceforth of this fruit of the vine, until that day when I drink it new with you in My Father's kingdom."*

"As we receive the bread and wine symbolizing Christ's broken body and spilled blood, we in imagination join in the scene of Communion in the upper chamber. We seem to be passing through the garden consecrated by the agony of Him who bore the sins of the world. We witness the struggle by which our reconciliation with God was obtained. Christ is set forth crucified among us.

"Looking upon the crucified Redeemer, we more fully comprehend the magnitude and meaning of the sacrifice made by the Majesty of heaven. The plan of salvation is glorified before us, and the thought of Calvary awakens living and sacred emotions in our hearts…"

"He who beholds the Savior's matchless love will be elevated in thought, purified in heart, transformed in character. He will go forth to be a light to the world, to reflect in some degree this mysterious love. The more we contemplate the cross of Christ, the more fully shall we adopt the language of the apostle when he said, *"God forbid that I should glory, save in the cross of our Lord Jesus Christ, by whom the world is crucified unto me, and I unto the world."* Galatians 6:14" (*Desire of Ages* 661).

PURGATORY

"Purgatory, according to Roman Catholic doctrine, the temporary abode and place of punishment for souls that have died in a state of grace but have not yet fully paid the penalty for their transgressions; a place of purification." *Compton's Encyclopedia*

"In Roman Catholicism, purgatory (from the Latin purgare, "to cleanse") is the place or state after death where those who have died in a state of grace but not free from imperfection expiate their remaining sins before entering paradise; the damned, on the other hand, go directly to hell. Purgatory is associated with the doctrine of indulgences.

"The living are encouraged to offer Masses, prayers, alms [money or goods given to the poor in charity- according to the American heritage Dictionary], and other acts of piety and devotion on behalf of those in purgatory." *The Grolier Multimedia Encyclopedia*

What does the Bible say? Psalm 49:6-8 declares: *"They that trust in their wealth, and boast themselves in the multitude of their riches; None of them can by any means redeem his brother, nor give to God a ransom for him: (For the redemption of their soul is precious, and it ceaseth for ever)."* Purgatory is another doctrine that is not found in the Bible. It is like saying that after you die you have a second chance. *"For to him that is joined to all the living there is hope: for a living dog is better than a dead lion"* (Ecclesiastes 9:4). There is no hope of salvation after death. Paul says in Hebrews 9:27 that after death comes judgment. It doesn't even consider purgatory as an alternative. Where are the wicked going to be punished? *"Behold, the righteous shall be recompensed in the earth: much more the wicked and the sinner"* (Proverbs 11:31). The wicked are going to be punished neither in hell, nor in purgatory, but on the surface of the earth.

TRADITION

In addition to the Bible, the Roman church holds as valid a long stream of tradition that began in the early centuries and was consolidated during the Middle Ages, in 1545 AD in the council of Trent, when the church leaders ruled that tradition has the same authority than the Bible.

"This 'deposit of faith,' as it is called, includes teachings transmitted by gatherings of bishops and church councils. These include certain dogmas that have no specific Biblical authority behind them such as the infallibility of the pope and the Assumption of the Virgin Mary." *Compton's Encyclopedia on line*. A dogma is a teaching proclaimed as a truth by a religious organization.

"As it is becoming that holy things he administered in a holy manner and of all things this Sacrifice is the most holy, the Catholic Church, to the end that it might be worthily and reverently offered and received, instituted many centuries ago the Holy Canon, which is so free from error that it contains nothing that does not in the highest degree savor of a certain holiness and piety and raise up to God the minds of those who offer. For it consists partly of the very words of the Lord, partly of the traditions of the Apostles, and also of pious regulations of holy Pontiffs." (*Acts of the Council of Trent*, session 22, chapter IV).

According to the previous paragraph, the Canon, or word of God, consist of: 1) the Bible,

2) the traditions, and

3) the regulations of the popes.

So for a real Catholic, the word of God alone is not enough to show them the way of salvation.

"Fundamental to Catholic belief in all ages has been the assumption that <u>God's love and grace are mediated to the world in a uniquely efficacious way through the ministry of the church</u>." *Encarta Encyclopedia 99* "It is essential, therefore, says cardinal Lefevre, that we remain loyal to Tradition, for <u>without Tradition there is no grace</u>, no continuity in the Church. If we abandon Tradition, we contribute to the destruction of the Church." The Bible teaches that we get grace from God, not from Tradition (Ephesians 2:8). We can only obtain grace directly from the source (Hebrews 4:16). Tradition mixed with the truth waters it down and it is no longer truth. Whether or not is pure tradition or it contains some Bible truth, you do not get the whole benefit that you could have enjoyed had you received the pure and complete truth. Do you prefer to get just watered down apple juice or a whole apple tree from where you can get all the pure apple juice you want to drink?

Cardinal Gibbons wrote: "<u>A Pope's letter is the most weighty authority in the Church</u>" (*The Faith of Our Fathers*, page 93). In page 89 of the same book, he says: "Now <u>the Scriptures alone do not contain all the truths which a Christian is bound to believe</u>, nor do they explicitly enjoin all the duties which he is obliged to practice." Tradition is an addition to the Divinely Inspired Canon. The last book of the Bible admonishes against such foolishness. *"For I testify to every man that hears the words of the prophecy of this book, If any man shall add to these things, God shall add to him the plagues that are written in this book"* (Revelation 22:18). What God said through His prophets is enough for teaching the way of salvation.

Tradition is a contradiction of what the Bible teaches. Psalm 119:105 says: *"Thy word is a lamp to my feet, and a light to my path."* *"All scripture is given by inspiration of God, and is <u>profitable for doctrine</u>, for reproof, <u>for correction</u>, <u>for instruction in righteousness</u>, <u>That the man of God may be perfect, thoroughly furnished to all good works</u>."* (2 Timothy 3:16,17). *"I charge you therefore before God, and the Lord Jesus Christ, who shall judge the quick and the dead at His appearing and His kingdom; <u>Preach the word</u>; be instant in season, out of season; reprove, rebuke, exhort with all longsuffering and doctrine. For <u>the time will come when they will not endure sound doctrine</u>; but after their own lusts shall they heap to themselves teachers, having itching ears; And **they shall turn** *away their ears from the truth, and shall be turned to fables"* (2 Timothy 4:1-4).

"*Knowing this first, that no prophecy of the scripture is of any private interpretation. For the prophecy came not in old time by the will of man: but holy men of God spake as they were moved by the Holy Ghost"* (2 Peter 1:20,21).

"*But there were false prophets also among the people, even as there shall be false teachers among you, who privily shall bring in damnable heresies, even denying the Lord that bought them, and bring upon themselves swift destruction. And many shall follow their pernicious ways; by reason of whom the way of truth shall be evil spoken of. And through covetousness shall they with feigned words make merchandise of you: whose judgment now of a long time lingereth not, and their damnation slumbereth not"* (2 Peter 2:1-3).

"*It is the spirit that quickens; the flesh profits nothing: the words that I speak to you, they are spirit, and they are life...Then Simon Peter answered Him, Lord, to whom shall we go? You have the words of eternal life."*(John 6:63,68). We don't need tradition. We need Jesus and His word abiding in our hearts.

"Men are taking sides, according to their choice. Those that are feeding on the word of God will show this by their practice; they are on the Lord's side, seeking by precept and example to reform the world. ALL THAT HAVE REFUSED TO BE TAUGHT OF GOD, HOLD THE TRADITIONS OF MEN. THEY AT LAST PASS OVER ON THE SIDE OF THE ENEMY, AGAINST GOD, AND ARE WRITTEN, "ANTICHRIST." The people of God, who understand our position in this world's history, are, with ears open and hearts softened and subdued, pressing together in unity - one with Jesus Christ. Those who will not practice the lessons of Christ, but keep themselves in hand to mold themselves, find in antichrist the center of their union. While the two parties stand in collision, the Lord will appear, and shine before his ancients gloriously. He will set up a kingdom that shall stand forever." *Special Testimonies for Ministers and Workers* - No. 9 p. 55

Talking to the church worldwide in 1998, the pope said that to preachers, he recommended better familiarity with the church fathers and with the Catechism of the Catholic Church. He did not recommend familiarity with the Scriptures. They are not as important to him as tradition is because he fears that they would discover what the Bible says about the institution that he heads.

"Theologians also held that certain truths or practices (such as infant baptism), although not found in Scripture, were validated by the tradition of the church." *Microsoft Encarta Encyclopedia 99*

Something that caught my attention was that "great theologians such as the 13th-century Italian St. Thomas Aquinas taught that 'Scripture alone' was the source for theology." *Encarta Encyclopedia 99*. This shows how full of contradictions is this church that pretends to teach the truth.

CONFESSION TO THE PRIEST

St. Alphonsus de Liguori, in his *Dignity and Duties of the Priest*, pages 34-36, wrote "The priest holds the place of the Savior Himself, who, by saying, 'Ego te absolvo', absolves from sin...To pardon a single sin requires all the omnipotence of God...But what only God can do by His Omnipotence, the Priest can do also by saying, 'Ego te absolvo a peccatis tuis [Latin 'I absolve you sinner']."

"The church's claim to the right to pardon leads the Romanist to feel at liberty to sin; and the ordinance of confession, without which her pardon is not granted, tends also to give license to evil. He who kneels before fallen man, and opens in confession the secret thoughts and imaginations of his heart, is debasing his manhood and degrading every noble instinct of his soul. In unfolding the sins of his life to a priest,--an erring, sinful mortal, and too often corrupted with wine and licentiousness,--his standard of character is lowered, and he is defiled in consequence. His thought of God is degraded to the likeness of fallen humanity, for the priest stands as a representative of God. This degrading confession of man to man is the secret spring from which has flowed much of the evil that is defiling the world and fitting it for the final destruction. Yet to him who loves self-indulgence, it is more pleasing to confess to a fellow mortal than to open the soul to God. It is more palatable to human nature to do penance than to renounce sin; it is easier to mortify the flesh by sackcloth and nettles and galling chains than to crucify fleshly lusts. Heavy is the yoke which the carnal heart is willing to bear rather than bow to the yoke of Christ.

"There is a striking similarity between the Church of Rome and the Jewish Church at the time of Christ's first advent. While the

Jews secretly trampled upon every principle of the law of God, they were outwardly rigorous in the observance of its precepts, loading it down with exactions and traditions that made obedience painful and burdensome. As the Jews professed to revere the law, so do Romanists claim to reverence the cross. They exalt the symbol of Christ's sufferings, while in their lives they deny Him whom it represents.

(*The Great Controversy*, pages 567, 568).

"Have mercy upon me, O God, according to thy lovingkindness: according to the multitude of thy tender mercies blot out my transgressions" (Psalm 51:1). Who blots out transgressions? It's God, not the priest. *"Wash me thoroughly from mine iniquity, and cleanse me from my sin"* (Psalm 51:2). When David sinned against God he said, *"I will confess my transgressions __to the LORD__; and thou forgavest the iniquity of my sin"* (Psalm 32:5). He did not confess to the priest, but to God.

"If we confess our sins, <u>He is faithful</u> and just <u>to forgive us our sins, and to cleanse us from all unrighteousness"</u> (1 John 1:9). Note that <u>the one that forgives us is Jesus</u> and not the priest. <u>Jesus is our Priest</u> (Hebrews 8:1,2). Let us run to Jesus. *"Who is a God like to thee, that pardoneth iniquity, and passeth by the transgression of the remnant of his heritage? He retaineth not his anger for ever, because <u>He delighteth in mercy</u>"* (Micah 7:18).

In my opinion, confession is only religious gossip. It satisfies the desires of the voyeur priests that want to know how many of their parishioners are in illicit relationships and everything else they do, etc. It serves also another purpose: it is good for blackmailing. The Jesuits had infiltrated practically every political entity in the world. There are a great intelligence gathering system with the world leaders telling priests everything they want to know in the confessionals.

Thank God we are to confess to Jesus only, because his motives are different and because real forgiveness comes not from any man but from God alone. I am glad that we can trust Him.

Sacraments

The Roman Catholic Church practices seven sacraments. In addition to their version of baptism and the counterfeit Lord's Supper (also called Eucharist and Holy Communion), these are confirmation, penance, marriage, ordination of priests, and anointing of the sick (or last rite). The number of sacraments was finalized in the 16th century- which was about 14 centuries after the last book of the Bible was written. Again, Rome introduced non-biblical doctrines in some of these, and in others, twisted the Holy Writings. Confirmation, penance (the prayers that people have to say after they confess to the priest) and ordination of the priest are not mentioned or required in the Bible. Penance is another way to say that you can help to work your own salvation.

BAPTISM, BY ASPERSION OR SPRINKLING?

Cardinal Gibbons, in his book the *Faith of Our Fathers,* talking about baptism, says that "…the church exercises her discretion in adopting the most convenient mode, according to the circumstances of time and place" Page 277. In the same page he adds: "For several centuries after the establishment of Christianity Baptism was **usually** conferred by immersion; but since the twelfth century the practice of baptizing by infusion has prevailed in the Catholic Church, as this manner is attended with **less inconvenience** than baptism by immersion."

Convenience???? What a way to treat the instructions of the Lord!!!! A religion made to fit. Just like the religion of the Pharisees and Sadducees. Cardinal Gibbons chose to ignore that when Jesus sent His disciples to preach the Gospel, He told them to immerse those that believe, since the word baptize means to immerse. *"Go ye into all the world, and preach the gospel to every creature. He that believeth and is baptized* [immersed] *shall be saved; but he that believeth not shall be damned"* (Mark 16:15, 16). Following Jesus it is not a matter of convenience; it is a matter of love and faith. We don't question God's motives or his instructions. We follow His instructions because we love Him. Notice also that it is necessary to believe before being baptized. This rules out infant baptism, since babies cannot understand the gospel.

The Bible says that when Jesus was baptized, *"went up straightway out of the water"* Mat 3:16. This indicates that He was **under the water**. We should choose to follow Jesus' example, because by doing it, we will never be wrong. *"And John also was baptizing in Aenon near to Salim, **because there was much water there**: and they came, and* *were baptized"* (John 3:23). If baptism by aspersion (sprinkling) were valid, then John did not need to have "much water." A few containers would be enough to baptize a few hundred every day. Dear reader, Jesus will be pleased if you follow His example and are baptized by immersion. This represents the burial of your old lifestyle. *"Therefore **we are buried with him by baptism into death**: that like as Christ was raised up from the dead by the glory of the Father, even so **we also should walk in newness of life**"* (Romans 6:4).

MARRIAGE ANNULMENT

I have read and heard for several years that the Catholic Church condemns divorce. The pope had made several declarations on the subject. Some are calling it a tragedy, a terrible malady, and are campaigning to discourage people from divorcing so they stay married, which I find laudable. They mention all the statistics on broken homes, families that become homeless because of it, fatherless or motherless kids, juvenile delinquency, etc. All that is worthy of commendation, and I back them up 100% on that important issue for our society.

The problem comes when they teach that a marriage can be annuled (nullification, invalidation, cancellation, dissolution), which means that after an investigation by the church authorities, it can be declared that the marriage never happened. That means that you were never married. The biggest contradiction comes when they say that you kids are not illegitimate at all after the dissolution of your marriage. I don't get it. If you were never married, so where did the kids come from? Annulment is just another name for divorce. It is just like saying: "no, you can not divorce, but you can divorce (annul)." It is just another contradiction that is not backed by the Bible. It is a blasphemy. It is hypocrisy; because there is no way that we can violate our vows without offending God and causing pain to others.

Here are some of the doctrines of Babylon that have replaced the truths of God:

God's truths	Pagan ideas that replaced the truth
The Bible as source of authority and truth	Tradition and papal teachings
Jesus died once and for all	The mass- sacrifice everyday many times
Baptism by immersion	Baptism by sprinkling
Communion- the bread represents Jesus	Transubstantiation- the bread becomes Jesus
Death is a sleep	Consciousness in death
Soul is mortal, only God is immortal	The soul is immortal
We rest in the grave until Jesus returns	Souls go to heaven, purgatory or hell after death
Salvation by faith	Salvation by works- forgiveness is earned
Pray to God	Pray to the Virgin and saints
We are forgiven by God	Forgiveness by the priest
Every man should have his wife	Celibacy
Sabbath is the 7th day of the week	The day of rest was changed to the 1st day

PETER - THE FIRST POPE?

•

For Catholics, this is a very sensitive subject. It is said that Peter <u>received </u>from Jesus Christ <u>the supreme pontifical power to be transmitted</u> to his successors. Without this claim, the church leadership would loose its authority and the church organization would loose its cohesion. They base this doctrine on a Bible verse forced out of context: *"And I say also to thee, That thou art Peter, and upon this rock I will build my church; and the gates of hell shall not prevail against it"* (Matthew 16:18). Jesus, when referring to His disciple, called him <u>Petros</u> (PetroV), which means a piece of a rock. The word that Jesus used for rock was <u>Petra</u> (Πετρα), which means a massive rock. The *Matthew Henry Commentary* says: "The word translated "rock," is not the same word as Peter, but is of a similar meaning. Nothing can be more wrong than to suppose that Christ meant the person of Peter was the rock. Without doubt Christ himself is the Rock, the tried foundation of the church; and woe to him that attempts to lay any other!"

The book *The Desire of Ages* says: "Jesus continued: 'I say also to thee, That thou art Peter, and upon this rock I will build My church; and the gates of hell shall not prevail against it." The word Peter signifies a stone,--a rolling stone. Peter was not the rock upon which the church was founded. The gates of hell did prevail against him when he denied his Lord with cursing and swearing. The church was built upon One against whom the gates of hell could not prevail' (Pages 412,413).

Paul, in 1 Corinthians 10:4 wrote: *"And did all drink the same spiritual drink: for they drank of that spiritual Rock that followed them: and **that Rock** (Petra) **was Christ**."* By saying that Peter is the foundation upon which the church was established is to contradict the

Bible. Paul wrote in the same letter: *"For other foundation can no man lay than that is laid, which is Jesus Christ"* (1 Corinthians 3:11). *"And are built upon the foundation of the apostles and prophets, Jesus Christ himself being the chief corner stone; In whom all the building fitly framed together grows to a holy temple in the Lord: In whom you also are built together for a habitation of God through the Spirit."* (Ephesians 2:20-22).

"Centuries before the Savior's advent Moses had pointed to the Rock of Israel's salvation. The psalmist had sung of "the Rock of my strength." Isaiah had written, "Thus saith the Lord God, Behold, I lay in Zion for a foundation a stone, a tried stone, a precious cornerstone, a sure foundation." Deut. 32:4; Ps. 62:7; Isaiah 28:16. Peter himself, writing by inspiration, applies this prophecy to Jesus. He says, "If ye have tasted that the Lord is gracious: to whom coming, a living stone, rejected indeed of men, but with God elect, precious, ye also, as living stones, are built up a spiritual house." 1 Peter 2:3-5, R. V. (*The Desire of Ages*, page 413)." Jesus is the Rock, no doubt about it. It is not Peter. It is not any other man. Thank God for Jesus, He is the living Rock and we need no other to save us.

When Jesus said that upon this Rock I will build my church, He was referring to Himself, shifting away from Peter. Was Peter infallible? Just a few seconds after Jesus' declaration, He had to rebuke Peter. *"From that time forth Jesus began to show to his disciples, how that he must go to Jerusalem, and suffer many things from the elders and chief priests and scribes, and be killed, and be raised again on the third day. Then Peter took Him aside, and began to rebuke Him, saying, Be it far from You, Lord: this shall not happen to you. But He turned, and said to Peter, Get behind Me, Satan: you are an offense to Me: for you are not mindful of the things of God, but those that are of men"* (Mathew 16:21-23). Peter wanted to stop the plan of salvation! He was not infallible.

Jesus also said to His disciple *"And I will give you the keys of the kingdom of heaven: and whatsoever you shall bind on earth shall be bound in heaven: and whatsoever you shall loose on earth shall be loosed in heaven."* (Mathew 16: 19). Was Jesus really giving Peter the right to decide who will go to heaven, like Catholics are taught by their leaders? Paul, in Galatians 2: 11-14 Says: *"But when Peter came to Antioch, I withstood him to the face, because he was to be blamed* [**condemned**]. *For before that certain men came from James, he would eat with the Gentiles: but when they came, he withdrew and separated himself, fearing them*

128

which were of the circumcision. And the other Jews dissembled likewise with him; in such way that Barnabas also was carried away with their hypocrisy. But when I saw that they walked not straightforward according to the truth of the gospel, I said to Peter before them all, 'If you, being a Jew, live after the manner of Gentiles, and not as do the Jews, why do you compel the Gentiles to live as do the Jews?'" Peter played favorites, he made some people superior to others.

Could this person had been entrusted with the keys of heaven, to grant or prohibit access to the kingdom as he pleased? Then those poor gentiles would have been lost! What Jesus meant was that <u>by preaching the message of salvation through the blood of Christ to the world, he would set people free of the shackles of sin and in that way open for then the door of heaven</u>. The Geneva Study Bible comments about the keys: "A <u>metaphor taken from stewards who carry the keys</u>: and here is set forth the power of the ministers of the word, as Isaiah 22:22 says, and that power is common to all ministers, as Matthew 18:18 says, and therefore the ministry of the gospel may rightly be called the key of the kingdom of heaven."

The last book of the Bible shows that ALL the keys are in Jesus' hands. He never gave them away to anybody. *"I am he that lives, and was dead; and, behold, I am alive for evermore, Amen; and **have the keys** of hell and of death."* (Revelation 1:18). *"And to the angel of the church in Philadelphia write; These things says He that is holy, He that is true, <u>He that has the key</u> of David, <u>He that opens, and no man shuts; and shuts, and no man opens</u>"* (Revelation 3:7). Only Jesus has the right to decide to whom He will grant the privilege of going to heaven.

Again the great *Matthew Henry Commentary* comes to our help: "Our Lord next declared the authority with which Peter would be invested. He spoke in the name of his brethren, and this related to them as well as to him. They had no certain knowledge of the characters of men, and were liable to mistakes and sins in their own conduct; but they were kept from error in stating the way of acceptance and salvation, the rule of obedience, the believer's character and experience, and the final doom of unbelievers and hypocrites. In such matters their decision was right, and it was confirmed in heaven. But <u>all pretensions of any man, either to absolve or retain men's sins, are blasphemous and absurd. None can forgive sins but God only</u>. And <u>this binding and loosing, in the common language of</u>

the Jews, signified to forbid and to allow, or to teach what is lawful or unlawful."

What were the keys? Luke 11:52 reads: *"Woe unto you, lawyers! for ye have taken away **the key of knowledge**: ye entered not in yourselves, and them that were entering in ye hindered."* So the keys that Jesus gave to Peter and the other disciples are a symbol of the knowledge of the plan of salvation.

"The keys of the kingdom of heaven" are the words of Christ. All the words of Holy Scripture are His, and are here included. These words have power to open and to shut heaven. They declare the conditions upon which men are received or rejected. Thus the work of those who preach God's word is a savor (flavor, taste, fragrance) of life to life or of death to death. Theirs is a mission weighted with eternal results." *The Desire of Ages*, pages 413,414.

Commenting on Matthew 16:19, the *Geneva Study Bible* says: "They are bound whose sins are retained; heaven is shut against them, because they do not receive Christ by faith: on the other hand, how happy are they to whom heaven is open, who embrace Christ and are delivered by him, and become fellow heirs with him!"

Another passage used to confuse people is John 20:23: *"Whosoever sins ye remit, they are remitted unto them; and whosoever sins ye retain, they are retained."* The best way to explain this concept is with a letter that you send to another person. In that case, you are the remittent. The word remit in Greek means "to send." When we tell sinners about Jesus, all we can do is remit them to the Savior and if they confess, their sins will in turn be remitted by Jesus to the depths of the sea (Micah 7:19).

Now, was Peter the leader of the church? Acts 12:17 says that Peter, after being released miraculously, went to a friend's house. *"But he, motioning to them with the hand to keep silent, he declared to them how the Lord had brought him out of the prison. And he said, Go tell these things to James, and to the brethren. And he departed and went to another place."* If he had to report to James (Jesus' brother) Peter was not the leader. In Acts 15 we read about the problem that the young church was having with the teachings of some people. They were disturbing the gentiles that had just accepted Jesus as Savior and Lord. Peter was in that council (verse 7). After Peter finished talking, Paul and Barnabas spoke to the Multitude. When they finished, James took the word and said: *"Therefore my sentence [judgment] is, that we trouble not them, which from among the Gentiles are turned to God"* (Acts 15:19). Only the leader could pronounce sentence. Please, read the whole chapter and see by yourself that Peter was not the leader; it was James. Later on, in the same record book of the primitive church says: *"And when we were come to Jerusalem, the brethren received us gladly. And the following day Paul went in with us to James; and all the elders were present. And when he had saluted them, he declared particularly what things God had wrought among the Gentiles by his ministry"* (Acts 21:17-19). Did they report to Peter, as they were supposed to do if he were the "pope"? No, absolutely not. They reported to James, the council leader.

"The Savior did not commit the work of the gospel to Peter individually. At a later time, repeating the words that were spoken to Peter [Mathew 18:18], He applied them directly to the church. And the same in substance was spoken also to the twelve as representatives of the body of believers. <u>If Jesus had delegated any special authority to one of the disciples above the others, we should not find them so often contending as to who should be the greatest. They would have submitted to the wish of their Master, and honored the one whom He had chosen.</u>" *Ibid*

In his letter to the church in Galatia, Paul wrote: *"And when James, Cephas, and John, who seemed to be pillars, perceived the grace that was given to me, they gave to me and Barnabas the right hands of fellowship; that we should go to the heathen, and they to the circumcision."* (Galatians 2:9). By placing James' name first, indicates that Peter was not the church leader.

"'<u>The head of every man is Christ.' God, who put all things under the Savior's feet, 'gave Him to be the head over all things to the church</u>, which is His body, the fullness of Him that fills all in all.' 1 Corinthians 11:3; Eph. 1:22, 23. The church is built upon Christ as its foundation; it is to obey Christ as its head. It is not to depend upon man, or be controlled by man. Many claim that a position of trust in the church gives them authority to dictate what other men shall believe and what they shall do. This claim God does not sanction. The Savior declares, 'All ye are brethren.' All are exposed to temptation, and are

131

liable to error. Upon no finite being can we depend for guidance. The Rock of faith is the living presence of Christ in the church. Upon this the weakest may depend, and those who think themselves the strongest will prove to be the weakest, unless they make Christ their efficiency. 'Cursed be the man that trusts in man, and makes flesh his arm.' The Lord 'is the Rock, His work is perfect.' 'Blessed are all they that put their trust in Him.' Jer. 17:5; Deut. 32:4; Ps. 2:12." (*The Desire of Ages*, page 414).

How does Peter calls himself? *"The elders which are among you I exhort, <u>who am also **an elder**</u>, and a witness of the sufferings of Christ, and also a partaker of the glory that shall be revealed"* (1 Peter 5:1). No, Peter was never a pope. After living for 3 ½ years with the one that did not have where to rest his head (Matthew 8:20), he would have never agreed to live in a sumptuous palace with 1,200 rooms and servants. The book of Acts records that when he went to the temple with John, he found a lame man begging. *"Then Peter said, <u>Silver and gold have I none</u>; but such as I have give I thee: In the name of Jesus Christ of Nazareth rise up and walk"* (Acts 3:6). The Catholic Church today is the richest kingdom on earth. How they contrast with Jesus and His teachings!

THE PAPACY

Since Peter was not a pope, and Jesus never appointed a man to rule as a prince over His church, the church instituted the papacy through fraud. A papal aide produced a false document (so it has been proven, but still is treasured by the church) known as The Donation of Constantine in which declared that the Roman emperor gave Rome, the great patriarchates and temporal sovereignty over Italy and the Western Empire, along with the Lateran Palace, and the islands of the seas to the popes perpetually. The following quote is from a Catholic website:

"...Constantine is made to confer on Sylvester and his successors the following privileges and possessions: the pope, as successor of St. Peter, has the primacy over the four Patriarchs of Antioch, Alexandria, Constantinople, and Jerusalem, also over all the bishops in the world. The Lateran basilica at Rome, built by Constantine, shall surpass all churches as their head, similarly the churches of St. Peter and St. Paul shall be endowed with rich possessions. The chief Roman ecclesiastics (*clerici cardinales*), among whom senators may also be received, shall obtain the same honours and distinctions as the senators. Like the emperor the Roman Church shall have as functionaries *cubicularii, ostiarii*, and *excubitores*. The pope shall enjoy the same honorary rights as the emperor, among them the right to wear an imperial crown, a purple cloak and tunic, and in general all imperial insignia or signs of distinction; but as Sylvester refused to put on his head a golden crown, the emperor invested him with the high white cap (*phrygium*). Constantine, the document continues, rendered to the pope the service of a *strator*, i.e. he led the horse upon which the pope rode. Moreover, the emperor makes a present to the pope and his successors of the Lateran palace, of Rome and the provinces, districts, and towns of Italy and all the Western regions (*tam palatium nostrum, ut prelatum est, quamque Romæ urbis et omnes Italiæ seu occidentalium regionum provincias loca et civitates*). The document goes on to say that for himself the emperor has established in the East a new capital which bears his name, and thither he removes his government, since it is inconvenient that a secular emperor have power where God has established the residence of the head of the Christian religion. The document concludes with maledictions against all who dare to violate these donations and with the assurance that the emperor has signed them with his own hand and placed them on the tomb of St. Peter." Quoted taken from http://www.newadvent.org/cathen/05118a.htm

It's interesting that the document contains the phrase "...Petrus in terris VICARIUS FILII DEI...", which claims that Peter on earth was the vicar of the Son of God. The definition of vicarious is representative or substitute. So this document is claiming that the pope is substituting Christ.

The document is dated March 30, 315 AD, but it was really created in the eighth century and of course, by then Constantine was dead and could not tell the truth. Lorenzo Valla, a rhetoric professor at the University of Pavia, in his *Declamatio* (*Treatise on the Donation of Constantine*), which he wrote in 1440, attacked the crude Latin of its anonymous author and from that observation he argued that the document could not possibly have dated from the time of Constantine. Even with this proof Rome kept its churches, properties and influence almost intact.

The Catholic power enjoyed such influence in world affairs after the end of the Western Roman Empire in AD 476, that it is called by some the resurrected Roman Empire or a continuation of it. The alliances between the popes of Rome and the kings of Europe made the papacy a powerful force in European politics and culture during the Middle Ages. The church became so strong that for a time the popes were able to command the submission of the great European monarchs. One of the occasions when the papacy used this power even to depose a king happened in 1213 AD when Pope Innocent III forced English King John to acknowledge the pope as feudal lord. The pope ordered the king's subjects to disobey him, forcing the monarch to beg the pope for forgiveness, and to promise total submission to him. Pope Gregory VII stated that of the pope alone all princes shall kiss the feet and that it may be permitted to him to depose emperors. Another pope, Innocent III wrote:

"The creator of the universe set up two great luminaries in the firmament of heaven; the greater light to rule the day, the lesser light to rule the night. In the same way for the firmament of the universal Church, which is spoken of as heaven, he appointed two great dignities; the greater to bear rule over souls (these being, as it were, days), the lesser to bear rule over bodies (those being, as it were, nights). These dignities are the pontifical authority and the royal power. Furthermore, the moon derives her light from the sun, and is in truth inferior to the sun in both size and quality, in position as well as effect. In the same way the royal power derives its dignity from the pontifical authority: and the more closely it cleaves to the sphere of that authority the less is the light with which it is adorned; the further it is removed, the more it increases in splendor" (*Empire and Papacy* 'The Moon and the Sun' *Sicut universitatis conditor*, October 1198).

Pope Boniface VIII (1294-1303) issued his bull Unam Sanctam in 1302AD, asserting supreme authority over secular state and every human creature. In other words, he owned the people and everything they had.

"But the supreme teacher in the Church is the Roman Pontiff. Union of minds, therefore, requires, together with a perfect accord in the one faith, complete submission and obedience of will to the Church and to the Roman Pontiff, **as to God Himself**." *The Great Encyclical Letters of Pope Leo XIII* (New York: Benziger, 1903).

Jesus said to Pilate that His kingdom was not of this world (John 18:36) but the papacy has done its best through the centuries to settle on this earth, uniting with the state, fulfilling in that way the description presented in Revelation 18:3: *"For all nations have drunk of the wine of the wrath of her fornication, and the kings of the earth have committed fornication with her, and the merchants of the earth are waxed rich through the abundance of her delicacies."* Riches unjustly taken from the people are treasured in the Vatican. They have gold, precious stones, silver, art, etc. *"How much she has glorified herself, and lived deliciously... The merchandise of gold, and silver, and precious stones, and of pearls, and fine linen, and purple, and silk, and scarlet, and all citron wood, and all manner vessels of ivory, and all manner vessels of most precious wood, and of brass, and iron, and marble, And cinnamon,* and incense, and ointments, and frankincense, and wine, and oil, and fine flour, and wheat, and beasts, and sheep, and horses, and chariots, and slaves, and souls of men" (Revelation 18:7,12,13). What an accurate description!

In a passage that appropriately applies to the popes and cardinals, the book of Revelation presents them as *"clothed in fine linen, and purple, and scarlet, and decked with gold, and precious stones, and pearls!"* (Revelation 18:16). I can not imagine Jesus dressed like that, ministering to the poor, to those that starve.

The rich clothing of the Catholic clergy and the luxury of the Catholic Churches can be appreciated on a painting by Claudio Coello, in which King Charles II of Spain is represented while receiving Holy Communion. See *Microsoft Encarta Encyclopedia 99.*

"But Romanism as a system is no more in harmony with the gospel of Christ now than at any former period in her history. The Protestant churches are in great darkness, or they would discern the signs of the times. The Roman Church is far-reaching in her plans and modes of operation. She is employing every device to extend her influence and increase her power in preparation for a fierce and determined conflict to <u>regain control of the world</u>, to <u>re-establish persecution</u>, and to <u>undo all that Protestantism has done</u>. Catholicism is gaining ground upon every side. See the increasing number of her churches and chapels in Protestant countries. Look at the popularity of her colleges and seminaries in America, so widely patronized by Protestants. Look at the growth of ritualism in England and the frequent defections to the ranks of the Catholics. These things should awaken the anxiety of all who prize the pure principles of the gospel.

"Protestants have tampered with and patronized popery; they have made compromises and concessions which papists themselves are surprised to see and fail to understand. Men are closing their eyes to the real character of Romanism and the dangers to be apprehended from her supremacy. The people need to be aroused to resist the advances of this most dangerous foe to civil and religious liberty.

"Many Protestants suppose that the Catholic religion is unattractive and that its worship is a dull, meaningless round of ceremony. Here they mistake. While Romanism is based upon deception, it is not a coarse and clumsy imposture. The religious service of the Roman Church is a most impressive ceremonial. Its gorgeous display and solemn rites fascinate the senses of the people and silence the voice of reason and of conscience. The eye is charmed. Magnificent churches, imposing processions, golden altars, jeweled shrines, choice paintings, and exquisite sculpture appeal to the love of beauty. The ear also is captivated. The music is unsurpassed. The rich notes of the deep-toned organ, blending with the melody of many voices as it swells through the lofty domes and pillared aisles of her grand cathedrals, cannot fail to impress the mind with awe and reverence"

"This outward splendor, pomp, and ceremony, that only mocks the longings of the sin-sick soul, is an evidence of inward corruption. The religion of Christ needs not such attractions to recommend it. In the light shining from the cross, true Christianity appears so pure and lovely that no external decorations can enhance its true worth. It is the beauty of holiness, a meek and quiet spirit, which is of value with God.

"Brilliancy of style is not necessarily an index of pure, elevated thought. High conceptions of art, delicate refinement of taste, often exist in minds that are earthly and sensual. They are often employed by Satan to lead men to forget the necessities of the soul, to lose sight of the future, immortal life, to turn away from their infinite Helper, and to live for this world alone.

"A religion of externals is attractive to the unrenewed heart. The pomp and ceremony of the Catholic worship has a seductive, bewitching power, by which many are deceived; and they come to look upon the Roman Church as the very gate of heaven. None but those who have planted their feet firmly upon the foundation of truth, and whose hearts are renewed by the Spirit of God, are proof against her influence. Thousands who have not an experimental knowledge of Christ will be led to accept the forms of godliness without the power. Such a religion is just what the multitudes desire. ...

"Papists place crosses upon their churches, upon their altars, and upon their garments. Everywhere is seen the insignia of the cross. Everywhere it is outwardly honored and exalted. But the teachings of Christ are buried beneath a mass of senseless traditions, false interpretations, and rigorous exactions. The Savior's words concerning the bigoted Jews, apply with still greater force to the leaders of the Roman Catholic Church: "They bind heavy burdens and grievous to be borne, and lay them on men's shoulders; but they themselves will not move them with one of their fingers." Matthew 23:4. Conscientious souls are kept in constant terror fearing the wrath of an offended God, while many of the dignitaries of the church are living in luxury and sensual pleasure.

"The worship of images and relics, the invocation of saints, and the exaltation of the pope are devices of Satan to attract the minds of the people from God and from His Son. To accomplish their ruin, he endeavors to turn their attention from Him through whom alone they can find salvation. He will direct them to any object that can be substituted for the One who has said: "Come to Me, all ye that labor and are heavy-laden, and I will give you rest." Matthew 11:28. (*The Great Controversy*, pages 565- 569).

Pope John Paul II and others before him had called for a better distribution of riches (sounds like Socialism), but they are not willing to obey Jesus and sell everything that they have and share it with the poor (Mathew 19:21). I recognize that there had been cases where the poor had been taken care of, like Mother Teresa did in Calcutta, India, and I think that it has been admirable. What causes me to worry is the fact that I never saw that humble woman talking to those poor souls about the free salvation that we have through Christ. Never did I see her carrying a Bible to read the Good News of the Gospel to the lost, so they could find salvation. Only the temporary needs were supplied.

The papacy has been plagued with conspiracies and scandals, one intrigue after the other. Pope Adrian IV (1154-1159 AD), the only Englishman to ascend to the papacy, almost immediately confronted Arnold of Brescia, an Italian monk and reformer who opposed the temporal power of the papacy. At Pope Adrian's request, the German king Frederick I seized Arnold and turned him over to the Roman Curia for trial as a political rebel. He was found guilty, of course, and condemned to death. After Arnold's execution in 1155, Pope Adrian crowned Frederick Holy Roman Emperor as a reward for his services.

Jesus had a very different way to treat those that where not part of His group of disciples. *"And John answered him, saying, Master, we saw one casting out devils in thy name, and he does not follow us: and we forbade him, because he does not follow us. But Jesus said, Do not forbid him: for there is no man which shall do a miracle in my name, that can lightly speak evil of me. For he that is not against us is on our part"* (Mark

9:38-40). In no place in the New Testament are we told to execute those that don't think alike.

Just to give you an idea of how much power the popes pretend to have, just look at this coin and observe that the triple crown that represents the papacy is <u>above the cross</u>, just as Paul had said in 2 Thessalonians 2:4 that this power "exalteth himself above all that is called God, or that is worshipped; so that he as God sitteth in the temple of God, showing himself that he is God."

Above photo from *The Prophetic Faith of Our Fathers*, Volume II, page 556, by Le Roy E. Froom, published by Review and Herald Publishing Association, Washington D.C., Copyright 1948.

The inscription reads: "OMNES REGES SERVIENTEI", which translated is "ALL KINGS ARE ITS SERVANT." What a contrast with Jesus who came as servant of servants! *"For even the Son of man came not to be ministered unto, but to minister, and to give his life a ransom for many"* (Mark 10:45).

Let's look once more at this coin from a previous page, in which a woman holds a cup, just as Revelation 17 describes the great harlot. Notice also that the rising sun is shown coming out of the cup.

Will Durant, one of the most reliable sources of church history, in his Story of Civilization, Volume 4, page 680 wrote about the rebuke of king Edward II by Pope Clement V: "We hear that you forbid torture as contrary to the laws of your land. But no state law can override the canon law, our law. Therefore I command you at once to submit those men to torture."

Pope Martin V gave the commandment to the king of Poland to destroy the heretics:

"Know that the interest of the Holy See, and those of your crown, make it a duty to exterminate the Hussites. Remember that those impious persons dare to proclaim principles of equality; they maintain that all Christians are brethren, and that God has not given to privileged men the right of ruling nations; they hold that Christ came on earth to abolish slavery; they call the people to liberty, that is to the annihilation of kings and priest.

"While there is still time, then, turn your forces against Bohemia; burn, massacre, make deserts everywhere, for nothing could be more agreeable to God, or more useful to the cause of kings, than the extermination of the Hussites" R.W. Thompson, *The Papacy and Civil Power*, page 553.

Describing the effort to conquer England, William P. Grady wrote in his book *Final Authority*: "On July 19th, the vanguard of Spain's "invincible armada" was spotted. A mere thirty-four warships and fifty-eight support vessels under the command of Charles, Lord Howard, assisted by Sir Francis Drake prepared to engage her. What happened next has constituted one of the most remarkable displays of Divine intervention in all of recorded history.

"The year before, Drake had led a surprise attack on the Spanish ships in Cadiz Harbor and discovered firsthand the Armada's construction project. Having been reared in the home of a Puritan minister, the undaunted "P.K." assured his Queen:

"God increase your most excellent Majesty's forces both by sea and land daily,... for this I surely think: there was never any force so strong as there is now ready or making ready against your Majesty and true religion; but . . . the Lord of all strengths is stronger and will defend the truth of his Word.

"Outmaneuvered by the smaller British vessels, the Spanish admiral, Medina-Sidonia, wrote in desperation:

"'The enemy pursued me, they fire on me from morn till dark, but they will not grapple...There is no remedy, for they are swift and we are slow.

"Sustaining over 8,000 casualties on the twenty-seventh alone, Medina-Sidonia had had enough! However, the Northern seas would devour many thousands more along the stormy route of retreat. Twenty-three ships were wrecked off the rocky coast of Ireland alone. Over 1,100 drowned Spaniards were washed up on the beach of Sligo. And those who made it to the shore alive had their throats cut by the Kernes (poorer class of Irishmen).

"Only fifty-one ships bearing 10,000 survivors were able to limp back to Spain. The Jesuit-educated Durant could only say that, 'The winds favored Elizabeth.' However, a total count of English losses placed at *60 men and 0 ships* would divert the attention of sober men to Him Who *'createth the wind.'* (Amos 4:13) Not a single hole was made below any English waterline!'"

I did not understand as a Catholic child why the Armada was destroyed until I read the History accounts and found out that it was just a religious war intended to conquer England for the pope. I was always taught in school that Sir Francis Drake was the bad guy in that defeat. Thanks God now I know the truth. He was just fighting for the freedoms that his country was enjoying without a pope. The Quakers should have considered themselves in Paradise, compared to the countries under the papacy.

These days, the Jesuits are working in the distortion of the Bible translations in different languages. The Greek texts Vaticanus and Sinaiticus are being used as the base of many modern translations such as the NIV (*New International Version*), RSV (*Revised Standard Version*) and others like the Spanish 1960 *Reina-Valera*. In this last version, the change on behalf of Catholic doctrine is very evident. In Spanish, the fourth commandment requires the observance of Saturday, for that is the way how Sabbath is translated into that language. The 1960 revision says "Remember to keep the <u>day of rest</u>," which is not the correct translation of the passage. Evidently the intent was to make this Bible circulate for several years until all the copies of the 1909 version disappeared. Then another version that would say "Remember to keep Sunday holy" would do just great for Rome's interest. We can praise the name of God, because again He intervened on behalf of the seekers of truth. In 1997, the Editorial Clie from Spain published a version more faithful to the originals and the truth was preserved once again.

I can not say that the Jesuits would not attempt again to change the Scriptures, because I owned a New Testament that says in Revelation 1:10 "I went in the Spirit **on Sunday**...." They need to remember, for the sake of their souls, what John wrote in the book of Revelation 22:18, 19: *"For I testify unto every man that heareth the words of the prophecy of this book, If any man shall add unto these things, God shall add unto him the plagues that are written in this book: And if any man shall take away from the words of the book of this prophecy, God shall take away his part out of the book of life, and out of the holy city, and from the things which are written in this book."* May God have mercy of their souls and may they allow Him to save them before is too late. Jesus died for them too. It makes me so sad to see how they are closing their ears and eyes to the evidence on behalf of the truth!

INFALLIBILITY?

What would Paul answer to that? *"God forbid: yes, let God be true, but **every man a liar**; as it is written, That you might be justified in your sayings, and might overcome when you are judged"* (Romans 3:4). To say that a man is infallible is to say that such a man does not lie, that there are not contradictions among such men that claim that attribute. One of the church fathers, Augustine, wrote: "…for that reason, whoever reads this, in whatever is in agreement with me, walk with me; in whatever doubts as I doubt, investigate with me; where he sees his error, turn to me; where sees mine, take me away from it." De Trinitate I 2,5. No pope now would listen to St. Augustine regarding that quote.

How did that doctrine creep into the Catholic Church? The historical context of Vatican I indicates that the pope of that time (Pius IX) was doing a desperate attempt to restore the prestige and power of the Catholic Church. At the end of the 18th century (1798), fulfilling the prophecy of Daniel 7 and Revelation 11 and 13, one of the generals of Napoleon kidnapped the pope, ending thus the arbitrary dominion of the papacy over the consciences of the people. Around that time, the world saw the excesses of the French Revolution, when the Catholic properties where confiscated and the priests persecuted and killed (as they themselves did for over a thousand years to the innocent and inoffensive Sabbath keepers and those who believed in righteousness by faith). The French Revolution bred the spreading of humanistic teachings at the beginning of the 19th century: socialism, masonry and democratic ideas. All this represented a threat for the authority of the pope. It was, as Dr. Hans Küng- Catholic theologian- says, a reaction of fear.

Who was Pope Pius IX? His name was Giovanni Maria Mastai-Ferretti (1792 –1878). He was Pope from 1846-78. His reign was the longest in Catholic papacy. During his pontificate the Papal States and Rome were annexed to a unified Italy (1870). He is known for enforcing the dogma of the Immaculate Conception in 1854 and he presided over the First Vatican Council (1869- 70), which was interrupted by the capture of Rome in October 1870 by Italian troops. The council upheld the pope as supreme leader of the Catholics, declared that God could be known by reason, and approved the dogma of papal infallibility when speaking ex-cathedra on matters of faith or morals. When the Pope speaks "ex-cathedra", which means *from the chair* [of Peter], Catholic's are bound to believe his decree as though it was given from God himself, since he claims that he alone has authority from God.

The first Vatican council was the 20th ecumenical council of the Catholic Church. It was convened on December 8, 1869 at the Vatican by Pope Pius IX.

In the way he acted and treated his subordinates, that pope left no doubts in many minds about his mental sanity and competitiveness. He once saw a lame man and pretended to heal him. The man was told by the pope to stand up and walk. He tried, but collapsed. This pope also applied John 14:6 to himself (*"I am the way, the truth, and the life"*), indicating in that way that he saw himself as Jesus. In his Syllabus of Errors (December 8, 1864), the pope listed a comprehensive compendium of modern errors that included progress, liberalism, and modern civilization. He also condemned the Biblical societies for distributing Bibles (so he could keep the consciences chained by ignorance) and demanded total subordination of the nations and scientific investigation (remember Galileo?) to the authority of the Catholic Church. He was a very emotional (and irrational) man of very little theological training. During the Council, some of the attendees complained about the excessive pressure received, the lack of freedom of conscience and the coercion to vote on favor of the dogma (several of the attendees wrote about the threats of excommunication if they did not vote on favor of the dogma).

The document started excommunicating whoever says that Peter was not constituted as prince over the church, and that Peter would not have perpetual successors, or that the pope is not a successor of Peter. Also, it excommunicated everybody who dared to say that "the Roman pontiff alone has duty of inspection and direction, but not full and supreme power of jurisdiction on the universal church, not alone in the matters that belong to the faith and morals, but also in those of regime and discipline of the church, widespread all over the orb, or that has the principal part, but with all the fullness of this supreme authority; or that this his authority is not ordinary and immediate, above all and each one of the churches, as well as above all and each one of the shepherds and faithful."

It was said that "all the directly doctrinal instructions of all the encyclicals, of all the letters directed to the particular bishops and all the allocutions [=harangue, address] pronounced by the popes, are declarations ex cathedra and ipso facto [by that very fact, or for that reason] infallible." W.G. Ward director of the Dublin Review as quoted by Hans Küng in his book *Infallible?*

This dogma reaffirmed the idea that the pope was not a mere man. It was said that "the infallibility of the pope is the infallibility of Jesus himself" (C.Butler and C. Lang in Das Vatkanische Koncil, page 68).

"The papal church will never relinquish her claim to infallibility. All that she has done in her persecution of those who reject her dogmas she holds to be right; and would she not repeat the same acts, should the opportunity be presented? Let the restraints now imposed by secular governments be removed and Rome be reinstated in her former power, and there would speedily be a revival of her tyranny and persecution" (*The Great Controversy*, Page 564.

We can not fall asleep before these errors, since Jesus says that we are to be watchful. Rome imitates God and falsifies or copies everything that God does or says. I think that their attitude is: "I the church don't change, just as God said in Malachi 3:6: 'For I am the LORD, I change not.'"

IMPURITY ABOUNDS

In Revelation 18:2, Babylon is presented as "a cage of every unclean and hateful bird." This is very interesting for me, because in Puerto Rico, where I lived for so many years, gays are called ducks and the Church is being plagued by the homosexual priests' scandals.

One of the church problems that have been brought to public attention in recent years is the high number of priests that are sexually abusing or fondling boys all around the world. I am not saying that this is an exclusive Catholic problem, but it is one caused by the obstinate perpetuation of a custom that is not biblically based: celibacy. Peter was married (Matthew 8:14). Millions of dollars had been awarded to victims that were abused when they were altar boys or students in Catholic institutions. Recently, I read that training is offered to Catholic high school faculty and administrators, that teaches that gay, lesbian, bisexual and transgender people deserve to be respected and treated with dignity. God loves gays and lesbians. This, however, does not imply that He approves of their lifestyle. I see that the only reason the Catholic Church has to show respect to gay teachers is to give them the opportunity to have kids to prey on.

The Dallas Morning News reported in 1998 cases of two individuals who accused Father Kenneth J. Roberts, a retired priest of the Dallas Diocese, of sexual molestation. They received, according to the paper, funds for treatment or settlement from the Dallas Diocese. The diocese has not confirmed or denied the reports. But there are hundreds of other cases. One of them was in Germany (March 2010) where even Pope Benedict was mentioned as looking the other way when he was still a cardinal. It is said that he even approved the transfer of an accused predator priest instead of removing him from the church. That priest went on to abuse children in his new church, just as many more priests did in so many places. The worst thing is that instead of dealing with the problem in a way that would protect future possible victims, the church bishops just transferred the accused predators to other parishes where they would just find a fresh supply of new victims. It seems like they were just as guilty of the same crimes and that is why they were so lenient (as a matter of fact, some of the leaders have been also accused). Thousands of children have been abused worldwide and more cases are being brought to light by victims and the governments of different nations, such as Ireland, were the abuse investigation concentrated in the 1930's to the 1990's. The real number of abused children will never be known because the majority will not dare to come forward.

While the pope presents his opinion, totally against any sexual deviation, the bishops and priests defend their practice, because some of them are involved in the "lifestyle" that caused the destruction of Sodom and Gomorrah, Adma, Seboim and Zoar. A practice that is condemned in different parts of the Bible inspired by One that does not change. Let's read some of those passages. *"**Thou shalt not lie with man, as with woman**: it is abomination. Do not defile yourselves in any of these things: for in all these the nations are defiled which I cast out before you"* (Leviticus 18:22,24). *"There shall be no whore of the daughters of Israel, nor a sodomite of the sons of Israel."* (Deut. 23:17). *"The men, leaving the natural use of the woman, burned in their lust one toward another; **men with men** working that which is unseemly, and receiving in themselves that recompense of their error which was meet. And even as they did not like to retain God in their knowledge, God gave them over to a reprobate mind, to do those things which are not convenient; Being filled with all unrighteousness, fornication, wickedness, covetousness, maliciousness; full of envy, murder, debate, deceit, malignity; whisperers, backbiters, haters of God, despiteful, proud, boasters, inventors of evil things, disobedient to parents, without understanding, covenant breakers, without natural affection, implacable, unmerciful: who knowing the judgment of God, that they which commit such things are worthy of death, not only do the same, but have pleasure in them that do them."* (Romans 1:27-32)

SUPERSTITION

Rome had a great deal of superstitions that crept into the church and where adopted and taught by the priests in the Middle Ages. "For centuries Europe made no progress in learning, arts, or civilization. A moral and intellectual paralysis had fallen upon the Christendom" (*What's Behind The New World Order*, page 10). The people, as they lacked the Scriptures, just accepted what the priests were telling them as truths from heaven. A quote that is found in several books describes well this period: "the noon of the papacy was the midnight of the world" (J.A. Wylie, *The Story of the Reformation*). By keeping the people ignorant, they were successful in keeping them subject to the will of the church leaders. The minds were chained. A modern example of mind control is what happened in the killing fields of Cambodia, where 2 million people were killed in just 4 years because they went to school, in order to keep the nation in ignorance, and consequently submitted to the authorities.

Believers were taught among other things, to trust that by looking at, or touching the churches' relics, they could win the favor of God.

One bizarre example of how superstitious the people were because of church influence was the belief in werewolves. "In the Middle ages, the church had stigmatized the wolf as the personification of evil and a servant of Satan himself. The Church courts managed to put so much pressure on schizophrenics, epileptics and the mentally disabled, that they testified to be werewolves and admitted to receive their orders directly from Satan. After 1270 it was even considered heretical not to believe in the existence of werewolves" (*Encyclopedia Mythica*- Article: Werewolf).

I was told when I was a kid that if I worked on Good Fridays, my tools would make the objects bleed (meaning that if I cut wood with my saw I would see blood). This was just superstition and when I was about 12 years old I purposely made a cut on a tree to see if it was true- it was not. I was lied to and that set me on a research adventure to see in what else they lied to me.

Superstition plays a roll on weird customs the world over. Take for example what happens in January every year when hundreds of pet owners bring their animals to be blessed on the day of San Anton, Spain's patron saint of animals. Jesus blessed children, not animals.

CHANGING THEOLOGY

The Catholic Church is like a chameleon. It is something in one place and another thing in a different place. For example, In United States, they uphold democracy; in Latin America, they are Marxists. In most countries they promote selfish practices like their famous fundraiser called bingo, while in Italy, they are condemning the lottery, because it can throw some people into a continual anticipation of a win, ruining families and replacing the responsibility of daily work according to Capuchin Father Raniero Cantalamessa, preacher of the papal household. Is it that bingo can not do that too?

Some priests interviewed by Italian media even declared that it was immoral for the state, in this case the Italian government, to be promoting lottery participation, and they argued that when "lotto fever" becomes a social addiction, it's not much different than selling drugs. Many lotto players were turning to the saints for help in choosing the winning numbers and also for a hand in winning. A magazine survey found that one in three Italian lottery players prayed to a saint for help. Other lotto hopefuls pray to the souls of their love ones in purgatory, in the belief that they can do each other a favor, because they believe that dead souls need prayers to ease their suffering (another belief that is not founded in the Bible), and the living need supernatural help from the dead to win a jackpot. The Catholic Church got the people hooked on lotto with their greedy example and now they try to look innocent, just as the drug pusher says about his client: "I did not make him use it".

THE INQUISITION

"Waves of opposition to the Roman Catholic Church swept over Europe in the 13th century. The church established a tribunal called the Inquisition to try persons accused of being heretics, that is, of revolting against religious authority... At a grand ceremonial, called sermo generalis or auto-da-fé, the names of the guilty were announced and punishments inflicted, ranging from fines and excommunication to imprisonment for life or burning at the stake for incorrigible heretics. Since canon law forbade the clergy to participate in bloodshed, the severer penalties were carried out by the state.

"The Inquisition was chiefly active in southern Europe and in parts of Latin America. It continued in modified form in Spain until 1820. Pope Paul III established the Congregation of the Holy Office in 1542 to review the judgments of the Inquisition courts and to examine charges of heresy. It was supplanted during Vatican Council II (1962-1965) by the *Congregation for the Doctrine of the Faith. Compton's Encyclopedia on line*

"The Inquisition was a medieval church court instituted to seek out and prosecute heretics. The term is applied to the institution itself, which was episcopal or papal, regional or local; to the personnel of the tribunal; and to the judicial procedure followed by the court. Notoriously harsh in its procedures, the Inquisition was defended during the Middle Ages by appeal to biblical practices and to the church father Saint Augustine, who had interpreted Luke 14:23 as endorsing the use of force against heretics." *The Grolier Multimedia Encyclopedia*

"Problems with sects like the Albigenses (Cathari) and Waldenses in the 12th century first led to the Episcopal Inquisition. Often at the instigation of secular rulers, bishops were urged to investigate and

151

deal locally with heretics, since they were seen as a threat to both the ecclesiastical and the social order. Papal documents as well as the Second, Third, and Fourth Lateran councils (1139, 1179, 1215) prescribed imprisonment and confiscation of property as punishment for heresy and threatened to excommunicate princes who failed to punish heretics.

"The papal Inquisition was formally instituted by Pope Gregory IX in 1231. Following a law of Holy Roman Emperor Frederick II, enacted for Lombardy in 1224 and extended to the entire empire in 1232, Gregory ordered convicted heretics to be seized by the secular authorities and burned." *The Grolier Multimedia Encyclopedia*

The Waldenses observed that under the guidance of popes and priest, multitudes were going to the grave without peace, oppressed by the weight of their sins, without hope. They decided then to dedicate their lives to bring to people the great news of a loving savior that wanted to give them eternal life just for the asking. The promises of Jesus were told to the penitent, sin stricken souls, bringing them joy and hope like they never dreamed possible. *"Come to me, all ye that labor and are heavy laden, and I will give you rest"* (Mat 11:28). They taught sinners to go directly to Jesus the Heavenly Priest and that they did not need an earthly one.

Hundreds, probably thousands of these lay preachers made their way to other countries. Several of them ended their lives in dungeons; others- the majority- sealed their testimony with their blood. Pope Innocent VIII ordered in 1487 to destroy that venomous snake, "that malicious and abominable sect of malignants," referring to the preachers of righteousness by faith that were bringing so much hope to the spiritually hungry.

"During the 13th century, the typical procedure began with the arrival of the inquisitors in a specific locality. A period of grace was proclaimed for penitent heretics, after which time denunciations were accepted from anyone, even criminals and other heretics. Two informants whose identity was unknown to the victim were usually sufficient for a charge. The court then summoned the suspect, conducted an interrogation, and tried to obtain the confession that was necessary for conviction. In order to do this, assisting secular authorities frequently applied physical torture. This practice probably started in Italy under the impact of rediscovered Roman civil law and made use of such painful procedures as stretching of limbs on the rack, burning with live coals, squeezing of fingers and toes, or the strappado, a vertical rack. *The Grolier Multimedia Encyclopedia.*

"In the days of Rome's supremacy there were instruments of torture to compel assent to her doctrines. There was the stake for those who would not concede to her claims. There were massacres on a scale that will never be known until revealed in the judgment. Dignitaries of the church studied, under Satan their master, to invent means to cause the greatest possible torture and not end the life of the victim. In many cases the infernal process was repeated to the utmost limit of human endurance, until nature gave up the struggle, and the sufferer hailed death as a sweet release" (*The Great Controversy*, page 569).

I saw one of the chairs used to torture the "heretics." It had a device to force the mouth of the victim opened. Why was it needed to keep the mouth opened? Because they used to pour melted lead through their victims' throats.

"Denial of the charges without counterproof, obstinate refusal to confess, and persistence in the heresy resulted in the most severe punishments: life imprisonment or execution accompanied by total confiscation of property. Since the church was not permitted to shed blood, the sentenced heretic was surrendered to the secular authorities for execution, usually by burning at the stake. When the Inquisition had completed its investigations, the sentences were pronounced in a solemn ceremony, known as the sermo generalis ('general address') or, in Spain, as the auto-da-fe ('act of faith'), attended by local dignitaries, clergy, and townspeople. Here the penitents abjured their errors and received their penalties; obstinate heretics were solemnly cursed and handed over to be burned immediately in public." *The Grolier Multimedia Encyclopedia*

The Spanish Inquisition was organized in 1483 AD throughout all the Spanish possessions, being most active in Spain, Perú and México.

As recently as Nov. 5, 1938, the spirit of the Inquisition showed in *The Tablet*: "Heresy is an awful crime against God, and those who start a heresy are more guilty than they who are traitors to the civil government. If the State has the right to punish treason with death, the principle is the same that concedes to the spiritual authority the power of life and death over the archtraitor."

A group that works with that spirit is the Knight of Columbus. They progress in the organization from step to step called degrees. This group was founded in 1882 in New Haven, Connecticut, in the basement of St. Mary's Catholic Church, when Father Michael McGivney and a small group of pioneering Catholics started a society designed to provide much-needed security for widows and orphans of Catholic parishioners. The Knights of Columbus has become an international society of more than 1.5 million Catholic men in some 10,000 councils who have dedicated themselves to present before the public the ideals of Columbianism: Charity, Unity, Fraternity and Patriotism. They organize fund raisers for charity, which is praiseworthy, but that is not the real purpose of their existence.

This organization has been called "the strong right arm of the Church." Dedication to the Church interest is a keystone of the Order's identity. The highest degree open to members of the Knights of Columbus is that of the Fourth (or Patriotic) Degree. The Color Corps of the Knights of Columbus are the uniformed members of the Fourth Degree. They are the ones that are most noticeable at church and public functions, parades, etc.

Have you ever heard about the secret oath of the Knights of Columbus? I got my hands on a copy several years ago and, asking a frightened former member of that organization if it was real, he read it and very nervously said to me that it was all true, but that he could not talk about it. He feared for his life. Before the people, they do charitable work. Inside, they are a sinister organization. It is sad to say it but the inquisition is still alive and active, just waiting for the right moment to come back stronger than ever. It is active now working behind the curtains to avoid criticism and exposure by the media. The name change from *Inquisition* to the *Congregation for the Doctrine of the Faith* has not changed its sinister actions- just the *modus operandi*.

I want you to see by yourself how much hate for Protestants is in that oath that <u>some select members</u> of the Knights of Columbus <u>sign with their own blood</u> (I want to emphasize that <u>only a chosen few are presented with this oath</u>- since the majority of them are kept doing humanitarian work):

OATH OF THE KNIGHTS OF COLUMBUS

"I, _____ in the presence of the Almighty God, and of the Blessed Virgin Mary, and of the blessed Saint John the Baptist, of the holy apostles Saint Peter and Saint Paul, of all the saints, sacred hosts of heaven, and of you my Father Holy Superior General of the Company of Jesus, founded by Saint Ignacio de Loyola in the pontificate of Pablo III and continued until the present by the womb of the Virgin Mary and the matrix of God, and the staff of Jesus Christ, I declare and I swear that His Holiness the Pope is the Vice regent of Christ and that it is the only one and real head of the universal Catholic Church in all the earth; and that by virtue of the keys to tie and unleash given to His Holiness by my Savior Jesus Christ, has power to depose heretic kings, princes, states, communities and governments and to destroy them without any prejudice. Therefore, with all my forces I will defend these doctrines and the rights and customs of His Holiness against all the heretical usurpers or special Protestant authorities of the Lutheran church in Germany, Holland, Denmark, Sweden and Norway, and now the intended authority of the Church of England, Scotland, and of the other of the same established in Ireland and in the American continent and of all the adherents, to whom is considered as usurping heretic enemies of the Holy Mother Roman Catholic Church.

"I resign and do not acknowledge any allegiance as a duty with any heretic king, prince or state, be it called Protestant or liberal and the obedience to any of their laws, magistrates and officials.

"I declare furthermore that the doctrines of the Church of England and Scotland, of the Calvinists, Huguenots, and others of Protestant name or Masons are damnable and all those which do not abandon them. I also declare that I will help, I will assist, and I will advise to all and to anyone of the agents of His Holiness in any place where it be, either in Switzerland, Germany, Holland or America or in any other kingdom or territory to where I go, and I will make all that I could to extirpate the Protestant or Masonic heretical doctrines and to destroy all their pretended legal powers of any kind whatever they will be.

"I promise and I declare, nevertheless that it is permitted me to pretend in any heretical religion in order to propagate the interest of the Mother Church, to keep the secret and not to reveal all the secrets of the agents, according to their instructions and not to divulge them directly neither indirectly by written word or any other manner, but to execute all what will be proposed me or entrusted and what is ordered to me through my Holy Father or by anyone of this Sacred Order.

"I declare furthermore and I promise that I will neither have opinion, nor own will, nor any moral reservation, but as a corpse I will obey unconditionally each one of the orders that I receive from my Superior in the Pope's militia and from Jesus Christ.

"I promise that I will go to any part of the world where I am sent, to the frigid regions of the north, to the thick mountains of India, to the centers of the European civilization, or to the wild cabins of the America barbarians without backbiting or complaint, and I will be submissive to all that will be communicated to me.

"I promise and declare that I will make, when the opportunity is presented to me, war without quarter, secret and openly against all the Protestant heretics and Masons, such as is ordered me to make; to extirpate them all from the face of the earth; and I will not take into account age neither sex, nor condition, and that I will hang, I will burn, I will destroy, I will boil, skin, I will strangle and I will bury alive these infamous heretics; I will open the stomachs and abdomens of their women and with the head of their infants I will strike against the stones, in order to annihilate this detestable race.

"That when this war could not be made openly, I will employ covertly the poison glass, the strangulation, the steel of the dagger, or the lead bullet without having in consideration the honor, the range, the dignity, or the authority of the persons, whatever be their condition in the public or private life, such as will be ordered to me in any time and place by the agents of the Pope or of the Superior General of the Brotherhood, of the Holy Father of the Society of Jesus.

"If I show falsehood or weakness in my determination, my brothers and companion soldiers in the militia of the Pope can cut my hands and my feet and my neck ear to ear, to open my abdomen and to burn sulfur in it and to apply to me all the punishments that could be on this earth, and that my soul will be tortured by the demons in the eternal hell forever.

"I promise that I will give my vote always to one of the Knights of Columbus with preference over a Protestant, especially over a Mason, and cause that all my party do the same; that if the Catholics are fighting, I will convince myself of who defends more the Holy Mother Catholic Church and I will give my vote to him.

"ALL OF WHICH I SWEAR BY THE BLESSED TRINITY AND THE BLESSED SACRAMENT THAT I AM ABOUT TO RECEIVE."

The above quoted oath of blood is a fulfillment of the prophecy of Revelation 13, where it describes the beast like a bear (cruel). The bear represents the Medo Persians- one of the cruelest conquering nations that this world had seen in the past. They also cut opened the womb of the pregnant women and did other things that the Catholics had done for over a thousand years. How accurate is the Bible prophecy!

Thank God there are so many good Catholics that are not like that, that are loving and kind and live close to God. I am sure that there are going to be several millions of them saved in heaven, that loved the Protestants and everybody else, even if those people were different and were not Catholics. "It is true that there are real Christians in the Roman Catholic communion. Thousands in that church are serving God according to the best light they have. ... They have never seen the contrast between a living heart service and a round of mere forms and ceremonies. God looks with pitying tenderness upon these souls, educated as they are in a faith that is delusive and unsatisfying. He will cause rays of light to penetrate the dense darkness that surrounds them. He will reveal to them the truth as it is in Jesus, and many will yet take their position with His people" (*The Great Controversy*, page 565).

MORE ON THE INQUISITION

A few years ago the pope issued an apology to the Jews and to the rest of the world, for the excesses of the inquisition during the dark ages. The pope pronounced a formal "mea culpa (=my fault)" on Ash Wednesday in the year 2000 for the past faults of Christians. It's too bad that those people burned alive will never hear that "apology." The statement avoided accusations against individuals and groups- typical practice of politicians and of those with ulterior motives.

The pope said during a symposium on the inquisition, that the church ultimately wants to make a <u>theological appraisal</u> of the Inquisition, and it "certainly cannot consider making an ethical judgment like the request for forgiveness without first being accurately informed about the <u>situation of that time.</u> Why a theological appraisal, instead of historical? If those theologians were allowed, they would be re-write history. If God doesn't change, His church should not change the way in which it treats the sinners either. We are not supposed to be chameleon Christians. The social and historical circumstances should have nothing to do with the way we treat those that dissent. How come people can not read their real purpose? All we have to do is to read between the lines.

They want to take into consideration the "mentality of the times." One of the theologians said that in some cases, the people cannot be held responsible for actions that today we consider sinful in themselves because they did not recognize the evil in committing them. This means that if we get to develop a similar mentality, the same actions will be repeated and called correct, rightfully done. Those monstrosities will be perpetrated again in the name of religion. The Bible presents the spirit of intolerance abiding in the beast from Revelation 13.

The pope called for acknowledgment of intolerance in the churches' own history, and even the use of "violence in the service of truth." Did Jesus whip the Pharisees? No! He made a whip but no where in the Bible mentions that anyone was stricken by it.

The pope added that "neither can it rely on images of the past that are circulated by public opinion, since these images are often overloaded with a passionate emotionalism that prevents a calm and objective diagnosis." Do Catholics ignore that those are the emotions of those that had counted the dead, the victims of the Inquisition?

The pope also said that the Vatican had "convened the experts to help lay a factual foundation about the Inquisition -- its activities, its methods and its mentality as seen in historical context. Now the church can ponder the results, and examine how 'methods of intolerance and even violence in the service of the truth' fell short of the Gospel." I would not say that the how is what it matters, but the **WHY**. Why was it ever there an Inquisition? Why Christians and Jews were killed in the name of religion? It was because of Rome's hunger for power and money. If more people got converted their coffers would suffer and eventually they would lose their influence over both the powerful of the earth and the masses.

Swiss Dominican Father Georges Cottier said that "by clarifying the historical record on the Inquisition, the symposium could also help free the collective memory from 'distortions,' discarding unfounded criticisms and 'eliminating myths.'" The preceding comments appeared in the *Catholic News Service* web site. In my humble opinion, this will be only an effort to erase the tracks after a crime has been committed. This revision of facts seems like the criminal has returned to the crime scene to make sure he can remove all incriminating evidence.

During the symposium, a participant said that he did not notice any attempt to whitewash the past. That is not the opinion of Jeremiah. He wrote: *"Can the Ethiopian change his skin, or the leopard his spots? Then may ye also do good, that are accustomed to do evil"* (Jer. 13:23). This persecuting power has not changed. Beware of its teeth. Remember the story of Little Red Riding Hood? That was a wolf posing as sweet innocent old grandma.

PROTESTANTS' BLOOD

It would be convenient to mention here how the church that pretended to represent Jesus treated those that preached the doctrine of salvation by faith.

"Century after century the blood of the saints had been shed. While the Waldenses laid down their lives upon the mountains of Piedmont "for the word of God, and for the testimony of Jesus Christ," similar witness to the truth had been borne by their brethren, the Albigenses of France. In the days of the Reformation its disciples had been put to death with horrible tortures. King and nobles, highborn women and delicate maidens, the pride and chivalry of the nation, had feasted their eyes upon the agonies of the martyrs of Jesus. The brave Huguenots, battling for those rights which the human heart holds most sacred, had poured out their blood on many a hard-fought field. The Protestants were counted as outlaws, a price was set upon their heads, and they were hunted down like wild beasts." The Great Controversy, page 271

"The 'Church in the Desert,' the few descendants of the ancient Christians that still lingered in France in the eighteenth century, hiding away in the mountains of the south, still cherished the faith of their fathers. As they ventured to meet by night on mountain-side or lonely moor, they were chased by dragoons, and dragged away to life-long slavery in the galleys. "The purest, the most refined, and the most intelligent of the French, were chained, in horrible torture, amidst robbers and assassins." Others, more mercifully dealt with, were shot down in cold blood, as, unarmed and helpless, they fell upon their knees in prayer. Hundreds of aged men, defenseless women, and innocent children were left dead upon the earth at their place of meeting. In traversing the mountain-side or the forest, where they had been accustomed to assemble, it was not unusual to find 'at every four paces dead bodies dotting the sward, and corpses hanging suspended from the trees.' Their country, 'laid waste with the sword, the ax, the fagot, was converted into a vast, gloomy wilderness.' These atrocities were not committed during the Dark Ages, but in that brilliant era 'when science was cultivated, and letters flourished; when the divines of the court and the capital were learned and eloquent men, who greatly affected the graces of meekness and charity.'" *The Great Controversy* [1888 edition], pages 271,272.

"But blackest in the black catalogue of crime, most horrible among the fiendish deeds of all the dreadful centuries, was the St. Bartholomew Massacre. The world still recalls with shuddering horror the scenes of that most cowardly and cruel onslaught. The king of France, urged on by Romish priests and prelates, lent his sanction to the dreadful work. The great bell of the palace, tolling at dead of night, was a signal for the slaughter. Protestants by thousands, sleeping quietly in their homes, trusting to the plighted honor of their king, were dragged forth without a warning, and murdered in cold blood.

"Satan, in the person of the Roman zealots, led the van. As Christ was the invisible leader of his people from Egyptian bondage, so was Satan the unseen leader of his subjects in this horrible work of multiplying martyrs. For seven days the massacre was continued in Paris, the first three with inconceivable fury. And it was not confined to the city itself, but by special order of the king extended to all provinces and towns where Protestants were found. Neither age nor sex was respected. Neither the innocent babe nor the man of gray hairs was spared. Noble and peasant, old and young, mother and child, were cut down together. Throughout France the butchery continued for two months. Seventy thousand of the very flower of the nation perished.

"The pope, Gregory XIII., received the news of the fate of the Huguenots with unbounded joy. The wish of his heart had been gratified, and Charles IX, was now his favorite son. Rome rang with rejoicings. The guns of the castle of St. Angelo gave forth a joyous salute; the bells sounded from every tower; bonfires blazed throughout the night; and Gregory, attended by his cardinals and priests, led the magnificent procession to the church of St. Louis, where the cardinal of Lorraine chanted a *Te Deum*. The cry of the dying host in France was gentle harmony to the court of Rome. A medal was struck to commemorate the glorious massacre; a picture, which still exists in the Vatican, was painted, representing the chief events of St. Bartholomew. The pope, eager to show his gratitude to Charles for his dutiful conduct, sent him the Golden Rose; and from the pulpits of Rome eloquent preachers celebrated Charles, Catherine, and the Guises as the new founders of the papal church.'" *Ibid.*

Below is the medal minted by order of the pope to commemorate the massacre:

C.H. Spurgeon, one of the greatest preachers from England, describes the massacre like this:

"NOT until the day of universal restitution will the infamous atrocity perpetrated on the eve of St. Bartholomew, 1572, by the Roman Catholics on the unoffending Huguenots or Protestants of France, cease to be remembered with the most intense horror. The coolness of the proceedings which instigated such a carnage, and the devilish passions which led Catholic nobles and statesmen to burst the bounds of humanity by heading the massacre, make the event unparalleled in the history of gigantic crimes. There, is no shadow of doubt as to who the originators of the plot were. The Roman Catholics had conceived the bitterest hatred to the Huguenots, and were determined that the land should be rid of them. Catherine de Medicis, whose furious enmity to Protestantism made her an admirable mover in the dreadful design, controlled her son, Charles IX. sufficiently to make him a mere puppet in her hands. Admiral Coligny, one of the most prominent advisers of the King of Navarre, who was then at the head of the Huguenots, was invited to attend the Parisian court. Coligny was the especial object of the Catholics' resentment, and an unsuccessful attempt was therefore made upon his life. The Queen-mother, finding that this part of her scheme had failed, represented to the king that the Huguenots were clamorous for revenge upon the nobles of the court for the attack upon Coligny. These representations had the effect of frightening the weak-minded king, who at once authorized the massacre of the offending Protestants._____

"Our illustration represents the first attack of the murderous Catholics in the streets of Paris. Charles IX. is in the act of giving the first signal by firing a gun from the window of his palace. Coligny with his household was murdered, and his body thrown out to the mob. Everywhere the cry was heard, 'Kill every man of them! Kill the Huguenots!' The streets were reeking with the blood of men, women, and children. Not an individual suspected of a leaning towards the Reformed religion was suffered to escape. While this scene was going on, the Protestants of Lyons, Rouen, and other cities, fell victims to the savage fury of the Catholics. The massacre was carefully planned so as to break out at the same hour in various cities and in their suburbs. By some it is supposed that at least 100,000 persons suffered death. The estimate given by Sully at 70,000, has, however, been adopted. It is pretty certain that at least 10,000 were destroyed in Paris alone, and this estimate does not include the 500 who belonged to the higher orders. It is said that 'the roads were rendered almost impassable, from the corpses of men, women, and children,—a new and appalling barricade.'

"The monstrous deed received the high approval of the Pope and his Cardinals, and thanks were impiously made to Heaven for the distinguished favor that had been rendered to the Church. The then head of the English Church by law established (Queen Elizabeth) seemed to take the matter equally well; for we find her immediately afterwards receiving the French Ambassador, and accepting thankfully a love-letter from the Duke of Alençon; and, in a few months, standing at the font as godmother to the child of the murderous King of France.

"By the side of these facts we ought to place a few computations which will show that the unexampled outrage on St. Bartholomew's Eve is only a part of a line of policy which the Church on the Seven

Hills has carried out during the twelve hundred years of its existence. Mr. D. A. Doudney, the incumbent of Bedminster, near Bristol, recently mentioned at a public meeting that at least fifty millions have been put to death by the Romish Church. That estimate gives us the number of martyrs *annually at* 40,000, or more than 100 a day for the last twelve hundred years. Spain especially has had her share in the responsibility of this iniquity, for under forty-five Inquisition trials, between the years 1481 and 1808, 31,658 were burnt alive, 18,049 were burnt in effigy, and 225,214 were condemned to galleys or imprisonment. It must not be supposed that in consequence of the respectable appearance which Catholicism is now necessitated to put on that the nature of Popery is changed. It is, and from its organization must continue to be, ambitious of supremacy. Even the *Times,* which looks upon the proselytizing schemes of the Romanists with cynical indifference, believes that it is impossible not to recognize in the recent complaints of English priests and dignitaries 'something of that perverse ambition which has always been the bane of Roman Catholicism. A purely religious power the Roman Catholic Church never has been, is not now, and it seems to have made up its mind that it never will be. Though it still embraces half Europe in its spiritual sway, it laments the loss of a few petty provinces in Italy with a bitterness far keener than that of the exiled dukes.' That this ever-increasing ambition will not rest satisfied until England shall bow before the Beast may be readily believed; and that all the efforts now being put forth to weaken the progress of Protestantism in this country have as their central object the humiliation of a liberty-loving people is too plain a fact to withstand. To obtain its ends Popery would not despise the most atrocious and abominable means. If our Savior's words, 'By their fruits shall ye know them,' have any significance whatever, they may be appropriately used in reference to this insidious Church. What have been the fruits of this fearful heresy during the period of its almost unlimited sway, but spiritual and political oppression as well as persecution in its grossest and most multifarious forms? Looking at the atrocities of this Church, one would feel tempted to question whether its character of being 'Drunken with the blood of the saints' is not too mildly drawn. The only defense of God's true Church is in God. By the constant preaching of his Word, and by the uplifting of the cross, we hope the day will come when no invectives will be required to denounce the gross imposture which has for so long a time 'made the people to sin.'" From The Massacre of St. Bartholomew by C. H. Spurgeon From the April 1866 *Sword and Trowel*

Let me tell you a couple of stories from recent years. A priest in the Dominican Republic hired a person to be the church's janitor. This individual was told to clean everything in the church, but he was prohibited to enter a room whose door was always closed, except that one day, the priest, being drunk, forgot to close it. Noticing that the door was not closed that day, and that the priest was not around, he ventured to get in the room. To his surprise, he discovered <u>torture instruments kept in good shape</u>. Another person in the USA was renovating a building, property of the Catholic Church, and was told to retrieve something from the basement (which was a multilevel). He was surprised to see a guard in front of one of the doors in an empty building. After befriending the guy, he told him that the room was a weapons warehouse. The worker asked: "Weapons? Why?" <u>The answer from the guard was: "to kill the Adventists."</u>

The persecutors are just waiting for the right moment. The enemies of God's people will accuse the children of God of causing the maladies that this planet is suffering, because they are obstinate in keeping Saturday, instead of Sunday. The people that had lost family members in natural disasters, or as victims of crime, wars, etc., will then hate the Sabbath keepers. The Bible talks about the hate for those that keep the commandments of God- the original ten repeated to Moses on Sinai *"And the dragon was wroth with the woman, and went to make war with the remnant of her seed, which <u>keep the commandments of God</u>, and have the testimony of Jesus Christ."* (Revelation12: 17). Very soon it is going to be war time. The battle of Armageddon is about to start. Please, make your decision to be on the right side before it is too late. Don't let fear for the persecution rob you of eternal blessings. Trust God who loves you and will keep you (see Psalm 91).

Spiritism and the Union of the Churches

"So-called out-of-body experiences are yet another evidence of the increasing importance that Westerners at the end of the twentieth century are placing on spirituality at the expense of rationalism. Interest in angels and appearances of the Virgin Mary also fit in as evidences of the paradigm shift." Marvin Moore in *The coming Great Calamity*

"Modern spiritualism, resting upon the same foundation, is but a revival in a new form of the witchcraft and demon worship that God condemned and prohibited of old. It is foretold in the Scriptures, which declare that 'in the latter times some shall depart from the faith, giving heed to seducing spirits, and doctrines of devils.' (1 Timothy 4:1). Paul, in his second letter to the Thessalonians, points to the special working of Satan in spiritualism as an event to take place immediately before the Second Advent of Christ. Speaking of Christ's Second Coming, he declares that it is 'after the working of Satan with all power and signs and lying wonders' (2 Thessalonians 2:9). And Peter, describing the dangers to which the church was to be exposed in the last days, says that as there were false prophets who led Israel into sin, so there will be false teachers, 'who privily shall bring in damnable heresies, even denying the Lord that bought them. . . . And many shall follow their pernicious ways'" (2 Peter 2:1, 2) *Patriarchs and Prophets* p. 686

EMPHASIS ON THE HOLY SPIRIT

Pope John Paul II declared 1998 as the year of the Spirit. He had mentioned several times how important is the Holy Spirit to the individual, to the church and to the whole world. Who is the Holy Spirit? He is known as the third person of the Divinity. We are told by Paul: *"And grieve not the Holy Spirit of God, whereby ye are <u>sealed to the day of redemption</u>"*(Eph 4:30). He seals us for salvation. Talking to Nicodemus, *"Jesus answered, Verily, verily, I say to thee, Except a man be <u>born of</u> water and of <u>the Spirit</u>, he cannot enter into the kingdom of God"* (John 3:5). If the pope was serious, he would allow the Holy Spirit to use him to clean the house by reforming the doctrines of the church discarding all paganism and exalting the Bible truths only. He would have even resigned as pope after that. The pope's emphasis on the Holy Spirit is just a trick to attract trusting Protestants, just like Hansel and Gretel were attracted to the house of the witch because of the candies.

PHILOSOPHY

Philosophy is defined as love for wisdom. Pope John Paul II said in November 1998, that by studying philosophy and theology together, those preparing to preach the Gospel would have the tools they need. Why is it that so much emphasis is given by this power to human wisdom? Does the Bible have anything to say about the subject? Lets check God's opinion. First, lets read about the origin of human wisdom (philosophy).

"This wisdom descendeth not from above, but is earthly, sensual, devilish" (James 3:15). So according to that passage, Satan inspires human wisdom. It is true that some philosophers are Christians, but when the word of God is neglected, or put aside, human wisdom is good for nothing. The problem is that in the case of the Catholic Church, philosophy is sometimes elevated far above the authority of the Scriptures. James adds: *"But the wisdom that is from above is first pure, then peaceable, gentle, and easy to be entreated, full of mercy and good fruits, without partiality, and without hypocrisy"* (James 3:17). For James, real wisdom is more of an action than it is a thought.

St. Thomas Aquinas is the best known theologian and philosopher of the Catholic Church. He adopted the philosophy of the Greeks and "Christianized it." His adaptation of Aristotle became official Catholic philosophy in 19th cent. A man that wants to become a priest is required to study more years of philosophy than he is required to study the Bible. Why so much fear of getting to know the Scriptures?

THE WOUND IS BEING HEALED

The healing of the papacy's deadly wound has been a gradual recuperation; but the most significant step was taken with the Lateran Treaty in February 11, 1929, when Premier Mussolini restored the 110 acre territory to the Vatican and allowed them to be autonomous. The Lateran Treaty guaranteed papal independence in the city-state of the Vatican, located mostly within the city of Rome. The unification of Italy in 1870 had deprived the pope of the former Papal States, by which the popes had endeavored to maintain their independence from any secular ruler and to get substantial income. On March 9th, 1929, the pope, Pius XI (1922-39) said: "The peoples of the entire world are with us." Almost repeating what the Bible says in Revelation 12, when John describes the world following the beast. The San Francisco Chronicle actually said that this pact healed "the wound of many years."

"By the time Pius XII died, in October 1958- twenty years to the month before John Paul II took his own place in the Apostolic Chair- the Holy See and its Church were seen as a single, supranational entity, one that had attained a georeligious status and stature eliciting from the world a geopolitical recognition that was unique." Malachi Martin, *The Keys of this Blood, page 137*

In a Newspaper from England (as quoted by Dwight K. Nelson in Net '98), there was an article written regarding the new dreamed leader for Europe:

"Europe's new emperor? With European 'federalism' on the agenda of both Western and Eastern governments, speculations are abroad as to who may become the political leader of the united European Community. A profile in '*The Sunday Telegraph*' on John Paul II is suggesting that he is the best choice in the new Holy European

Empire. The article speaks of the increasing role of the Roman Catholic political power since the fall of Napoleon and even since the Counter Reformation. The moral authority of the papacy becomes the apparent winner of the day. If European federalism triumphs, the EC will indeed be an empire. It will lack an emperor; but it will have the pope. It is difficult not to think that Wojtyla realizes this,' *The Sunday Telegraph* suggests." *Light Magazine.*

The papacy is gaining momentum. The number of pilgrims attending papal audiences and public events was up by 61 percent in 1998, indicating a renovated interest in religion and more trust in the leadership of the church.

A GLOBAL COURT

Pope John Paul II gave his blessing to a worldwide conference meant to establish the first permanent, global criminal court. They also had the encouragement from the head of the United Nations. The five-week meeting that started June 15, 1998 had opening remarks from U.N. secretary-general Kofi Annan and delegates of more than 150 states and observers from 235 non-governmental organizations.

In what would sound like the innocent intent to help the justice system of the nations to catch criminals and terrorist, the pontiff voiced his support for the creation of a world criminal court and the work of other investigative bodies. For the careful observer of history and prophecy, this looks more like the resurrection of the power of the inquisition. The group was to spend its first days defining which war crimes; acts of genocide and crimes against humanity would come under its jurisdiction.

The following weeks were intended to determine how much control individual governments will have over the court, its relationship to the United Nations and how independent would be the prosecutors.

It would also have jurisdiction when a state is unwilling to try its own citizens for alleged crimes and when government officials may be implicated in crimes. In what is a case of international intervention in the affairs of people from another country, Spain is trying to bring Chilean former dictator Augusto Pinochet to trial. He is being accused of genocide and torture. A report from the government of Chile says that some 3,000 people were murdered or simply disappeared. The secret police under Pinochet's command it's being blamed for the crimes. Pinochet was dictator from 1973-1990, when protests from Chilean groups and international pressure forced him to resign. He cut a deal by which he would remain a senator for life. As we say in America, he committed the crimes and walked, or got away with it.

International law is also intervening with the Bosnian Serbs and the Rwandan Hutus for their war crimes. As I write this, I think that it is right to bring criminals to justice, but I worry that as when this kind of intervention happened in the past, centuries ago, also innocent people were brought to justice for "crimes" against an established religion.

Do we have historical evidence that those crimes will include disobedience to the rules of the Catholic Church? In the Middle Ages, kings trembled at the power of the popes. Remember the king that stood on the snow for three days before he was allowed to go on his knees to ask the pope to forgive him, so his subjects would obey him again?

Since there is no agreement on regards of what nation the court will be accountable to, guess who will have control of it? The Vatican will. The pope is presenting himself as the paladin of peace and justice. The leaders of the nations often ask him to intercede on behalf of righteous causes, in favor of peace (like when Sadam Hussein asked the pope for intervention to finish with the United Nations embargo), but it is just a wolf dressed on sheep clothes. My fear is that the pope will use this power to persecute those that keep the commandments of God (Revelation 12:17). I repeat: this could well be the next inquisition. Jesus said: "Then shall they deliver you up to be afflicted, and shall kill you: and ye shall be <u>hated of all nations</u> for my name's sake" (Mat 24:9).

Recently, the pope declared that "<u>the notion of freedom</u> as personal autonomy is <u>superficially attractive</u>; endorsed by intellectuals, the media, legislatures and the courts, it becomes a powerful cultural force. Yet it ultimately <u>destroys the personal good of individuals and the common good of society</u>." That's frightening! This reminds me of a picture that I saw years ago, presenting a young man with a chain and a padlock around his head, representing the people that are not free to express their opinion. Just like in the Middle Ages. The pope made the comments June 27 in a written address handed to bishops from Texas, Oklahoma and Arkansas, who were making their "ad limina" (the "ad limina" visits are made once every five years by heads of dioceses) visits to the Vatican.

He also said that constitutional and statutory law are to be held accountable to the <u>objective</u> moral law. Guess whose law it will be. The Catholic law of course.

THE POOR "VICTIM"

In a talk with the pope, Archbishop Patrick F. Flores of San Antonio referred to the "pain" felt by the bishops over several ongoing problems, among them:

The "horrendous lawsuits" faced by several dioceses, an apparent reference to sexual abuse cases. (Who is the real victim, the church, or the kids molested by the "celibate" priests?).

The "bad publicity we receive" on TV and in the printed press. (What is the duty of the press if the church leaders generate a scandal? Don't we have the right to know if the wolf is on the lose so we can protect the remaining lambs?)

"Bishop Joseph A. Fiorenza of Galveston-Houston told Catholic News Service that in talks with the Vatican congregations for doctrine and clergy, the bishops were told that the Vatican was working on a document that will outline procedures for <u>dispensing</u> priests guilty of sexual impropriety from their priestly obligations."

This bishop said "the procedure would be <u>administrative rather than juridical</u>- something many U.S. bishops have been requesting in recent years. He called the development 'welcome news.'" I see it only as a great way of walking away after committing a crime, as a cover up. A pat on the back. It's like telling the guilty: "sorry, but you got caught, and we have to let you go to another city."

PROTESTANTS EXTEND THE HAND TO THE PAPACY

The book *The Great Controversy* says that the Protestants of the US will extend the hand to the Catholics. All you have to do to believe it is to listen to Billy Graham, Chuck Colson, Pat Robertson, Jack Van Impe, Jerry Falwell and others, to express their opinion about the pope and his church.

In January 21,1997 in an interview with Larry King, Billy Graham said that he was very comfortable with the Vatican and with pope John Paul II. He also said that he had gone to see the pope several times. The day John Paul was made pope, Billy Graham was preaching in the pope's cathedral in Krakow, Poland. When the pope came to Columbia, South Carolina, the pope invited Billy Graham to be on the platform to speak with him. Mr. Graham sees the pope of Rome as the one who should be the **head** of the united churches. Billy Graham has been a great evangelist, bringing thousands of people to Jesus, but now....

For me, Dr. Graham is the greatest evangelist of the 20th century, a great soul winner, and I respect Him greatly. I consider him a man of God. However, <u>men of God also make mistakes</u>. I think that there is still hope for preachers sympathizers of the papacy. The Holy Spirit has a message for them: *"<u>Remember therefore from whence thou art fallen</u>, and <u>repent</u>, and do the first works; or else I will come to thee quickly, and will remove thy candlestick out of his place, except thou repent"* (Rev 2:5). Ecumenism is not God's plan. God cares about the truth. The churches behind the ecumenical movement teach opposing doctrines-that is confusion, what the Bible calls Babylon in Revelation 17. The union of those churches will not bring blessings from God, because they are denying the truth, and God cares about it. To reject the truth is to reject God Himself who gave it.

"But Romanism as a system is no more in harmony with the gospel of Christ now than at any former period in her history. The Protestant churches are in great darkness, or they would discern the signs of the times. The Roman Church is far-reaching in her plans and modes of operation. She is employing every device to extend her influence and increase her power in preparation for a fierce and determined conflict to regain control of the world, to re-establish persecution, and to undo all that Protestantism has done. Catholicism is gaining ground upon every side. See the increasing number of her churches and chapels in Protestant countries. Look at the popularity of her colleges and seminaries in America, so widely patronized by Protestants. Look at the growth of ritualism in England and the frequent defections to the ranks of the Catholics. These things should awaken the anxiety of all who prize the pure principles of the gospel.

"Protestants have tampered with and patronized popery; they have made compromises and concessions which papists themselves are surprised to see and fail to understand. Men are closing their eyes to the real character of Romanism and the dangers to be apprehended from her supremacy. The people need to be aroused to resist the advances of this most dangerous foe to civil and religious liberty.

"Many Protestants suppose that the Catholic religion is unattractive and that its worship is a dull, meaningless round of ceremony. Here they mistake. While Romanism is based upon deception, it is not a coarse and clumsy imposture. The religious service of the Roman Church is a most impressive ceremonial. Its gorgeous display and solemn rites fascinate the senses of the people and silence the voice of reason and of conscience. The eye is charmed. Magnificent churches, imposing processions, golden altars, jeweled shrines, choice paintings, and exquisite sculpture appeal to the love of beauty. The ear also is captivated. The music is unsurpassed. The rich notes of the deep-toned organ, blending with the melody of many voices as it swells through the lofty domes and pillared aisles of her grand cathedrals, cannot fail to impress the mind with awe and reverence" (The Great Controversy, pages 565, 566).

Protestants are trying to push religion in schools to open the door to Catholic teachers to teach our kids. In Columbia, South Carolina, the State Attorney said Monday, August 10, 1998, that public schools can display copies of the Ten Commandments. He said that religion has a <u>constitutional place</u> in the public schools. This can be a double edged sword. It can be a blessing, but unfortunately, the majority will use these laws, if approved, to promote and perpetuate the error. I fear that the Commandments that will be displayed will be the Catholic version, and not how they appear in the Bible.

Why are Protestants getting closer to Catholics? I see some reasons that could explain this approaching between these two. The first one is that in the Second Vatican Council, Pope John XXIII started to call Protestants "separated brethren" instead of heretics. Now, they are using terms coined in the bosom of the Protestant churches, so they sound like they are "Christians" The reason why I say it that way it's because for centuries, the Catholics had so many pagan ideas taught as dogmas, that they were not considered Christians. Some of the terms used now are:

"Born again,"
"Received the Holy Spirit,"
"Worship the Lord,"
"Praise the Lord,"
"Personal praying times,"
"Conversion,"
"She has receive Jesus," etc.

A second reason is that the Jesuits started <u>training people to "speak in tongues."</u> I know that for a fact. I personally interviewed a former Jesuit years ago (around 1983). The Catholic Church claims that he is a fake, but I, raised as a Catholic, knew that he was telling the truth. Today in the Internet, I found out with great sadness that he was poisoned. The Jesuits never forgive one that betrays them. His name was Dr. Alberto Rivera- a very powerful preacher who spoke from several years of experience as a Jesuit leader. He was in charge of training the faithful to "speak in tongues," so they could fool Protestants who started to say: "so, Catholics also speak in tongues. They are receiving the Holy Spirit." Today, the charismatic movement has softened the hearts of the most careful, faithful and watchful Protestant preachers. Miracles are accompanying the speaking in tongues. Readers beware because Jesus said: *"For false Christs and false prophets shall rise, and shall show signs and wonders, to seduce, if it were possible, even the elect*" (Mark 13:22). This prophecy is being fulfilled before our eyes. I saw those miracles personally. I went to check them out. But the day following the healing miracle, the healed person was sick again. The explanation was they lost their faith. Will God make a miracle if the person doesn't have the faith? We can not base our faith in miracles, because they don't provide conclusive evidence that the Holy Spirit is behind that movement. *"Not every one that saith to me, Lord, Lord, shall enter into the kingdom of heaven; but he that doeth the will of my Father which is in heaven. Many will say to me in that day, Lord, Lord, have we not prophesied in thy name? And in thy name have cast out devils? And in thy name done many wonderful works? And then will I profess to them, I never knew you: depart from me, ye that work iniquity"* (Mat 7:21).

The third important reason why the "separated brethren" are "coming home" is the rampant immorality and crime that is threatening to destroy all the societies on this planet, and Rome is showing itself as a champion of "human rights," pro-life, anti-gay, pro-family, etc. We see around us that even the government and church leaders are immoral, which reminds me of the Catholic ladies planted in Protestant churches to fake conversion, but having a sinister hidden agenda. Their spiritual leaders offered them generous indulgences if they seduce a pastor unwilling to join the charismatic movement. If that doesn't work, because the man of God is well connected with the Source of all strength, they recur to slander (remember the Biblical cases in which false witnesses were brought against a faithful Israelite in Ahab's time and also against Jesus?). I know because I not only read it, but I saw it happening. See 1 Kings 21:3; Matthew 26:59-62.

In 2014, Anglican Bishop Tony Palmer, a personal friend of Pope Francis, recorded an invitation from the pope to unite. Bishop Palmer even said that the protest was over, that we "might be all Catholics now." This video was presented at a meeting organized by Kenneth Copeland, who has been one of the most popular TV preachers for decades. How can we unite with error? How can we forget the millions of lives cut short because of the thirst for power of the popular, apostate church? How can we voluntarily place our heads inside the open mouth of the lion and expect him not to close its jaws and cut our freedoms, especially to worship God according to the dictates of our conscience? Dear reader, please, for the sake of your soul and the soul of those that you love and love you, do not fall in the snare of the enemy of the souls. The cat is wagging its tail, hypnotizing the world, presenting a benevolent, innocent image but it is only doing so to jump on its prey and devour it. Do not turn your back on Jesus by accepting the error or this union of all the churches. The ecumenical movement does not carry the seal of approval from God. Escape for your soul before is too late.

IS TRUTH IMPORTANT?

– Consider these excerpts from *The Great Controversy*, pp 520-524.

"The position that it is of no consequence what men believe is one of Satan's most successful deceptions. He knows that the truth, received in the love of it, sanctifies the soul of the receiver; therefore he is constantly seeking to substitute false theories, fables, another gospel. From the beginning the servants of God have contended against false teachers, not merely as vicious men, but as inculcators of falsehoods that were fatal to the soul. Elijah, Jeremiah, Paul, firmly and fearlessly opposed those who were turning men from the word of God. That liberality which regards a correct religious faith as unimportant found no favor with these holy defenders of the truth.

"The vague and fanciful interpretations of Scripture, and the many conflicting theories concerning religious faith, that are found in the Christian world are the work of our great adversary to confuse minds so that they shall not discern the truth. And the discord and division, which exist among the churches of Christendom, are in a great measure due to the prevailing custom of wresting the Scriptures to support a favorite theory. Instead of carefully studying God's word with humility of heart to obtain knowledge of His will, many seek only to discover something odd or original.

"In order to sustain erroneous doctrines or unchristian practices, some will seize upon passages of Scripture separated from the context, perhaps quoting half of a single verse as proving their point, when the remaining portion would show the meaning to be quite the opposite. With the cunning of the serpent they entrench themselves behind disconnected utterances construed to suit their carnal desires. Thus do many willfully pervert the word of God. Others, who have an active imagination, seize upon the figures and symbols of Holy Writ,

179

interpret them to suit their fancy, with little regard to the testimony of Scripture as its own interpreter, and then they present their vagaries as the teachings of the Bible.

"Whenever the study of the Scriptures is entered upon without a prayerful, humble, teachable spirit, the plainest and simplest as well as the most difficult passages will be wrested from their true meaning. The papal leaders select such portions of Scripture as best serve their purpose, interpret to suit themselves, and then present these to the people, while they deny them the privilege of studying the Bible and understanding its sacred truths for themselves. The whole Bible should be given to the people just as it reads. It would be better for them not to have Bible instruction at all than to have the teaching of the Scriptures thus grossly misrepresented.

"The Bible was designed to be a guide to all who wish to become acquainted with the will of their Maker. God gave to men the sure word of prophecy; angels and even Christ Himself came to make known to Daniel and John the things that must shortly come to pass. Those important matters that concern our salvation were not left involved in mystery. They were not revealed in such a way as to perplex and mislead the honest seeker after truth. Said the Lord by the prophet Habakkuk: "Write the vision, and make it plain, . . . that he may run that readeth it." Habakkuk 2:2. The word of God is plain to all who study it with a prayerful heart. Every truly honest soul will come to the light of truth. "Light is sown for the righteous." Psalm 97:11. And no church can advance in holiness unless its members are earnestly seeking for truth as for hid treasure.

"By the cry, Liberality, men are blinded to the devices of their adversary, while he is all the time working steadily for the accomplishment of his object. As he succeeds in supplanting the Bible by human speculations, the law of God is set aside, and the churches are under the bondage of sin while they claim to be free.

"To many, scientific research has become a curse. God has permitted a flood of light to be poured upon the world in discoveries in science and art; but even the greatest minds, if not guided by the word of God in their research, become bewildered in their attempts to investigate the relations of science and revelation....

"Those who are unwilling to accept the plain, cutting truths of the Bible are continually seeking for pleasing fables that will quiet the conscience...Too wise in their own conceit to search the Scriptures with contrition of soul and earnest prayer for divine guidance, they have no shield from delusion. Satan is ready to supply the heart's desire, and he palms off his deceptions in the place of truth. It was thus that the papacy gained its power over the minds of men; and by rejection of the truth because it involves a cross, Protestants are following the same path. All who neglect the word of God to study convenience and policy, that they may not be at variance with the world, will be left to receive damnable heresy for religious truth. Every conceivable form of error will be accepted by those who willfully reject the truth. He who looks with horror upon one deception will readily receive another. The apostle Paul, speaking of a class who "received not the love of the truth, that they might be saved," declares: "For this cause God shall send them strong delusion, that they should believe a lie: that they all might be damned who believed not the truth, but had pleasure in unrighteousness." 2 Thessalonians 2:10-12. With such a warning before us it behooves us to be on our guard as to what doctrines we receive.

"Among the most successful agencies of the great deceiver are the delusive teachings and lying wonders of spiritualism. Disguised as an angel of light, he spreads his nets where least suspected. If men would but study the Book of God with earnest prayer that they might understand it, they would not be left in darkness to receive false doctrines. But as they reject the truth they fall a prey to deception.

The same book, in page 525 says: "The errors of popular theology have driven many a soul to skepticism who might otherwise have been a believer in the Scriptures. It is impossible for him to accept doctrines which outrage his sense of justice, mercy, and benevolence; and since these are represented as the teaching of the Bible, he refuses to receive it as the word of God." Doctrines like an eternal hell not only fill churches with people that serve God for the wrong reason (fear), but also keep unbelievers away from such an angry and revengeful God.

In page 528 it says: "There is but one course for those to pursue who honestly desire to be freed from doubts. Instead of questioning and caviling concerning that which they do not understand, let them give heed to the light, which already shines upon them, and they will receive greater light. Let them do every duty which has been made plain to their understanding, and they will be enabled to understand and perform those of which they are now in doubt.

"Satan can present a counterfeit so closely resembling the truth that it deceives those who are willing to be deceived, who desire to shun the self-denial and sacrifice demanded by the truth; but it is impossible for him to hold under his power one soul who honestly desires, at whatever cost, to know the truth. Christ is the truth and the "Light, which lighteth every man that cometh into the world." John 1:9. The Spirit of truth has been sent to guide men into all truth. And upon the authority of the Son of God it is declared: "Seek, and ye shall find." "If any man will do His will, he shall know of the doctrine." Matthew 7:7; John 7:17.

What the Bible says about truth? Let's see some verses:

"Who changed the truth of God into a lie, and <u>worshipped and served the creature more than the Creator</u>, who is blessed for ever. Amen" (Rom 1:25). This verse alone should discourage people from their devotion to Mary. In the rosary, there are more prayers to her than to God.

Here is the proof to the last statement, taken from instructions on how to pray the rosary:

1. Make the **Sign of the Cross** and say the <u>"Apostle's Creed."</u>
2. Say the <u>"Our Father."</u> Say 3 <u>"Hail Marys."</u>
3. Say the <u>"Glory be to the Father."</u>
4. Announce the First Mystery; then say the <u>"Our Father."</u>
5. Say <u>10 "Hail Marys,"</u> while meditating on the Mystery.
6. Say the <u>"Glory be to the Father."</u>
7. Announce the Second Mystery; then say the <u>"Our Father."</u>

Six and seven are repeated and continued with Third, Fourth and Fifth Mysteries in the same manner.

Now read the Hail Mary and see how she is exalted more than Jesus, for there is no Catholic prayer addressed to the Savior that compares to this one: "**HAIL, HOLY QUEEN,** Mother of Mercy, our life, our sweetness and our hope! To thee do we cry, poor banished children of Eve; to thee do we send up our sighs, mourning and weeping in this valley of tears. Turn then, most gracious advocate, thine eyes of mercy toward us, and after this our exile, show unto us the blessed fruit of thy womb, Jesus. O clement, O loving, O sweet Virgin Mary!"

It was not Jesus' plan that we make repetitious prayers when He taught the disciples to pray. His prayer was intended to be just an example of how we should address the Father. When He himself was taking to the Father, as registered in John 17, He did not repeat the prayer that he taught His disciples. *"But you, when you pray, enter into your closet, and when you have shut your door, pray to your Father which is in secret; and your Father which sees in secret shall reward you openly. But <u>when you pray</u>, <u>do not use vain repetitions</u>, as the pagans do: for they think that they shall be heard for their much speaking."* (Matthew 6:6,7).

The truth is to be obeyed: *"But to them that are contentious, and do not <u>obey the truth</u>, but obey unrighteousness, indignation and wrath"* (Romans 2:8).

"For we can do nothing against the truth, but for the truth" (2 Corinthians 13:8).

"O foolish Galatians, who has bewitched you, that you should not <u>obey the truth</u>, before whose eyes Jesus Christ has been evidently set forth, crucified among you?" (Galatians 3:1).

"Ye did run well; who did hinder you that ye should not <u>obey the truth</u>?" (Galatians 5:7).

"And with all deceivableness of unrighteousness in them that perish; because <u>they received not the love of the truth</u>, that they might be saved" (2 Thessalonians 2:10).

"That they all might be <u>damned who believed not the truth</u>, but had pleasure in unrighteousness" (2 Thessalonians 2:12).

"...God hath from the beginning chosen you to <u>salvation through sanctification of the Spirit and belief of the truth</u>" (2 Thessalonians 2:13).

"Who will have all men to be saved, and to <u>come to the knowledge of the truth</u>" (1 Timothy 2:4).

"...the church of the living God, the pillar and ground of the truth" (1 Timothy 3:15).

"<u>Forbidding to marry</u>, and <u>commanding to abstain from meats</u>, which God hath created to be received with thanksgiving of them which believe and know the truth" (1 Timothy 4:3). This verse refers to the practice of celibacy and not eating meat on Fridays.

"Study to <u>show thyself approved to God</u>, a workman that needeth not to be ashamed, <u>rightly dividing the word of truth</u>" (2 Timothy 2:15).

"In meekness instructing those that oppose themselves; if God peradventure will give them repentance to the <u>acknowledging of the truth</u>" (2 Timothy 2:25).

"<u>Ever learning, and never able to come to the knowledge of the truth</u>. Now as Jannes and Jambres withstood Moses, so do <u>these also resist the truth</u>: men of corrupt minds, reprobate concerning the faith" (2 Timothy 3:7,8).

*"I charge thee therefore before God, and the Lord Jesus Christ, who shall judge the quick and the dead at his appearing and his kingdom; Preach the word; be instant in season, out of season; reprove, rebuke, exhort with all longsuffering and doctrine. For **the time will come when they will not endure sound doctrine; but after their own lusts shall they heap to themselves teachers, having itching ears; And they shall turn away their ears from the truth, and shall be turned to fables**"* (2 Timothy 4:1-4).

"Paul, a servant of God, and an apostle of Jesus Christ, according to the faith of God's elect, and the <u>acknowledging of the truth which is after godliness</u>" (Titus 1:1).

"Not giving heed to Jewish fables, and <u>commandments of men, that turn from the truth</u>" (Titus 1:14).

*"For <u>if we sin willfully after that we have received the knowledge of the truth</u>, **there remaineth no more sacrifice for sins**"* (Hebrews 10:26). This is one of the most terrible verses in the Bible. God does consider the truth important.

"Brethren, if any of you do err from the truth, and one convert him; Let him know, that he which <u>converts the sinner from the error</u> of his way shall save a soul from death, and shall hide a multitude of sins" (James 5:19,20). Catholics and Protestants alike now attack proselytism, but the Bible teaches in this passage about helping people come back to the truth.

"Seeing ye have <u>purified your souls in obeying the truth</u> through the Spirit to unfeigned love of the brethren, see that ye love one another with a pure heart fervently" (1 Pet 1:22).

Three times God advises in the Bible to avoid deception.

1. *"<u>Let no man deceive you</u> with vain words: for because of these things cometh the wrath of God upon the children of disobedience. Be not ye therefore partakers with them. For ye were sometimes darkness, but now are ye light in the Lord: walk as children*

of light: (For the fruit of the Spirit is in all goodness and righteousness and truth;) Proving what is acceptable to the Lord. And have no fellowship with the unfruitful works of darkness, but rather reprove them" (Eph 5:6-11).

2. *"<u>Let no man deceive you</u> by any means: for that day shall not come, except there come <u>a falling away</u> first, and that man of sin be revealed, the son of perdition; Who opposes and exalts himself above all that is called God, or that is worshipped; so that he as God sitteth in the temple of God, <u>showing himself that he is God</u>. Remember ye not, that, when I was yet with you, I told you these things? And now ye know what withholds that he might be revealed in his time. For the mystery of iniquity is already at work: only he who now lets will let, until he be taken out of the way. And then shall that Wicked be revealed, whom the Lord shall consume with the spirit of his mouth, and shall destroy with the brightness of his coming: Even him, whose coming is after the working of Satan <u>with all power and signs and lying wonders</u>, And with all deception and unrighteousness in them that perish; because <u>they do not received the love of the truth</u>, that they might be saved. And for this reason God shall send them strong delusion, that they should believe a lie: That they all might be <u>damned who believed not the truth</u>, but had pleasure in unrighteousness. But we are bound to give thanks always to God for you, brethren beloved of the Lord, because God has chosen you to salvation from the beginning through <u>sanctification of the Spirit and belief of the truth</u>"* (2 Thessalonians2:3-13)- free translation (paraphrase).

3. *"Little children, **<u>let no man deceive you</u>**: he that doeth righteousness is righteous, even as he is righteous"* (1 John 3:7).

As we just read, 3 times God presented the same phrase; "**<u>let no man deceive you</u>**". Whenever He wants to put emphasis in something He repeats it at least 3 times. Every day there is a battle of loyalties, for the truth, in our hearts. Rejecting the truth, for insignificant or unimportant that it may look, is equivalent to rejecting God.

"<u>I have no greater joy than to hear that my children walk in truth</u>" (3 John 1:4).

185

THEY ADMIT THE TRUTH

As predicted in Daniel 7:25, the law of God was going to be tampered with. The Catholic power candidly admits to the alteration:

"I have repeatedly offered $1,000.00 to anyone who can prove me from the Bible alone that I am bound to keep Sunday holy. There is no such law in the Bible. It is a law of the Holy Catholic Church alone. The Bible says Remember that thou keep holy the Sabbath day. The Catholic Church says No, by my divine power I abolish the Sabbath day, and command you to keep holy the first day of the week. And lo! the entire civilized world bows down in reverent obedience to the command of the Holy Catholic Church." Priest Enright. C.S.S.R, Kansas City, MO

"Of course the Catholic Church claims the change was her act. And the act is a **mark** of her ecclesiastical power and **authority** in religious matters." C.F. Thomas, Chancellor of Cardinal Gibbons, November 11, 1895.

The Catholic Church admits that they don't teach the truth in different publications. One of the most authoritative of them is the quote from James Cardinal Gibbons in his book *The Faith of Our Fathers*, page 89: "But you may read the Bible from Genesis to Revelation, and <u>you will not find a single line authorizing the sanctification of **Sun**day</u>. The Scriptures enforce the religious observance of Saturday, a day which we never sanctify."

"Nowhere in the Bible is it stated that worship should be changed from Saturday to **Sun**day.

"<u>We Catholics do not accept the Bible as the only rule of faith</u>. Besides the Bible we have the living church, the authority of the church, as a rule to guide us…. we accept her change of the Sabbath to **Sun**day. <u>We frankly say, yes, the church made this change, made this</u>

law, as she made many other laws, for instance, the Friday abstinence, the unmarried priesthood…and a thousand other laws.

"It is always somewhat laughable, to see the Protestant churches, in pulpit and legislation, demand the observance of Sunday, of which there is nothing in their Bible." Peter R. Kraemer, Catholic Church Extension Society (1975) Chicago, Illinois.

I consider the following statement proof of the fulfillment of the prophecy of Daniel 7:11 *("I beheld then because of the voice of the great words which the horn spoke:").* "**Sun**day is our **mark** of authority… **The church is above the Bible**, and this transference of Sabbath observance is proof of that fact." *The Catholic Record*, London, Ontario, September 1ˢᵗ 1923.

"**Sun**day is a Catholic institution, and its claim to observance can be defended only on Catholic principles…From beginning to end of Scripture there is not a single passage that warrants the transfer of weekly public worship from the last day of the week to the first." *Catholic Press*, Sydney, Australia, August, 1900.

"Reason and sense demand the acceptance of one or the other of these alternatives: either Protestantism and the keeping holy of Saturday or Catholicity and the keeping holy of Sunday. Compromise is impossible." Cardinal Gibbons, *The Catholic Mirror*, December 23, 1893.

"The observance of **Sun**day by Protestants is an homage they pay, in spite of themselves, to the authority of the (Roman Catholic) Church." Monsignor Segur in *Plain Talk About the Protestantism of Today*, page 213.

"Nothing is said in the Bible about a change of the Lord's day from Saturday to **Sun**day. We know of the change only from the **tradition** of the Church- a fact handed down to us from earliest times by the living voice of the Church. That is why we find so illogical the attitude of so many non-Catholics, who say that they will believe nothing unless they can find it in the Bible and yet will continue to keep Sunday as the Lord's day on the say-so of the Catholic Church" (Leo G. Trese in *The Faith Explained*, page 243).

The *Doctrinal Catechism* of Stephen Keenan, says in page 174:

"Question: Have you any other way to proving that the church has power to institute festivals of precept?

"Answer: Had she not such power, she could not have done that in which all modern religionist agree with her- she could not have substituted the observance of Sunday, the first day of the week, for the observance of Saturday the seventh day, a change for which there is no Scriptural authority."

The converts Catechism of Catholic Doctrine, 1957 edition, reads:

"Question: Which day is the Sabbath day?

"Answer: Saturday is the Sabbath day.

"Question: Why do we observe **Sun**day instead of Saturday?

"Answer: We observe Sunday instead of Saturday because the Catholic Church transferred the solemnity form Saturday to **Sun**day."

Now consider this questions from a Catholic priest to the Protestants:

"Nothing can be more plain and easy to understand than this; there is nobody who attempts to deny it. It is acknowledged by everybody that the day which Almighty God appointed to be kept holy was Saturday, not **Sun**day. Why do you then keep holy the **Sun**day and not Saturday?

"You will tell me that Saturday was the Jewish Sabbath, but that the Christian Sabbath has been changed to Sunday. Changed! But by whom? Who has authority to change an express commandment of Almighty God? When God has spoken and said, 'thou shalt keep holy the Seventh day,' who shall dare to say, 'Nay, thou shalt keep holy the first day in its instead?' This is a most important question, which I know not how you answer.

"You are a Protestant, and you profess to go by the Bible and the Bible only; and yet, in so important matter as the observance of one day in seven as the holy day, you go against the plain letter of the Bible, and put another day in the place of that day which the Bible has commanded. The command to keep holy the Seventh day is one of the Ten Commandments; you believe that the other nine are still binding. Who gave the authority to tamper with the fourth? If you are consistent with your own principles, if you really follow the Bible, and the Bible only you ought to be able to produce some portion of the New Testament in which this fourth commandment is expressly altered." Excerpts form *Why don't you keep holy the Sabbath Day?*, pages 1-15, in the Clifton Tract, volume 4, Published by the Roman Catholic Church in 1869 (quoted in a handout by the www.sundaylaw.org).

The great Alexander Campbell, founder of the Disciples of Christ, wrote:

"For example, nowhere in the Bible do we find that Christ or the Apostles ordered that the Sabbath be changed from Saturday to **Sun**day. We have the commandment of God given to Moses to keep holy the Sabbath day, that is the 7th day of the week, Saturday. Today most Christians keep **Sun**day because <u>it has been revealed</u> to us by the church <u>outside the Bible</u>." Catholic Virginian, October 3, 1947, p.9 Notice that the authority to change the Sabbath was a so called revelation "<u>outside the Bible</u>." It is just a tradition, not a biblical truth.

"It is old wives' fables to talk of the change of the Sabbath from the seventh to the first day. If it was changed, it was that august personage changed it who changes times and laws ex officio- I think his name is Doctor antichrist." Alexander Campbell, in *The Christian Baptist*, February 2, 1824, vol. 1, no 7, page 164.

There was an admission of the change published in the *Sentinel*, a Catholic bulletin from Algonac, Michigan on May 21st, 1995 that reads:

"Perhaps the boldest thing, the most revolutionary change the church ever did, happened in the first century. The holy day, the Sabbath, was changed from Saturday to Sunday. 'The day of the Lord' (dies Dominica) was chosen, not from any directions noted in the Scriptures, but from the church's sense of its own power. The day of resurrection, [and] the day of Pentecost, fifty days later, came on the first day of the week. So this would be the new Sabbath. People who think that the Scriptures should be the sole authority, should logically become 7th Day Adventist, and keep Saturday holy."

"Think not that I am come to destroy the law, or the prophets: I am not come to destroy, but to fulfil. For verily I say to you, <u>Till heaven and earth pass</u>, <u>one jot or one tittle shall in no wise pass from the law</u>, till all be fulfilled. Whosoever therefore shall break one of these least commandments, and shall teach men so, he shall be called the least in the kingdom of heaven: but whosoever shall do and teach them, the same shall be called great in the kingdom of heaven" Mat 5:17-19. Is this world passed? **NO**! Jesus never abolished any part of the law. *"The LORD is well pleased for his righteousness' sake; <u>he will magnify the law, and make it honorable</u>"* Isaiah 42:21.

God will do nothing of such importance without prophesizing it. *"Surely the Lord GOD will do nothing, but he reveals his secret to his servants the prophets"* Amos 3:7.

We have an immutable God. *"For I am the LORD, I change not; therefore ye sons of Jacob are not consumed"* Mal 3:6. *"Jesus Christ the same yesterday, and to day, and forever"* Hebrews 13:8.

The world is beginning to make changes to accommodate what the church has initiated. Right now there over 30 countries that have change their calendar to show Sunday as the last or seventh day of the week. "The International Standards Organization (ISO) specifies that the week begins with Monday, a usage that is becoming more widespread, for instance in airline timetables. One recent Vietnamese dictionary (Tự Điển Tiếng Việt), ignoring (or ignorant of) the traditional usage, goes out of its way to point out that, thứ ba, the 'third day' or Tuesday, is really only the second day of the week!" (*from http://cjvlang.com/Dow/dowviet.html*)

**Now let's consider the change in the law
that Daniel 7:25 prophesied:**

THE LAW OF GOD

AS GIVEN BY JEHOVA:	AS CHANGED BY MAN:
I	**I**
Thou shalt have no other gods before me.	I am the Lord thy God; thou shalt not have strange gods before me.
II	**II**
Thou shalt not make to thee any graven image, or any likeness of any thing that is in heaven above, or that is in the earth beneath, or that is in the water under the earth: thou shalt not bow down thyself to them, nor serve them: for I the Lord thy God am a jealous God, visiting the iniquity of the fathers upon the children to the third and fourth generation of them that hate me; and showing mercy to thousands of them that love me, and keep my commandments.	Thou shalt not take the name of the Lord thy God in vain.
III	**III**

Thou shalt not take the name of the Lord thy God in vain; for the Lord will not hold him guiltless that taketh his name in vain.

IV

Remember the Sabbath day, to keep it holy. Six days shalt thou labour, and do all thy work: but the seventh day is the Sabbath of the Lord thy God: in it thou shalt not do any work, thou, nor thy son, nor thy daughter, thy manservant, nor thy maidservant, nor thy cattle, nor thy stranger that is within thy gates: for in six days the lord made heaven and earth, the sea, and all that in them is, and rested the seventh day: wherefore the Lord blessed the Sabbath day, and hallowed it.

V

Honour thy father and thy mother: that thy days may be long upon the land which the Lord thy God giveth thee.

VI

Thou shalt not kill

VII

Thou shalt not commit adultery.

VIII

Thou shalt not steal.

IX

Thou shalt not bear false witness against thy neighbor.

Remember thou keep holy the Sabbath day.

IV

Honour thy father and thy mother.

V

Thou shalt not kill

VI

Thou shalt not commit adultery.

VII

Thou shalt not steal.

VIII

Thou shalt not bear false witness against thy neighbor.

IX

Thou shalt not covet thy neighbor's wife.

X	X
Thou shalt not covet thy neighbor's house, thou shalt not covet thy neighbor's wife, nor his manservant, nor his maidservant, nor his ox, nor his ass, nor any thing that is thy neighbor's. *(Exodus 20:3-7)*	Thou shalt not covet thy neighbor's goods. (Peter Geiermann. *The Convert's Catechism of Catholic Doctrine (1946 Edition*, pages 37, 38.)

THE WOLF IS STARTING TO WEAR A CUSTOM TO TRAP THE SHEEP

"Romanism is now regarded by Protestants with far greater favor than in former years. In those countries where Catholicism is not in the ascendancy, and the papists are taking a conciliatory course in order to gain influence, there is an increasing indifference concerning the doctrines that separate the reformed churches from the papal hierarchy; the opinion is gaining ground that, after all, we do not differ so widely upon vital points as has been supposed, and that a little concession on our part will bring us into a better understanding with Rome. The time was when Protestants placed a high value upon the liberty of conscience which had been so dearly purchased. They taught their children to abhor popery and held that to seek harmony with Rome would be disloyalty to God. But how widely different are the sentiments now expressed!

"The defenders of the papacy declare that the church has been maligned, and the Protestant world are inclined to accept the statement. Many urge that it is unjust to judge the church of today by the abominations and absurdities that marked her reign during the centuries of ignorance and darkness. They excuse her horrible cruelty as the result of the barbarism of the times and plead that the influence of modern civilization has changed her sentiments.

"Have these persons forgotten the claim of infallibility put forth for eight hundred years by this haughty power? So far from being relinquished, this claim was affirmed in the nineteenth century with greater positiveness than ever before. As Rome asserts that the "church *never erred;* nor will it, according to the Scriptures, *ever err* "(John L. Von Mosheim, *Institutes of Ecclesiastical History,* book 3, century

II, part 2, chapter 2, section 9, note 17), how can she renounce the principles which governed her course in past ages?
(*The Great Controversy*, pages 563, 564).

The Catholic Church is making several changes to attract Protestants. According to Cardinal Lefebvre (French rebel that wants a more traditional liturgy), the following is a list of things that are being changed:

1) The abolition of the minor orders and the sub-diaconate
2) The creation of a married diaconate
3) The abandonment of clerical and religious dress
4) The sharing of liturgical functions formerly reserved to the Priesthood.
5) The mass as is called today by the faithful no longer make reference to the Sacrifice, but rather to the Liturgy of the Word, to the Lord's Supper and to the breaking of bread, or to the Eucharist, thus reflecting a clear Protestant orientation.
6) The suppression of the altar stone.
7) The use of a single altar cloth.
8) The priest facing the people.
9) The Host remaining on the paten rather than on the corporal.
10) The introduction of ordinary bread and sacred vessels of less noble substances.
11) Communion in the hand and its distribution by lay men and lay women.
12) The reduced number of genuflections, which many priests have discontinued altogether.
13) There is no excommunication for Catholics who become Freemasons.

The previous 13 points are from *Luther's Mass- An Examination of the Shocking Similarities Between the "New Mass" and Luther's "Mass"* from a lecture given by His Grace Archbishop Marcel Lefebvre.
In a mass before believers from Oceania, the pope ignored the strict rules regarding dress code and shared the stage with barefooted and bare-chested people. Everything that can be done to make it look like he is one of the boys is being done. I never heard Jesus establishing

dress codes to approach God. I don't deny that in a church service we need to dress with our best clothes, but Jesus came into this world as a poor to rescue the poor. The clothes of the church hierarchy are in great contrast with the clothes that Jesus wore when he was on earth. The Savior dressed plainly like those around Him. John, the greatest prophet according to Jesus, dressed with skins. Elijah did too. There wasn't gold on Jesus' head, and He said that He didn't even have a place to rest His head.

Some famous people had been called heretics in the past. Now, the Catholic Church is apologizing. Remember Galileo? The church admitted that it was sorry, that they made a mistake, that Galileo was right. What about Joan of Arc? She was burned at the stake as a witch. Centuries later, she was declared a saint of the same church that ordered to execute her.

Recently Cardinal Willebrands, speaking in his capacity as the Holy See's envoy to the World Council of Churches at Geneva, declared solemnly that we should have to rehabilitate Martin Luther! All this is a mere attempt to look sorry or appear penitent, so the sheep will walk into the open jaws of the wolf.

On the other hand, some Catholic leaders are active in politics, and in most cases, they even take up the arms. Pope John Paul acknowledged that some members of the priesthood might be among the guilty parties in the 1994 violence, that killed so many people in Africa. The pope now talks about genocide, but he does not remember that that has been precisely the style of the church for centuries. It is hard to teach new tricks to the old wolf. Those priests are just practicing to be ready when the time comes to enforce the observation of **Sun**day. They will be the leaders of the new concentration camps and gas chambers.

Another way to clean up their image is to intervene in every conflict as peace negotiators. The pope himself had made several calls for peace. He wants to stop bloodshed here and stop threats of war there, looking tender and compassionate. I remember how I was taught to catch pigeons. I was supposed to put corn or another grain or seed that those birds like and make a line all the way to the inside of a box held by a stick. To that stick I was to tie a string and when the pigeon was under the box, I would pull and the pigeon was trapped. That is what its happening now. The people of the world are that pigeon.

They are enjoying being fed by the beautiful words of encouragement coming from the Catholic side. They just don't realize that there is a string attached to the stick (did you see the one that the popes carry, claiming that it was St. Peter's).

The pope is being universally recognized as primary defender of human rights. He also had apologized several times for the abuses of the past. He is just presenting a screen to distract the mouse with the tail of the cat. According to Navarro -Vals, the pope spokesman, this pope has traveled to 119 countries on more than 80 trips, with millions listening to him, using the world as a pulpit to preach the Gospel and denounce injustice.

In the book *The Great Controversy*, pages 464,465 says: "A well-known writer speaks thus of the attitude of the papal hierarchy as regards freedom of conscience, and of the perils which especially threaten the United States from the success of her policy:

"There are many who are disposed to attribute any fear of Roman Catholicism in the United States to <u>bigotry or childishness</u>. Such see nothing in the character and attitude of Romanism that is hostile to our free institutions, or find nothing portentous in its growth. Let us, then, first compare some of the fundamental principles of our government with those of the Catholic Church.

"The Constitution of the United States guarantees *liberty of conscience* . Nothing is dearer or more fundamental. Pope Pius IX, in his Encyclical Letter of August 15, 1854, said: '<u>The absurd and erroneous doctrines or ravings in defense of liberty of conscience are a most pestilential error--a pest, of all others, most to be dreaded in a state</u>.' The same pope, in his Encyclical Letter of December 8, 1864, <u>anathematized 'those who assert the liberty of conscience and of religious worship</u>,' also '<u>all such as maintain that the church may not employ force</u>.'

"The pacific tone of Rome in the United States does not imply a change of heart. <u>She is tolerant where she is helpless</u>. Says Bishop O'Connor: '<u>Religious liberty is merely endured until the opposite can be carried into effect without peril to the Catholic world</u>.'. . . The archbishop of St. Louis once said: 'Heresy and unbelief are crimes; and in Christian countries, as in Italy and Spain, for instance, where all the people are Catholics, and where the Catholic religion is an essential part of the law of the land, they are punished as other crimes.'. . .

"Every cardinal, archbishop, and bishop in the Catholic Church takes an oath of allegiance to the pope, in which occur the following words: 'Heretics, schismatics, and rebels to our said lord (the pope), or his aforesaid successors, I will to my utmost persecute and oppose.'"-- Josiah Strong, *Our Country,* ch. 5, pars. 2-4.

Beautiful words were said to Eve in the Garden of Eden. The Bible shows that she was deceived (ensnare). *"But I fear, lest by any means, as the serpent beguiled Eve through his craftiness, so your minds should be corrupted from the simplicity that is in Christ"* (2 Cor 11:3). *"And Adam was not deceived, but the woman being deceived was in the transgression"* (1 Timothy 2:14). Rome always tried to have people commit debauchery (seduction from allegiance or duty) against God. Satan himself can appear as a heavenly messenger: *"And no marvel; for Satan himself is transformed into an angel of light. Therefore it is no great thing if his ministers also be transformed as the ministers of righteousness; whose end shall be according to their works."* (2 Cor 11:14,15).

THE JESUITS

The Society of Jesus is the largest religious order of the Roman Catholic Church. Founded in 1540 by Saint Ignatius Loyola, a Spanish nobleman, the Society now numbers some 25,000 members on six continents and in 112 nations throughout the world. Soon after the Society was founded it started to bring not only fear but also death to people. Their symbol is a sun (Catholicism has perpetuated the pagan worship of the sun) with the letters HIS (the same initials of the Egyptian trinity-Isis, Horub and Seb) in the middle, as seen above. The candidates have to pronounce perpetual vows of poverty, chastity and obedience. With these vows, if he plans to prepare for priestly ordination, he becomes a scholastic of the Society and begins his study of **philosophy** and theology. Notice that philosophy goes first. What they call theology is the writings of the saints, almost no Bible.

Probably the most famous phrase coined by Loyola was "the end justifies the means." In this way, lying, stealing, killing (even family members) are allowed if they are to promote the principles and serve the interest of the church. Thousands of Jesuits had become counselors to the kings of the earth. Innumerable others had infiltrated the most closed systems of government as spies (the Vatican has one of the most efficient and powerful intelligence systems on the planet). They had founded some of the best universities in the world, in order to train the kids of both the noble and the common peasant to accept Roman heresy. After all, they are training the men that in the near future will handle the economy and the government.

You have probably heard about the Jesuits' activism in the so called "Theology of Liberation," which has caused so much bloodshed in South America, mostly in Nicaragua. "The new mission of the Society- for it is nothing less than that- suddenly places them in

199

actual and, in some instances, willing alliance with Marxist in their class struggle." Malachi Martin in *The Jesuists*, page 8. "In …Central American countries…Jesuits not only participated in guerrilla training of Marxist cadres, but some became guerrilla fighters themselves.… Jesuits found that all was permitted- even encouraged- as long as it furthered the concept of the new 'people's church.'" Ibid., pages 17,18.

"*Webster Third New International Dictionary*, having given the basic meaning of Jesuit as a member of the Order, then supplies the negative meanings: 'one given to intrigue or equivocation; a crafty person'; terms that are amplified by *Dornseif's Dictionary* into 'two-faced, false, insidious, dissembling, perfidious…insincere, dishonorable, dishonest, untruthful.' A Spanish proverb admonished people not to trust a monk with your wife or a Jesuit with your money." Ibid., page 28.

Some of their most famous students were: Voltaire, Hitler, Fidel Castro and Alfred Hitchcock, just to name a few.

Always thirsty for world power, "They had a part in every political alliance in Europe- an influential post with every government, an advisory capacity with every great man and each powerful woman." *The Jesuits*, page 31.

Their leader today is known as the "black Pope" and some say that his power is above the power of the pope in the Catholic Church, being the later just a screen, a puppet in the hands of the former.

"The Society of Jesus was established by the papacy in 1540 as a very special 'fighting unit' at the total and exclusive disposal of the Roman pope- whoever he might be. From their beginnings, the Jesuits were conceived in a military mode. Soldiers of Christ, they were given only two purposes: to propagate the religious doctrine and the moral law of the Roman Catholic Church as taught by the Roman Pope, and to defend the rights and prerogatives of that same Roman pope." *The Jesuits*, page 41.

The high Hierarchy of the church and the Jesuits had some battles during the 20th century, so John Paul I, as soon as he was elected pope, decided to confront this powerful group with an ultimatum. The day before he was to deliver his message to the leadership of the Congregation, he was found dead in bed, and as I remember clearly that day in 1978, no autopsy was allowed to be performed.

Explaining the training of a Jesuit novice, A.H. Newman wrote: "He is now excluded formal communication with his relatives and former friends. Every earthly tie is broken. He is to have no will of his own as to his future course, but is to put himself into the hands of the director as the interpreter of heaven towards him. He is to be as a corpse or as a staff. Absolute obedience is the thing most insisted upon. His conscience must not assert itself in opposition to the will of his superiors. Absolute destruction of individual will and conscience is aimed at and to a great extent accomplished. The director studies with the greatest care the condition of the novice from day to day. He is allowed to read nothing but a little devotional matter. He may not converse with other novices. His obedience is fully tested by the requirements of the most disagreeable and arduous services. The novitiate usually last about 2 years, and if the novice is found to possess great energy and tact, and absolute obedience, he is accepted as a scholar." Manual of Church history, page 371.

"Originality and independence of mind, love of truth for its own sake, the power of reflecting, and of forming correct judgments, were not merely neglected,- they were suppressed in the Jesuit's system." *Essays on Educational Reformers*, R.H. Quick, page 23. Please, refer to the appendix for more information- considered secret, first hand information, right from the bosom of the Jesuits' high hierarchy.

As *Pilgrim's Rest* published years ago, the Jesuits become "(1) priest to the royalty, leaders, and wealthy of the nations. (2) As teachers in schools and especially in the universities of the land. These would either be Catholic schools, government schools, or as secret agents in Protestant schools. (3) As secret agents working directly within governments, Protestant church organizations, or pagan religious organizations such as Hinduism. Their role would be that of minister, teacher or a highly trained professional, such as an accountant, lawyer, etc."

The same publication published some of the 65 propositions of the Jesuit Order. While you read them, keep in mind the saying of the founder: "the end justifies the means" ("If it helps the Society, the Church of Rome, or the individual Jesuit serving it- it is permissible, though it may involve theft, bribery, embezzlement, rape, treason, adultery, or murder"- Newman, page 378). These are some of those propositions:

13. "Keeping the required moderation, you can, without mortal sin, feel grieved about the life of a person; rejoice at his natural death, wish it, hope for it, with an inefficacious desire, not through hate for that person but in view of a material advantage resulting to yourself.

14. "It is allowed to wish with an absolute desire, for the death of your father, not as an evil for him, but as an advantage to the wisher; for instance, if a large inheritance is to result from that death.

15. "It is permitted to a son, who has killed his father while in a state of drunkenness, to rejoice at his death, when a considerable inheritance results from his murder.

37. "Servants may steal secretly from their masters what they deem a compensation for extra work not sufficiently rewarded by their wages.

59. "Masturbation is not prohibited by natural right.

60. Connection with a married woman, when the husband consents, is not adultery.

61. "The servant who, by bending his shoulders, knowingly helps his master reach a window in order to violate a girl, and frequently assist him with a ladder, opening a door, and furnishing him co-operation in a similar manner, does not commit a mortal sin if he so acts through fear of a grave damage; as, for instance, to suffer ill treatment from his master, to be considered as a fool and discharged."

Translated by M. Paul Bert in *Doctrines of the Jesuits*, pages 416-421.

One thing that startled me years ago was the "doctrine of 'mental reservation' or restriction, whereby one may without burdening his conscience, tell a down-right falsehood, provided the word or clause that would make the statement true remains unpronounced in the mind. Thus, one accused of having committed certain act last week in a certain place may swear that he was not there, reserving the statement 'this morning'. He may promise to do something, reserving in his mind a condition of which the person concerned knows nothing." Newman, page 379.

When Abraham Lincoln was working as a lawyer, he defended a former Catholic priest, Charles Chiniquy (who later wrote a book entitled, *Fifty years in the Church of Rome*), and got an acquittal for him. Lincoln knew very well that he was gaining for himself free enemies because of that since the Jesuits would not forgive him for their defeat. Lincoln wrote: "We have the proof that the company which had been selected and organized to murder me was led by a rabid Roman Catholic named Byrne; it was almost entirely composed of Roman Catholics. More than that, there were two disguised priests among them to lead and encourage them. Professor Morse, the learned inventor of electric telegraphy, tells me that recently, when he was in Rome, he found the proofs of a most formidable conspiracy against this country and all its institutions. It is evident that it is to the intrigues and emissaries of the Pope we owe, in great part, the horrible civil war which is threatening to cover the country with blood and ruin."

Lincoln knew that the first settlers and more influential people of California, Louisiana, Texas, New Mexico, Florida, Missouri and South Carolina were Roman Catholics. He also knew that their first teachers were Jesuits who hated the institutions, laws, schools and liberties of the Northern States. He recognized also the influence that the convents, colleges and schools of the Jesuits had on the minds of the people from the South.

As Abraham Lincoln said: "If the Protestants of the North and the South could learn what the priests, nuns, and monks, who daily land on our shores, under the pretext of preaching their religion, were doing in our schools and hospitals, as emissaries of the Pope and the other despots of Europe, to undermine our institutions and alienate the hearts of our people from our Constitution and our laws, and prepare a reign of anarchy here, as they have done in Ireland, Mexico, Spain, and wherever there are people that wish to be free, they would unite in taking power out of their hands." *Fifty Years in the Church of Rome*, by Charles Chiniquy.

There are several books that show evidence that Lincoln's assassination was a religiously motivated crime and that the Vatican was backing the war on the side of the South. See the recommended reading section in the last page.

OUR ONLY SAFEGUARD

"Satan is well aware that the weakest soul who abides in Christ is more than a match for the hosts of darkness, and that, should he reveal himself openly, he would be met and resisted. Therefore he seeks to draw away the soldiers of the cross from their strong fortification, while he lies in ambush with his forces, ready to destroy all who venture upon his ground. Only in humble reliance upon God, and obedience to all His commandments, can we be secure.

"No man is safe for a day or an hour without prayer. Especially should we entreat the Lord for wisdom to understand His word. Here are revealed the wiles of the tempter and the means by which he may be successfully resisted. Satan is an expert in quoting Scripture, placing his own interpretation upon passages, by which he hopes to cause us to stumble. We should study the Bible with humility of heart, never losing sight of our dependence upon God. While we must constantly guard against the devices of Satan, we should pray in faith continually: 'Lead us not into temptation'" *The Great Controversy*, page 530

OBEDIENCE OR LEGALISM?

Some people argue that Sabbath keepers are legalist. Ask those people if abstaining from adultery or from killing or just being honest in business transactions is legalism. What about for a child to obey his parents? They will agree that it is not. So, why is keeping one commandment considered legalism and keeping the other nine it is not? Isn't that a great contradiction? James taught that keeping nine and violating one is not going to make God happy. "For whosoever shall keep the whole law, and yet offend in **one** point, he is guilty of all. For he that said, Do not commit adultery, said also, Do not kill. Now if thou commit no adultery, yet if thou kill, thou art become a transgressor of the law. So speak ye, and so do, as they that shall be judged by the law of liberty" (James 2:10-12).

DOES IT REALLY MATTER WHICH DAY WE KEEP?

Some people argue that it really does not matter which day we choose to worship God. He is not as picky as we are, some say. This is the passage that they use:

"Him that is weak in the faith receive ye, but not to doubtful disputations. For <u>one believes that he may eat all things: another, who is weak, eats herbs</u>. Let not him that eats despise him that eats not; and let not him which eats not judge him that eats: for God has received him. Who are you that judges another man's servant? To his own master he stands or falls. Yes, he will be held up: for God is able to make him stand. One man esteems one day above another: another esteems every day *alike*. Let every man be fully persuaded in his own mind. He that regards the day, regards it to the Lord; and he that regards not the day, to the Lord he does not regard it. He that eats, eats to the Lord, for he gives God thanks; and he that eats not, to the Lord he eats not, and gives God thanks" (Romans 14:1-6).

This passage does not refer to the keeping of the Sabbath holy at all. The context shows that it is talking about ceremonies, because it mentions food. It is undoubtedly referring to eating meats offered to idols, and to days that the Jews considered important. A parallel passage is found in 1 Corinthians 8:4-13: "As concerning therefore the <u>eating of</u> those <u>things that are offered in sacrifice to idols</u>, we know that an idol is nothing in the world, and that there is none other God but one. For though there be that are called gods, whether in heaven or in earth, (as there be gods many, and lords many,) But to us there is but one God, the Father, of whom are all things, and we in him; and one Lord Jesus Christ, by whom are all things, and we by him. Howbeit there is not in every man that knowledge: for some <u>with</u>

conscience of the idol to this hour eat it as a thing offered to an idol; and their conscience being weak is defiled. But meat commendeth us not to God: for neither, if we eat, are we the better; neither, if we eat not, are we the worse. But take heed lest by any means this liberty of yours become a stumbling block to them that are weak. For if any man see thee which hast knowledge sit at meat in the idol's temple, shall not the conscience of him which is weak be emboldened to eat those things which are offered to idols; And through thy knowledge shall the weak brother perish, for whom Christ died? But when ye sin so against the brethren, and wound their weak conscience, ye sin against Christ. Wherefore, if meat make my brother to offend, I will eat no flesh while the world stands, lest I make my brother to offend." As you can see, some had tried to force the passage as to say that it's OK to observe any day.

We still have the question unanswered (Does it really matter which day we keep?). Suppose that a rich father tells his 10 kids: "I want you to come this next Tuesday to a special celebration, and from then on, it will be every Tuesday. I will come to town to be with you. It will be a special time to meet as a family." Eight of the kids did not like Tuesday, because it was just "not convenient." So they decided to go on Wednesday instead. When they got there: they found no food, no cake, the musicians were gone and their father was not there either. How would you feel if you were the father in the story? Probably betrayed, discouraged, disappointed, ignored, rejected. How do you think that God feels after He specified that He wanted us to keep Saturday holy? People (the majority) don't find it convenient to go to church on Saturdays. They don't realize that it is just like in the times of Jesus when He said: "Behold, **your house is left to you desolate**" (Mat. 23:38). No blessings! Jesus is not there, because He declared that the day of worship, the day of friendship, the day to share time with Him as our Best Friend and Savior, is Saturday, but Christians insist in going the day after!

Evangelist Mark Finley has an illustration that goes something like this:

"Suppose that my wife has 6 sisters and is the day of our wedding. When we go to our honeymoon, I take one of the sisters in the limousine. My wife, in horror, says to me: 'she is not your wife; I am.' My answer is: 'honey, one in seven, what difference does it make?" The

Bible indicates that God is jealous. When we disobey Him, we make him jealous. We go away with the other sister.

"God has given men the Sabbath as a sign between Him and them as a test of their loyalty. Those who, after the light regarding God's Law comes to them, continue to disobey and exalt human laws above the Law of God in the great crisis before us, will receive the mark of the beast." *Evangelism* page 235

How to keep the Sabbath Holy

In the book *The Desire of Ages*, page 283 says:

"No other institution which was committed to the Jews tended so fully to distinguish them from surrounding nations as did the Sabbath. God designed that its observance should designate them as His worshipers. It was to be a token of their separation from idolatry, and their connection with the true God. But in order to keep the Sabbath holy, men must themselves be holy. Through faith they must become partakers of the righteousness of Christ. When the command was given to Israel, 'Remember the Sabbath day, to keep it holy,' the Lord said also to them, 'Ye shall be holy men to Me.' Ex. 20:8; 22:31. Only thus could the Sabbath distinguish Israel as the worshipers of God."

"This is the work that we are called upon to do. From the pulpits of the popular churches it is proclaimed that the first day of the week is the Sabbath of the Lord; but God has given us light, showing us that the fourth precept of the Decalogue is as verily binding as are the other nine moral precepts. It is our work to make plain to our children that the first day of the week is not the true Sabbath, and that its observance after light has come to us as to what is the true Sabbath, **is idolatry**, and in plain contradiction to the law of God. In order to give them instruction in regard to the claims of the law of Jehovah, it is necessary that we separate our children from worldly associations and influences, and keep before them the Scriptures of truth, by educating them line upon line, and precept upon precept, that they may not prove disloyal to God." *Fundamentals of Christian Education*, page 287.

"…If the true Sabbath had always been kept, there would never have been an infidel or an atheist [Charles Darwin, for example]. The observance of the Sabbath would have preserved the world from idolatry. The fourth commandment has been trampled upon; therefore we are called upon to repair the breach in the law, and plead for the downtrodden Sabbath. The man of sin, who exalted himself above God, and thought to change times and laws, brought about the change of the Sabbath from the seventh to the first day of the week. In doing this, he made a breach in the law of God. Just prior to the great day of God, a message is sent forth to warn the people to come back to their allegiance to the law of God which antichrist has broken down. By precept and example, attention must be called to the breach in the law. *Testimonies for the Church Volume One*, page 76.

AN INVITATION

"Two great opposing powers are revealed in the last great battle. On one side stands the Creator of heaven and earth. All on His side bear His signet. They are obedient to His commands. On the other side stands the prince of darkness, with those who have chosen apostasy and rebellion" (Review & Herald May 7, 1901).

"The present is a solemn, fearful time for the church. The angels are already girded, awaiting the mandate of God to pour their vials of wrath upon the world. Destroying angels are taking up the work of vengeance; for the Spirit of God is gradually withdrawing from the world. Satan is also mustering his forces of evil, going forth 'to the kings of the earth and of the whole world,' to gather them under his banner, to be trained for 'the battle of that great day of God Almighty.' Satan is to make most powerful efforts for the mastery in the last great conflict. Fundamental principles will be brought out, and decisions made in regard to them. Skepticism is prevailing everywhere. Ungodliness abounds. The faith of individual members of the church will be tested as though there were not another person in the world" (MS 1a, 1890).

"In the seventeenth chapter of Revelation is foretold the destruction of all the churches who corrupt themselves by idolatrous devotion to the service of the papacy, those who have drunk of the wine of the wrath of her fornication" S.D.A. Bible Commentary Vol. 7, page 983.

Today, being so close to the conclusion of the drama of the history of this world, we should pay attention to the advice of the apostle Paul: "Let no man deceive you" (2 Thessalonians 2:3), and to the invitation from God: "**get out of her my people**" (Revelation 18:4). God wants to save you and protect you like the hen does with her chicks. Like Jesus told Jerusalem of old, he also makes the same call to his children today: "O Jerusalem, Jerusalem, the one who kills the prophets and stones those who are sent to her! How often I wanted to gather your children together, as a hen gathers her chicks under *her* wings, but you were not willing!" How many times had Jesus called you through the reading of this book and you have not been willing to leave the error and come to the truth that has been so clearly revealed?

John admonishes us not to unite with those that teach the error:

"Look to yourselves, that we lose not those things which we have wrought, but that we receive a full reward. Whosoever transgresseth, and abideth not in the doctrine of Christ, hath not God. He that abideth in the doctrine of Christ, he hath both the Father and the Son. If there come any to you, and bring not this doctrine, receive him not into your house, neither bid him God speed: For he that biddeth him God speed is partaker of his evil deeds" (2 John 1:8-11).

Very soon the mark of the beast (**Sun**day) will be presented from the pulpits of the fallen churches (yes, it's coming soon to a church near you promoted by your very own pastor and elders) as something worth accepting, just as if it comes from God. It is up to you to make a decision for right or for wrong. It will be a matter of conscience, of following man or following God, of having a religion of convenience or obeying with faith what God ask so lovingly.

As R. J. Wieland wrote in his *Revelation* book, page 159: "**Shall we follow the 'beast', or shall we follow the 'Lamb'** "? For the sake of your soul, leave Babylon before is too late! Do not be like Lot's wife or the people from Noah's time. Get out now, come to the boat.

APPENDIX

The following material contains the Secret Instructions of the Society of Jesus or Secreta Monita of the Jesuits. Please be careful to whom you show this material. It can spell evil for you. It can be found in the Internet. I once had it in my hands in 3 languages (Spanish, English and Latin). The person who gave it to my acquaintance was drunk. Apparently he was use to get in that condition. The two of them used to live at that time in the same apartment building. Apparently the apartment was tapped, because that was the last time that anybody saw him alive. He disappeared, leaving behind all his belongings.

Someone that I never met, found out that I had read the material and sent me a letter from Texas telling me that he knew I had a copy. The thing that caught my attention was that instead of sending the letter to my house (like somebody else would by consulting the phone book), he sent it to my PLACE OF WORK. That was very scary, trust me. They even know where I worked!!!

La Monita Secreta (Latin)

"These particular instructions must be guarded and kept with careful attention by the superiors, communicated with prudent caution to a few of the professors; in the meantime there does not exist any other thing so good for the Society; but we are charged with the most profound silence, and to make a false show, should they be written by any one though founded in the experience we have had. As there are various professors who are in these secrets, the Society has fixed the rule, that those who know these reserved instructions that they cannot pass in any one religious Order, whether it be of the Carthusians, to cause them to retire from that in which they live, and the inviolable silence with which they are to be guarded, all of which has been confirmed by the Holy See. Much care must be taken that they do not get out; for these counsels in the hands of strange persons to the Society, because they will give a sinister interpretation invidious to our situation.

"If (unless God does not permit) we reach success, we must openly deny that the Society shelters such thoughts and to take care that it is so affirmed by those of the Society that they are ignorant by not having been communicated, which they can protest with truth, that they know nothing of such instructions; and that there does not exist other than the general printed or manuscripts, which they can present, to cause any doubt to vanish. The superiors must with prudence and discretion, inquire if any of the Society have shown these instructions to strangers; for neither for himself, or for another, they must be copied by no one, without permission of the General or of the Provincial; and when it is feared that anyone has given notice of these instructions, we shall not be able to guard so rigorous a secret; and we must assert to the contrary, all that is said in them, it will be so given to be understood, that they only show to all, to be proved, and afterwards they will be dismissed.

CHAPTER 1.
THE MANNER OF PROCEDURE WITH WHICH THE SOCIETY MUST BE CONDUCTED WHEN CONSIDERING THE COMMENCING OF SOME FOUNDATION.

1. To capture the will of the inhabitants of a country, it is very important to manifest the intent of the Society, in the manner prescribed in the regulations in which it is said, that the Society must labor with such ardor and force for the salvation of their neighbor as for themselves. For the better inducement of this idea, the most opportunely that we practice the most humble offices, visiting the poor, the afflicted, and the imprisoned. It is very convenient to confess with much promptness, and to hear the confessions, showing indifference, without teasing the penitents; for this, the most notable inhabitants will admire our fathers and esteem them; for the great charity they have for all, and the novelty of the subject.

2. To have in mind that it is necessary to ask with religious modesty, the means for exercising the duties of the Society, and that it is needful to procure and acquire benevolence, principally of the secular ecclesiastics, and of persons of authority, that may be conceived necessary.

3. When called to go to the most distant places, where alms are to be received, they are to be accepted, no matter how small they may be, after having marked out the necessities of ourselves. Notwithstanding, it will be very convenient at the moment to give those alms to the poor, for the edification of those who do not have an exact understanding of the Society; and, "but we must in advance be more liberal with ourselves."

4. All must labor as if we were inspired by the same spirit; and each one must study to acquire the same styles, with the object of uniformity among so great a number of persons, edifying the whole; those who do the contrary must be expelled as pernicious.

5. In a beginning it is not convenient to purchase property; but in case they can be found, some good sites may be bought,

saying that they are to belong to other persons, using the names of some faithful friends, who will guard the secret. The better to make our poverty apparent, the property nearest our college must belong to colleges the most distant, that we can prevent the princes and magistrates from ever knowing that the income of the Society has a fixed point.

6. We must not ourselves go out to reside to form colleges, except to the rich cities; for in this we must imitate Christ, who remained in Jerusalem; and as he alone, passed by the less considerable populations.

7. We must obtain and acquire of the widows all the money that we can, presenting ourselves at repeated times to their sight our extreme necessity.

8. The Superior over each province is the one to whom we must account with certainty, the income of the same; but the amount to the treasurer at Rome, it is, and must always be, an impenetrable mystery.

9. It is for us to preach and say in all parts and in all conversations, that we have come to teach the young and aid the people; and this without interest in any single species and without exception of persons, and that we are not so onerous to the people as other religious orders.

CHAPTER II.
THE MANNER WITH WHICH THE FATHERS OF THE ORDER MUST CONDUCT THEMSELVES TO ACQUIRE AND PRESERVE THE FAMILIARITY OF PRINCES, MAGNATES AND POWERFUL AND RICH PERSONS.

1. It is necessary to do all that is possible to gain completely the attentions and affections of princes and persons of the most consideration; for that, who, being on the outside, but in advance, all of them will be constituted our defenders.

2. As we have learned by experience that princes and potentates are generally inclined to the favor of the ecclesiastics, when these disseminate their odious actions, and when they give an interpretation that they favor, as is to be noted among the married, contract with their relations or allies; or in other similar things; assembling much with them, to animate those

who may be found in this case, saying to them that we confide in the assurance of the exemptions, that by intervention of us fathers, which the Pope will concede, if he is made to see the causes, and will present other examples of similar things, exhibiting at the same time the sentiments that we favor, under the pretext of the common good and THE GREATER GLORY OF GOD that is the object of the Society.

3. If at this same assembly the prince treats of doing something, that will not be agreeable to all the great men, for which we are to stir up and investigate, meanwhile, counseling others to conform with the prince, without ever descending to treat of particulars, for fear there may not be a successful issue of the matter, for which the Society will be imputed blame; and for this, if this action shall be disapproved, there will be advertences presented to the contrary that may be absolutely prohibited and put in jeopardy, the authority of some of the fathers, of whom it can be said with certainty, that they have not had notice of the Secret Instructions; for that, it can be affirmed with an oath, that the calumny to the Society, is not true in respect to that which is imputed to it.

4. To gain the good will of Princes, it will be very convenient to insinuate with skill; and for third persons, that we fathers, are a means to discharge honorable and favorable duties in the courts of other kings and princes, and more than any one else in that of the Pope. By this means we can recommend ourselves and the Society; for the same, no one must be charged with this commission but the most zealous persons and well versed in our institute.

5. Aiming especially to bring over the will of the favorites of princes and of their servants, by means of presents and pious offices, that they may give faithful notice to us fathers of the character and inclinations of the princes and great men. Of this manner the Society can gain with facility as much to one as to others.

6. The experience we have had, has made us acquainted with the many advantages that have been taken by the Society of its intervention in the marriages of the House of Austria, and of those which have been effected in other kingdoms, France,

Poland, and in various duchies. Forasmuch assembling, proposing with prudence, selecting choice persons who may be friends and families of the relatives, and of the friends of the Society.

7. It will be easy to gain the princesses, making use of their valets; by that, coming to feed and nourish with relations of friendship, by being located at the entrance in all parts, and thus become acquainted with the most intimate secrets of the familiars.

8. In regard to the direction of the consciences of great men, we confessors must follow the writers who concede the greater liberty of conscience. The contrary of this is to appear too religious; for that they will decide to leave others and submit entirely to our direction and counsels.

9. It is necessary to make reference to all the merits of the Society; to the princes and prelates, and to as many as can lend much aid to the Society, after having shown the transcendency of its great privileges.

10. Also, it will be useful to demonstrate, with prudence and skill, such ample power which the Society has, to absolve, even in the reserved cases, compared with that of other pastors and priests; also, that of dispensing with the fasts, and of the rights which they must ask and pay, in the impediments of marriage, by which means many persons will recur to us, whom it will be our duty to make agreeable.

11. It is not the less useful to invite them to our sermons, assemblies, harangues, declamations, etc., composing odes in their honor, dedicating literary works or conclusions; and if we can for the future, give dinners and greetings of divers modes.

12. It will be very convenient to take to our care the reconciliation of the great, in the quarrels and enmities that divide them; then by this method we can enter, little by little, into the acquaintance of their most intimate friends and secrets; and we can serve ourselves to that party which will be most in favor of that which we present.

13. If there should be some one at the service of a monarch or prince, and he were an enemy of our Society, it is necessary to procure well for ourselves better than for others, making him a

friend, employing promises, favors, and advances, which shall be in proportion to the same monarch or prince.

14. No one shall recommend to a prince any one, nor make advances to any who have gone out from us, being outside of our Society, and in particular to those who voluntarily verified, for yet when they dissimulate they will always maintain an inextinguishable hatred to the Society.

In fine, each one must procure and search for methods to increase the affection and favor of princes, of the powerful, and of the magistrates of each population, that whenever occasion is offered to support, we can do much with efficacy and good faith, in benefiting ourselves, though contrary to their relations, allies and friends.

CHAPTER III.
HOW THE SOCIETY MUST BE CONDUCTED WITH THE GREAT AUTHORITIES IN THE STATE, AND IN CASE THEY ARE NOT RICH WE MUST LEND OURSELVES TO OTHERS.

1. The care consigned to us, that we must do all that is possible, for to conquer the great; but it is also necessary to gain their favor to combat our enemies.

2. It is very conducive to value their authority, prudence and counsels, and induce them to despise wealth, at the same time that we procure gain and employ those that can redeem the Society; tacitly valuing their names, for acquisition of temporal goods if they inspire sufficient confidence.

3. It is also necessary to employ the ascendant of the powerful, to temper the malevolence of the persons of a lower sphere and of the rabble against our Society.

4.* It is necessary to utilize, whenever we can, the bishops, prelates and other superior ecclesiastics, according to the diversity of reason, and the inclination we manifest.

5. In some points it will be sufficient to obtain of the prelates and curates, that which it is possible to do, that their subjects respect the society; and that obstructing the exercise of its functions among those who have the greatest power, as in Germany, Poland, etc. It will be necessary to exhibit the most distinguished attentions for that, mediating its authority and

that of the princes, monasteries, parishes, priorates, patronates, the foundations of the churches and the pious places, can come to our power. Because we can with more facility where the Catholics will be found mixed with heretics. It is necessary to make such prelates see the utility and merit that we have in all this, and that never will they have so much valuation from the priests, friars, and for the future from the faithful. If making these changes, it is necessary to publicly praise their zeal, although written, and to perpetuate the memory of their actions.

6. For this it is necessary to labor, to the end, that the prelates will place in the hands of us fathers, as confessors and counselors; and if they aspire to more elevated positions in the Court of Rome, we must unite in their favor and aid their pretensions with all our forces, and by means of our influence.

7. We must be watchful that when the bishops are instituting principal colleges and parochial churches, that the faculties are taken from the Society, and placed in both vicarious establishments, with the charge of cures, and that the Superior of the Society to be, that all the government of these churches shall pertain to us, and that the parishioners shall be our subjects, of the method that all can be placed in them.

8. Where there are those of the academies who have been driven out from us, and are contrary; where the Catholics or the heretics obstruct our installation, we will compound with the prelates, and make ourselves the owners of the first cathedrals; for thus shall we make them to know the necessities of the Society.

9. Over all, we must be very certain to procure the protection and affection of the prelates of the Church, for the cases of beatification or canonization of ourselves; in whose subjects convened further, to obtain letters from the powerful and of the princes, that the decisions may be promptly attained in the Catholic Court.

10. If it shall be accounted that the prelates or magnates should send commissioned representatives, we must put forth all ardor, that no other priests, who are in dispute with us, shall be sent; for the reason, that they shall not communicate their

animadversion, discrediting us in the cities and provinces we inhabit; and that if they pass by other provinces and cities, where there are colleges, they will be received with affection and kindness, and be so splendidly treated as a religious modesty will permit.

CHAPTER IV.
OF THAT WHICH WE MUST CHARGE THE PREACHERS AND CONFESSORS OF THE GREAT OF THE EARTH.

1. Those of us who may be directed to the princes and illustrious men, of the manner in which we must appear before them, with inclination unitedly "to the greater glory of God," obtaining -- with its austerity of conscience, that the same princes are persuaded of it; for this direction we must not travel in a principle to the exterior or political government, but gradually and imperceptibly.

2. Forasmuch there will be opportunity and conducive notices at repeated times, that the distribution of honors and dignities in the Republic is an act of justice; and that in a great manner it will be offending God, if the princes do not examine themselves and cease carrying their passions, protesting to the same with frequency and severity, that we do not desire to mix in the administration of the State; but when it shall become necessary to so express ourselves thus, to have your weight to fill the mission that is recommended. Directly that the sovereigns are well convinced of this, it will be very convenient to give an idea of the virtues that may be found to adorn those that are selected for the dignities and principal public changes; procuring then and recommending the true friends of the Society; notwithstanding, we must not make it openly for ourselves, but by means of our friends who have intimacy with the prince that it is not for us to talk him into the disposition of making them.

3. For this watchfulness our friends must instruct the confessors and preachers of the Society near the persons capable of discharging any duty, that over all, they must be generous to the Society; they must also keep their names, that they may

insinuate with skill, and upon opportune occasions to princes, well for themselves or by means of others.

4. The preachers and confessors will always present themselves so that they must comport with the princes, lovable and affectionate, without ever shocking them in sermons, nor in particular conversations, presenting that which rejects all fear, and exhorting them in particular to faith, hope and justice.

5. Never receive gifts made to any one in particular, but that for the contrary; but picture the distress in which the Society or college may be found, as all are alike; having to be satisfied with assigning each one a room in the house, modestly furnished; and noticing that your garb is not over nice; and assist with promptness to the aid and counsel of the most miserable persons of the palace; but that you do not say it of them, but only those who have agreed to serve the powerful.

6. Whenever the death occurs of any one employed in the palace, we must take care of speaking with anticipation, that they fail in the nomination of a successor, in their affection for the Society; but giving no appearance to cause suspicion that it was the intent of usurping the government of the prince; for which, it must not be from us that it is said; take a part direct; but assembling of faithful or influential friends who may be found in a position of rousing the hate of one and another until they become inflamed.

CHAPTER V.
OF THE MODE OF CONDUCTING THE SOCIETY WITH RESPECT TO OTHER ECCLESIASTICS WHO HAVE THE SAME DUTIES AS OURSELVES IN THE CHURCH.

1. It is necessary to help with valor these persons, and manifest in their due time to the princes and lords that are always ours, and being constituted in power, that our Society contains essentially the perfection of all the other orders, with the exception of singing and manifesting an exterior of austerity in the mode of life and in dress; and that if in some points they excel the communities of the Society, this shines with greater splendor in the Church of God.

2. We must inquire into and note the defects of the other fathers (non-Jesuit priests), and when we find them, we must divulge them among our faithful friends, as condoling over them; we must show that such fathers do not discharge with certainty, that we do ourselves the functions, that some and others recommend.

3. It is necessary that the fathers of our Society oppose with all their power the other fathers who intend to found houses of education to instruct the youths among the populations where ours are found teaching with acceptation and approval; and it will be very convenient to indicate our projects to princes and magistrates, that such people will excite disturbances and commotions if they are not prohibited from teaching; and that in the last result, the damage will fall upon the educated, by being instructed by a bad method, without any necessity; posting them that the Society is sufficient to teach the youth. In case the fathers bear letters of the Pontificate, or recommendations from the Cardinals, we must work in opposition to them, making the princes and great men to point out to the Pope the merits of the Society and its intelligence for the pacific instruction of the youths, to which end, we must have and obtain certifications of the authorities upon our good conduct and sufficiency.

4. Having notwithstanding to form duties, our fathers in displaying singular proofs of our virtue and erudition, making them to exercise the alumni (graduates) in their studies in methods of functions, scholars of diversion, capable of drawing applause, making for supposition, these representations in the presence of the great magistrates and concurrence of other classes.

CHAPTER VI.
OF THE MODE OF ATTRACTING RICH WIDOWS.

1. We must elect effective fathers already advanced in years, of lively complexion and conversation, agreeable to visit these ladies, and whence they can promptly note in them appreciation or affection for our Society; making offerings of good works and the merits of the same; that, if they accept

them, and succeed in having them frequent our temples, we must assign to them a confessor, who will be able of guiding them in the ways that are proper, in the state of widowhood, **making the enumeration and praises of satisfaction that should accompany such a state; making them believe and yet with certainty that they who serve as such, is a merit for eternal life, being efficacious to relieve them from the pains of purgatory**.

2. The same confessor will propose to them to make and adorn a little chapel or oratory in their own house, to confirm their religious exercises, because by this method we can shorten the communication, more easily hindering those who visit others; although if they have a particular chaplain, and will content to go to him to celebrate the mass, making opportune advertencies to her who confesses, to the effect and treating her as being left to be overpowered by said Chaplain.

3. We must endeavor skillfully but gently to cause them to change respectively to the Order and to the method of the House, and to conform as the circumstances of the person will permit, to whom they are directed, their propensities, their piety, and yet to the place and situation of the edifice.

4. We must not omit to have removed, little by little, the servants of the house that are not of the same mind with ourselves, proposing that they be replaced by those persons who are dependent on us, or who desire to be of the Society; for by this method we can be placed in the channel of communication of whatever passes in the family.

5. The constant watch of the confessor will have to be, that the widow shall be disposed to depend on him totally, representing that her advances in grace are necessarily bound to this submission.

6. We are to induce her to the frequency of the sacraments, and especially that of penitency, making her to give account of her deeper thoughts and intentions; inviting her to listen to her confessor, when he is to preach particular promising orations; recommending equally the recitation each day of the litanies and the examination of conscience.

7. It will be very necessary in the case of a general confession, to enter extensively into all of her inclinations; for that it will be to determine her, although she may be found in the hands of others.

8. Insist upon the advantages of widowhood and the inconvenience of marriage; in particular that of a repeated one, and the dangers, to which she will be exposed, relatively to her particular businesses into which we are desirous of penetrating.

9. We must cause her to talk of men whom she dislikes, and to see if she takes notice of anyone who is agreeable, and represent to her that he is a man of bad life; procuring by these means disgust of one and another, and repugnant to unite with anyone.

10. When the confessor has become convinced that she has decided to follow the life of widowhood, he must then proceed to counsel her to dedicate herself to a spiritual life, but not to a monastic one, whose lack of accommodations will show how they live; in a word, we must proceed to speak of the spiritual life of Pauline and of Eustace, &c. The confessor will conduct her at last, that having devoted the widow to chastity, to not less than for two or three years, she will then be made to renounce a second nuptial forever.

    In this case she will be found to have discarded all sorts of relations with men, and even the diversions between her relatives and acquaintances, we must protest that she must unite more closely to God. With regard to the ecclesiastics who visit her, or to whom she goes out to visit, when we cannot keep her separate and apart from all others, we must labor that those with whom she treats shall be recommended by ourselves or by those who are devoted to us.

11. In this state, we must inspire her to give alms, under the direction, as she will suppose, or her spiritual father; then it is of great importance that they shall be employed with utility; more, being careful that there shall be discretion in counsel, causing her to see that inconsiderate alms are the frequent causes of many sins, or serve to torment at last, that they are not the fruit, nor the merit which produced them.

CHAPTER VII.
SYSTEM WHICH MUST BE EMPLOYED WITH WIDOWS AND METHODS OF DISPOSING OF THEIR PROPERTY.

1. It will be necessary to inspire her to continue to persevere in her devotion and the exercise of good works and of disposition, in not permitting a week to pass, to give away some part of her overplus, in honor of Jesus Christ, of the Holy Virgin and of the Saint she has chosen for her patron; giving this to the poor of the Society or for the ornamenting of its churches, until she has absolutely disposed of the first fruits of her property as in other times did the Egyptians.

2. When the widows, the more generally to practice their alms, must be given to know with perseverance, their liberality in favor of the Society; and they are to be assured that they are participants in all the merits of the same, and of the particular indulgences of the Provincial; and if they are persons of much consideration, of the General of the Order.

3. The widows who having made vows of chastity, it will be necessary for them to renew them twice per annum, conforming to the custom that we have established; but permitting them notwithstanding, that day some honest freedom from restraint by our fathers.

4. They must be frequently visited, treating them agreeably; referring them to spirited and diverting histories, conformable to the character and inclination of each one.

5. But that they may not abate, we must not use too much rigor with them in the confessional; that it may not be, that they by having empowered others of their benevolence, that we do not lose confidence of recovering their adhesion, having to proceed in all cases with great skill and caution, being aware of the inconstancy natural to woman.

6. It is necessary to have them do away with the habit of frequenting other churches, in particular those of convents; for which it is necessary to often remind them, that in our Order there are possessed many indulgences that are to be obtained only partially by all the other religious corporations.

7. To those who may be found in the case of the garb of mourning, they will be counseled to dress a little more

agreeable, that they may at the same time, unite the aspect of mourning with that of adornment, to draw them away from the idea of being found directed by a man who has become a stranger to the world. Also with such, that they may not be very much endangered, or particularly exposed to volubility, we can concede to them, as if they maintained their consequence and liberality, for and with the society, that which drives ensuality away from them, being with moderation and without scandal.

8. We must manage that in the houses of the widows there shall be honorable young ladies, of rich and noble families; that little by little they become accustomed to our direction and mode of life; and that they are given a director elected and established by the confessor of the family, to be permanently and always subject to all the reprehensions and habits of the Society; and if any do not wish to submit to all, they must be sent to the houses of their fathers, or to those from which they were brought, accusing them directly of extravagance and of glaring and stained character.

9. The care of the health of the widows, and to proportion some amusement, it is not the least important that we should care for their salvation; and so, if they complain of some indisposition, we must prohibit the fast, the hair cloth girdle, and the discipline, without permitting them to go to church; further continue the direction, cautiously and secretly with such, that they may be examined in their houses; if they are given admission into the garden, and edifice of the college, with secrecy; and if they consent to converse and secretly entertain with those that they prefer.

10. To the end that we may obtain, that the widows employ their utmost obsequiousness to the Society, it is the duty to represent to them the perfection of the life of the holy, who have renounced the world, estranged themselves from their relations, and despising their fortunes, consecrating themselves to the service of the Supreme Being with entire resignation and content. It will be necessary to produce the same effect, that those who turn away to the Constitutions of the Society, and their relative examination to the abandonment of all

things. We must cite examples of the widows who have reached holiness in a very short time; giving hopes of their being canonized, if their perseverance does not decay; and promising for their cases our influence with the Holy Father.

11. We must impress in their souls the persuasion that, if they desire to enjoy complete tranquility of conscience it will be necessary for them to follow without repugnance, without murmuring, nor tiring, the direction of the confessor, so in the spiritual, as in the eternal, that she may be found destined to the same God, by their guidance.

12. Also we must direct with opportunity, that the Lord does not desire that they should give alms, nor yet to fathers of an exemplary life, known and approved, without consulting beforehand with their confessor, and regulating the dictation of the same.

13. The confessors must take the greatest care that the widows and their daughters of the confessional do not go to see other fathers (i.e. non-Jesuit priests) under any pretext, nor with them. For this, we must praise our Society as the Order most illustrious of them all; of greater utility in the Church, and of greater authority with the Pope and with the princes; perfection in itself; then dismiss the dream of them, and menace them, that we can, and that we are no correspondents to them, we can say, that we do not consent to froth and do as among other monks who count in their convents many ignorant, stupid loungers who are indolent in regard to the other life, and intriguers in that to disorder, &c.

14. The confessors must propose and persuade the widows to assign ordinary pensions and other annual quotas to the colleges and houses of profession for their sustenance with especially to the professed house at Rome; and not forgetting to remind them of the restoration of the ornaments of the temples and replenishing of the wax, the wine, and other necessaries for the celebration of the mass.

15. If they do not make relinquishment of their property to the Society, it will be made manifest to them, on apparent occasion in particular, when they are found to be sick, or in danger of death; that there are many colleges to be

founded; and that they may be excited with sweetness and disinterestedness, to make some disbursements as merit for God, and in that they can found his eternal glory.

16. <u>In the same manner, we must proceed with regard to princes and other well doers, making them to see that such foundations will be made to perpetuate their memory in this world, and gain eternal happiness</u>, and if some malevolent persons adduce the example of Jesus Christ, saying, that then he had no place to recline his head, the Society bearing his name should be poor in imitation of himself, we must make it known and imprint it in the imagination of those, and of all the world, that the Church has varied, and that in this day we have become a State; and we must show authority and grand measures against its enemies that are very powerful, or like that little stone prognosticated by the prophet, that, divided, came to be a great mountain. <u>Inculcate constantly to the widows, who dedicate their alms and ornaments to the temples, that the greater perfection is in disposing of the affection and earthly things, ceding their possession to Jesus Christ and his companions.</u>

17. Being very little, that which we must promise to the widows, who dedicate and educate their children for the world, we must apply some remedy to it.

CHAPTER VIII.
METHODS BY WHICH THE CHILDREN OF RICH WIDOWS MAY BE CAUSED TO EMBRACE THE RELIGIOUS STATE, OR OF DEVOTION.

1. <u>To secure our object, we must create the custom that the mothers treat them severely, and show to them, that we are in love with them. Coming to induce the mothers to do away with their tastes, from the most tender age, and regarding, restraining, &c., &c., the children especially; prohibiting decorations and adornments when they enter upon competent age; that they are inspired in the vocation for the cloister, promising them an endowment of consideration, if they embrace a similar state; representing to them the insipidity that is brought with matrimony, and the disgust that has been</u>

experienced in it; signifying to them the weight they would sit under, for not having maintained in the celibate. Lastly, coming to direct in the conclusions arrived at by the daughters of the widows, so fastidious of living with their mothers, that their feet would be directed to enter into a convent.

2. We must make ourselves intimate with the sons of the widows, and if for them an object or the Society, and cause them to penetrate the intent of our colleges, making them to see things that can call their attention by whatever mode, such as gardens, vineyards, country houses, and the farm houses where the masters go to recreate; talk to them of the voyages the Jesuits have made to different countries, of their treating with princes, and of much that can capture the young; cause them to note the cleanliness of the refectory, the commodiousness of the lodges, the agreeable conversation we have among ourselves, the suavity of our rule, and that we have all for the object of the greater glory of God; show to them the preeminence of our Order over all the others, taking care that the conversations we have shall be diverting to pass to that of piety.

3. At proposing to them the religious state, have care of doing so, **as if by revelation**; and in general, insinuating directly with sagacity, the advantage and sweetness of our institute above all others; and in conversation cause them to understand the great sin that will be committed against the vocation of the Most High; in fine, induce them to make some spiritual exercises that they may be enlightened to the choice of this state.

4. We must do all that is possible that the masters and professors of the youth indicated shall be of the Society, to the end, of being always vigilant over these, and counsel them; but if they cannot be reduced, we must cause them to be deprived of some things, causing that their mothers shall manifest their censure and authority of the house, that they may be tired of that sort of life; and if, finally, we cannot obtain their will to enter the Society, we must labor; because we can remand them to other colleges of ours that are at a distance, that they may study, procuring impediment, that their mothers show endearment

and affection, at the same time, continuing for our part, in drawing them to us by suavity of methods.

CHAPTER IX.
UPON THE AUGMENTING OF REVENUE IN THE COLLEGES.

1. We must do all that is possible, because we do not know if bound with the last vow of him, who is the claimant of an inheritance, meanwhile we do not know if it is confirmed, to not be had in the Society a younger brother, or of some other reason of much entity. Before all, that which we must procure, are the augmentations of the Society with rules to the ends agreed upon by the superiors, which must be conformable: for that the Church returns to its primitive splendor for the greater glory of God; of fate that all the clergy shall be found animated by a united spirit. To this end, we must publish by all methods, that the Society is composed in part of professors so poor, that are wanting of the most indispensable, to not be for the beneficence of the faithful; and that another part is of fathers also poor, although living upon the product of some household property; but not to be grievous to the public, in the midst of their studies, their ministry, as are other ordinary mendicants. The spiritual directors of princes, great men, accommodating widows, and of whom we have abundant hope, that they will be disposed at last to make gifts to the Society in exchange for spiritual and eternal things, that will be proportioned, the lands and temporalities which they possess; for the same, carrying always the idea, that we are not to lose the occasion of receiving always as much as may be offered. If promises and the fulfillment of them are retarded, they are to be remembered with precaution, dissimulating as much as we can the coveting of riches. When some confessor of personages or other people, will not be apt, or wants subtility, that in these subjects is indispensable, he will be retired with opportunity, although others may be placed anticipatedly; and if it be entirely necessary to the penitents, it will be made necessary to take out the destitute to distant colleges, representing that the Society has need for them there; because it being known that some young widows, having

232

unexpectedly failed, the Society not having the legacy of very precious movables, having been careless by not accepting in due time. But to receive these things, we could not attend at the time, and only at the good will of the penitent.

2. To attract the prelates, canonicals and other rich ecclesiastics, it is necessary to employ certain arts, and in place procuring them to practice in our houses spiritual exercises, and gradually and energetically of the affection that we profess to divine things; so that they will be affectionate towards the Society and that they will soon offer pledges of their adhesion.

3. The confessors must not forget to ask with the greatest caution and on adequate occasions of those who confess, what are their names, families, relatives, friends, and properties, informing their successors who follow them, the state, intention in which they will be found, and the resolution which they have taken; that which they have not yet determined obtaining, having to form a plan for the future to the Society. When it is founded, whence directly there are hopes of utility; for it will not be convenient to ask all at once; they will be counseled to make their confession each week, to disembarrass the conscience much before, or to the title of penitence. They will be caused to inform the confessor with repetition, of that which at one time they have not given sufficient light; and if they have been successful by this means, she will come, being a woman, to make confession with frequency, and visit our church; and being a man, he will be invited to our houses and we are to make him familiar with ourselves.

4. <u>That which is said in regard to widows, must have equal application to the merchants and neighbors of all classes, as being rich and married, but without children, of that plan by which the Society can arrive to be their heirs, if we put in play the measures that we may indicate; but over all, it will be well to have present, as said, near the rich devotees that treat with us, and of whom the vulgar can murmur, when more, if they are of a class not very elevated.</u>

5. Procuring for the rectors of the colleges entrance for all the ways of the houses, parks, groves, forests, lawns, arable lands, vineyards, olive orchards, hunting grounds, and whatever

species of inheritances which they meet with in the end of their rectory; if their owners pertain to the nobility, to the clergy, or are negotiators, particulars, or religious communities, inquiring the revenues of each one, their loads and what they pay for them. All these dates or notices they are to seek for with great skill and to a fixed point, energetically yet from the confessional, then of the relations of friendship; or of the accidental conversations; and the confessor meets with a penitent of possibles, he will be placed in knowledge of the rector, obtaining by all methods the one conserved.

6. The essential point to build upon, is the following: that we must so manage, that in the ends we gain the will and affections of our penitents, and other persons with whom we treat, accommodating ourselves to their inclinations if they are conducive. The Provincials will take care to direct some of us to points, in which reside the nobility and the powerful; and if the Provincials do not act with opportunity, the rectors must notice with anticipation, the crops (the field of operations) that are there, which we go to examine.

7. When we receive the sons of strong houses in the Society, they must show whether they will be easy to acquire the contracts and titles of possession; and if so they were to enter of themselves, of which they may be caused to cede some of their property to the college, or the usufruct (profit) or for rent, or in other form, or if they can come for a time into the Society, the gain of which may be very much of an object, to give a special understanding to the great and powerful, the narrowness in which we live, and the debts that are pressing us.

8. When the widows, or our married devoted women, do not have more than daughters, we must persuade them to the same life of devotion, or to that of the cloister; but that except the endowment that they may give, they can enter their property in the Society gently; but when they have husbands, those that would object to the Society, they will be catechized; and others who desire to enter as religious in other Orders, with the promise of some reduced amount. When there may be an only son, he must be attracted at all cost, inculcating the

vocation as made by Jesus Christ; causing him to be entirely disembarrassed from the fear of its fathers, and persuading him to make a sacrifice very acceptable to the Almighty, that he must withdraw to His authority, abandon the paternal house and enter in the Society; the which, if he so succeeds, after having given part to the General, he will be sent to a distant novitiate; but if they have daughters, they will primarily dispose the daughters for a religious life; and they will be caused to enter into some monastery, and afterwards be received as daughters in the Society, with the succession of its properties.

9. The Superiors will place in the channel of the circumstances, the confessors of these widows and married people, that they on all future occasions may act for the benefit of the Society; and when by means of one, they cannot take our part he will be replaced with another; and if it is made necessary, he will be sent to great distances, of a manner that he cannot follow understandingly with these families.

10. If we succeed in convincing the widows and devoted persons, who aspire with fervor to a perfect life, and that the better means to obtain it is by ceding all their properties to the Society, supporting by their revenues, that they will be religiously administered until their death, conforming to the degree of necessity in which they may be found, and the just reason that may be employed for their persuasion is, that by this mode, they can be exclusively dedicated to God; without attentions and molestations, which would perplex them, and that it is the only road to reach the highest degree of perfection.

11. The Superiors craving the confidence of the rich, who are attached to the Society, delivering receipts of its proper hand writing whose payment afterwards will differ; not forgetting to often visit those who loan, to exhort them above all in their infirmities of consideration, as to whom will devolve the papers of the debt; because it is not so to be found mention of the Society in their testament; and by this course we must acquire properties, without giving cause for us to be hated by the heirs.

12. We must also in a grand manner ask for a loan, with payment of annual interest, and employ the same capital in other speculation to produce greater revenues to the Society; for at such a time, succeeding to move them with compassion to that which they will lend to us, we will not lose the interest in the testament of donation, when they see that they found colleges and churches.

13. The Society can report the utilities of commerce, and value the name of the merchant of credit, whose friendship we may possess.

14. Among the peoples where our fathers reside, we must have physicians faithful to the Society, whom we can especially recommend to the sick, and to paint under an aspect very superior to that of other religious orders, and secure direction that we shall be called to assist the powerful, particularly in the hour of death.

15. That the confessors shall visit with assiduity the sick, particularly those who are in danger, and to honestly eliminate the other fathers, which the superiors will procure, when the confessor sees that he is obliged to remove the other from the suffering, to replace and maintain the sick in his good intentions. Meanwhile we must inculcate as much as we can with prudence, the fear of hell, &c., &c., or when, the lesser ones of purgatory; demonstrating that as water will put out fire, so will the same alms blot out the sin; and that we cannot employ the alms better, than in the maintaining and subsidizing of the persons, who, by their vocation, have made profession of caring for the salvation of their neighbor; that in this manner the sick can be made to participate in their merits, and find satisfaction for their own sins; placing before them that charity covereth a multitude of sins; and that also, we can describe that charity, is as a nuptial vestment, without which, no one can be admitted to the heavenly table. In fine it will be necessary to move them to the citations of the scriptures, and of the holy fathers, that according to the capacity of the sick, we can judge what is most efficacious to move them.

16. We must teach the women, that they must complain of the vices of their husbands, and the disturbances which they

occasion, that they can rob them in secret of some amounts of money, to offer to God, in expiation of the sins of their husbands, and to obtain their pardon.

CHAPTER X.
OF THE PARTICULAR RIGOR OF DISCIPLINE IN THE SOCIETY.

1. If there shall be anyone dismissed under any protest, as an enemy of the Society, whatever may be his condition, or age; all those who have been moved to become the devotees of our churches; or of visiting ourselves; or who having been made to take the alms on the way to other churches; or who having been found to give to other fathers; or who having dissuaded any rich man, and well intentioned towards our Society, or giving anything; or in the time in which he can dispose of his properties, having shown great affection for his relations with this Society; because it is a great proof of a mortified disposition; and we conclude that the professions are entirely mortified; or also, that he having scattered all the alms of the penitents, or of the friends of the Society, in favor of his poor relations. Furthermore, that he may not complain afterwards of the cause of his expulsion, it will be necessary to thrust him from us directly; but we can prohibit him from hearing confessions, which will mortify him, and vex him by imposing upon him most vile offices, obliging him each day to do things that are the most repugnant; he will be removed from the highest studies and honorable employments; he will be reprimanded in the chapters by public censures; he will be excluded from the recreations and prohibited from all conversation with strangers; he will be deprived of his vestments and the uses of other things when they are not indispensable, until he begins to murmur and becomes impatient; then he can be expelled as a shameful person, to give a bad example to others; and if it is necessary to give account to his relatives, or to the prelates of the Church, of the reason for which he has been thrust out, it will be sufficient to say that he does not possess the spirit of the Society.

2. Furthermore, having also expelled all those who may have scrupled to acquire properties for the Society, we must direct

that they are too much addicted to their own judgment. If we desire to give reason of their conduct to the Provincials, <u>it is necessary not to give them a hearing</u>; but call for the rule, <u>that they are obligated to a blind obedience</u>.

3. It will be necessary to note, whence the beginning and whence their youth, those who have great affection for the Society; and those which we recognize their affection until the furthest orders, or until their relatives, or until the poor shall be necessarily disposed, little by little, as carefully said, to go out; **then they are useless**.

CHAPTER XI.
HOW WE MUST CONDUCT OURSELVES UNITEDLY AGAINST THOSE WHO HAVE BEEN EXPELLED FROM THE SOCIETY.

1. <u>As those whom we have expelled, when knowing little or something of the secrets, the most times are noxious to the Society for the same, it shall be necessary to obviate their efforts by the following method, before thrusting them out; it will be necessary to obligate them to promise, by writing, and under oath, that they will never by writing or speaking, do anything which may be prejudicial to the Society</u>; and it will be good that the Superiors guard a point of their evil inclinations, of their defects and of their vices; that they are the same, having to manifest in the discharge of their duties, following the custom of the Society, for that, if it should be necessary, this point can serve near the great, and the prelates to hinder their advancement.

2. Constant notice must be given to an the colleges of their having been expelled; and **we must exaggerate the general motives of their expulsion**; as the little mortification of their spirit; their disobedience; their little love for spiritual exercises; their self love, &c., &c. Afterwards, we must admonish them, that they must not have any correspondence with them; and they must speak of them as strangers; that the language of all shall be uniform, and that it may be told everywhere, that the Society never expels any one without very grave causes, and that as the sea casts up dead bodies, &c., &c. **We must**

insinuate with caution, similar reasons to these, causing them to be abhorred by the people, that for their expulsion it may appear plausible.

3. In the domestic exhortations, it will be necessary to persuade people that they have been turned out as unquiet persons; that they continue to beg each moment to enter anew into the Society; and **it will be good to exaggerate the misfortunes of those who have perished miserably, after having separated from the Society**.

4. It will also be opportune to send forth the accusations, that they have gone out from the Society, which we can formulate by means of grave persons, who will everywhere repeat that the Society never expels any one but for grave causes; and that they never part with their healthy members; the which they can confirm by their zeal, and show in general for the salvation of the souls of them that do not pertain to them; and how much greater will it not be for the salvation of their own.

5. Afterwards, the Society must prepare and attract by all classes of benefits, the magnates, or prelates, with whom those who have been expelled begin to enjoy some authority and credit. It will be necessary to show that the common good of an Order so celebrated as useful in the Church, must be of more consideration, than that if a particular one who has been cast out. If an this affliction preserves some affection for those expelled, it will be good to indicate the reasons which have caused their expulsion; and yet **exaggerate the causes the more that they were not very true**; with such they can draw their conclusions as to the probable consequences.

6. Of all modes, it will be necessary that they particularly have abandoned the Society by their own free will; not being promoted to a single employment or dignity in the Church; that they would not submit themselves and much that pertains to the Society; and that all the world should withdraw from them that desire to depend on them.

7. Procuring soon, that they are removed from the exercise of the functions celebrated in the Church, such as the sermons, confessions, publication of books, &c., &c., so that they do not win the love and applause of the people. For this, we

must come to inquire diligently upon their life and their habits; upon their occupations, &c., &c., penetrate into their intentions, for the which, we must have particular correspondence with some of the family in whose house they live, of those who have been expelled. In surprising something reprehensible in them or worthy of censure, which is to be divulged by people of medium quality; giving in following the steps conducive to reach the hearing of the great, and the prelates, who favor then, that they may be caused to fear that the infamy will relapse upon themselves. If they do nothing that merits reprehension, and conduct themselves well, we must curtail them by subtle propositions and captious phrases, their virtues and meritorious actions, causing that the idea that has been formed of them, and the faith that is had in them, may little by little be made to disappear; this is of great interest for the Society, that those whom we repel, and more principally those who by their own will abandon us, shall be sunk in obscurity and oblivion.

8. **We must divulge without ceasing the disgraces and sinister accidents that they bring upon them, notwithstanding the faithful, who entreat for them in their prayers, that they may not believe that we work from impulses of passion. In our houses we must exaggerate by every method these calamities, that they may serve to hinder others**. [**NOTE**: The Spanish version reads in this section: "**It shall be invented incessantly sinister and deplorable accidents, against those that in any sense abandon the Company; recommending simultaneously to the faithful to implore for them in their prayers and invocations the mercy of the Supreme Being; and in that way no one would think that we speak with passion. In our houses it will be exaggerated this inconveniences so they will be a hindrance to others**"].

CHAPTER XII.
WHO MAY COME THAT THEY MAY BE SUSTAINED AND PRESERVED IN THE SOCIETY.

1. The first place in the Society pertains to the good operators; that is to say, those who cannot procure less for the temporal

than for the spiritual good of the Society; such as the confessors of princes, of the powerful, of the widows, of the rich pious women, the preachers and the professors who know all these secrets.

2. Those who have already failed in strength or advanced in years; conforming to the use they have made of their talents in and for the temporal good of the Society; of the manner which has attended them in days that are passed; and further, are yet convenient instruments to give part to the Superiors of the ordinary defects which are to be noted in ourselves, for they are always in the house.

3. We must never expel but in case of extreme necessity, for fear of the Society acquiring a bad reputation.

4. Furthermore, it will be necessary to favor those who excel by their talent, their nobleness and their fortune; particularly if they have powerful friends attached to the Society; and if they themselves have for it a sincere appreciation, as we have already said before. They must be sent to Rome or to the universities of greater reputation to study there; or in case of having studied in some province, it will be very convenient that the professors attend to them with special care and affection. Meanwhile, they not having conveyed their property to the Society, we must not refuse them anything; for after confirming the cession, they will be disappointed as the others, notwithstanding guarding some consideration for the past.

5. Having also especial consideration on the part of the Superiors, for those that have brought to the Society, a young notable, placed so that they are given to know the affection made to it; but if they have not professed, it is necessary to take care of not having too much indulgence with them, for fear that they may return at another time, to carry away those whom they have brought to the Society.

CHAPTER XIII.

OF THE YOUTH WHO MAY BE ELECTED TO BE ADMITTED INTO THE SOCIETY, AND OF THE MODE OF RETAINING THEM.

1. It is necessary that much prudence shall be exercised, respecting the election of the Youth; having to be sprightly, noble, well liked, or at the least excellent in some of these qualities.

2. To attract them with greater facility to our institute, it is necessary in the meanwhile, to study that the rectors and professors of colleges shall exhibit an especial affection; and outside the time of the classes, to make them comprehend how great is God, and that some one should consecrate to his service all that he possesses; and particularly if he is in the Society of his Son.

3. Whenever the opportunity may arrive, conducive in the college and in the garden, and yet at times to the country houses, that in the company of ourselves, during the recreations, that we may familiarize with them, little by little, being careful, notwithstanding, that the familiarity does not engender disgust.

4. We cannot consent that we shall punish them, nor oblige them to assemble at their tasks among those who are the most educated.

5. We must congratulate them with gifts and privileges conforming to their age and encouraging above all others with moral discourses.

6. We must inculcate them, that it is for one divine disposition that they are favorites among so many who frequent the same college.

7. <u>On other occasions, especially in the exhortations, we must aim to terrify them with menaces of the eternal condemnation, if they refuse the divine vocation.</u>

8. Meanwhile frequently expressing the anxiety to enter the Society, we must always defer their admission, that they may remain constant; but if for these, they are undecided, then we must encourage them incessantly by other methods.

9. If we admonish effectively, that none of their friends, nor yet the fathers, nor the mothers discover their vocation before being admitted; because then, if then, they come to the temptation of withdrawing; so many as the Society desires to give full liberty of doing that which may be the most convenient; and in case of succeeding to conquer the temptation, we must never lose occasions to make them recover spirit; remembering that which we have said, always that this will succeed during the time of the novitiate, or after having made their simple vows.

10. With respect to the sons of the great, nobles, and senators, as it is supremely difficult to attract them, meanwhile living with their fathers, who are having them educated to the end, that they may succeed in their destinies, we must persuade, vigorously, of the better influences of friends that are persons of the same Society; that they are ordered to other provinces, or to distant universities in which there are our teachers; careful to remit to the respective professors the necessary instructions, appropriate to their quality and condition, that they may gain their friendship for the Society with greater facility and certainty.

11. When having arrived at a more advanced age, they will be induced to practice some spiritual exercises, that they may have so good an exit in Germany and Poland.

12. We must console them in their sadness and afflictions, according to the quality and dispositions of each one, making use of private reprimands and exhortations appropriate to the bad use of riches; inculcating upon them that they should depreciate the felicity of a vocation, menacing them with the pains of hell for the things they do.

13. It will be necessary to make patent to the fathers and the mothers, that they may condescend more easily to the desire of their sons of entering the Society, the excellence of its institute in comparison with those of other orders; the sanctity and the science of our fathers; its reputation in all the world; the honor and distinctions of the different great and small. We must make enumeration of the princes and the magnates, that, with great content, have lived until their death, and yet living

in the Society. We must show how agreeable it is to God, that the youth consecrate themselves to Him, particularly in the Society of his Son: and what thing is there so sublime as that of a man carrying the yoke of the Lord from his youth. That if they oppose any objections because of their extreme youth, then we must present the facility of our institute, the which not having anything to molest, with the exception of the three vows, and that which is most notable, that we do not have any obligatory rule, nor yet under penalty of venial sin.

CHAPTER XIV.
UPON RESERVED CASES AND MOTIVES THAT NECESSITATE EXPULSION FROM THE SOCIETY.

1. To most of the cases expressed in the Constitutions, and of which only the Superior or the ordinary confessor, with permission of this, can absolve them, where there is sodomy, unnatural crime, fornication, adultery, of the unchaste touch of a man, or of a woman; also if under the pretext of Zeal, or whatever motive, they have done some grave thing against the Society; against its honors and its gains; these will be just causes for reason of the expulsion of the guilty.

2. If anyone confesses in the confessional of having committed some similar act, he will not be promised absolution, until he has promised to reveal to the Superior, outside of the confessional, the same or by his confessor. The Superior will operate the better for it, in the general interests of the Society; further, if there is founded hope of the careful hiding of the crime, it will be necessary to impose upon the guilty a convenient punishment; if otherwise he can be expelled much before. With all the care that is possible, the confessor will give the penitent to understand that he runs the danger of being expelled.

3. If any one of our confessors, having heard a strange person say, that he had committed a shameful thing with one of the Society, he will not absolve such a person, without his having said, outside of his confession, the name of the one with whom he has sinned; and if he so says, he will be made to swear

that he will not divulge the same, without the consent of the Society.

4. If two of ourselves have sinned carnally, he who first avows it will be retained in the Society; and the other will be expelled; but he who remains permanent, will be after such mortification and bad treatment, of sorrow, and by his impatience, and if we have occasion for his expulsion, it will be necessary for the future of it that it be done directly.

5. The Society being a noble corporation and preeminent in the Church, it can dismiss those that will not be apt for the execution of our object, although giving satisfaction in the beginning; and the opportunity does not delay in presenting itself; if it procures continuous maltreatment; and if he is obliged to do contrary to his inclination; if they are gathered under the orders of gloomy Superiors; if he is separated from his studies and from the honorable functions, &c., &c., until be gets to murmuring.

6. In no manner must we retain in the Society, those that openly reveal against their Superiors, or that will complain publicly, or reservedly, of their companions, or particularly if they make them to strangers; nor to those who are among ourselves, or among persons who are on the outside, censure the conduct of the Society in regard to the acquisition or administration of temporal properties, or whatever acts of the same; for example, of crushing or oppressing many of those whom we do not wish well, or that they the same having been expelled, &c., &c. Nor yet those, that in conversation, who tolerate, or defend the Venetians, the French and others, that have driven the Society away from the territories, or that have occasioned great prejudices.

7. **Before the expulsion of any we must vex and harass them in the extreme**; depriving them of the functions that they have been accustomed to discharge, dedicating them to others. Although they may do well, it will be necessary to censure them, and with this pretext, apply them to another thing. Imposing by a trifling fault that they have committed the most severe penalties, that they blush in public, until they have lost all patience; and at last will be expelled as pernicious to all, for

which a future opportunity will present itself when they will think less.

8. When some one of the Society has a certain hope of obtaining a bishopric, or whatever other ecclesiastical dignity, to most of the ordinary vows of the Society he will be obliged to take another; and that is, that he will always preserve good sentiments towards the Society; that he will always speak favorably of it; that he will not have a confessor that will not be to its bosom; that he will do nothing of entity without having heard the justice of the same. Because in consequence of not having observed this, the Cardinal Tolet the Society had obtained of the Holy See, that no **swinish** descendants of Jews or Mahometans were admitted, that he did not desire to take such vows; and that for celebrity that is out, he was expelled as a firm enemy of the Society.

CHAPTER XV.
HOW THE SOCIETY MUST BE CONDUCTED WITH THE MONKS AND NUNS.

1. The confessors and preachers must guard well against offending the nuns and occasioning temptations contrary to their vocation; but on the contrary, having conciliated the love of the Lady Superiors, that we obtain to hear, when less, their extraordinary confessions, and that it is predicted that we may hope soon to receive some gratitude from them; because the abbesses, principally the rich and noble, can be of much utility to the Society, by themselves, and by their relatives and friends; of the manner with which we treat with them and influence of the principal monasteries, the Society will little by little arrive to obtain the knowledge of all the corporation and increase its friendship.

2. It will be necessary, notwithstanding, to prohibit our nuns from frequenting the monasteries of women, for fear that their mode of life may be more agreeable, and that the Society will see itself frustrated in the hopes of possessing all their properties. We must induce them to take the vow of chastity and obedience, at the hands of their confessors; and to show them that this mode of life will conform with the uses of

the Primitive Church, placed as a light to shine in the house, and that it cannot be hidden under a measure, without the edification of their neighbor, and without fruit for the souls; furthermore, that in imitation of the widows of the Gospel, doing well by giving themselves to Jesus Christ and to his Society. If they were to know how evil it can possibly be, of the life of the cloisters; but these instructions must be given under the seal of inviolable secrecy that they do not come to the ears of the monks.

CHAPTER XVI.
HOW WE MUST MAKE PROFESSION OF DESPISING RICHES.
["How we must pretend to despise wealth."]

1. <u>With the end of preventing the seculars from directing attention to our itching for riches, it will be useful to repel at times alms of little amount, by which we can allow them to do services for our Society; though we must accept the smallest amounts from people attached to us, for fear that we may be accused of avarice, if we only receive those that are most numerous.</u>

2. <u>We must refuse sepulture to persons of the lowest class in our churches,</u> though they may have been very attached to our Society; for we do not believe that we must seek riches by the number of interments, and we must hold firmly the gains that we have made with the dead.

3. In regard to the widows and other persons who have left their properties to the Society, we must labor with resolution and greater vigor than with the others; things being equal, and not to be made apparent, that we favor some more than others, in consideration of their temporal properties. The same must be observed with those that pertain to the Society, after that they have made cession of their property; and if it be necessary to expel them from the Society, it must be done with discretion, to the end that they leave to the Society a part for the less of that which they have given, or that which they have bequeathed at the time of their death.

CHAPTER XVII.
METHODS TO EXALT THE COMPANY.

1. Treating principally all, though in things of little consequence, we must have the same opinion, or at least exterior dignity; for by this manner we may augment and strengthen the Society more and more; to overthrow the barrier we have overcome in the business of the world.

2. Thus strengthening all, it will shine by its wisdom and good example, that we shall excel all the other fathers, and particularly the pastors, &c., &c., until the people desire us to all. Publicly divulging that the pastors do not need to possess so much knowledge; with such they can discharge well their duties, stating that they can assist them with the counsels of the Society; that for this motive they can dedicate themselves to all classes of studies.

3. **We must inculcate this doctrine with kings and princes, THAT THE CATHOLIC FAITH CANNOT SUBSIST IN THE PRESENT STATE, WITHOUT POLITICS; but that in this, it is necessary to proceed with much certainty. Of this mode, we must share the affection of the great, and BE ADMITTED TO THE MOST SECRET COUNSELS**.

4. We must entertain their good will, by writing from all parts interesting facts and notices.

5. It will be no little advantage that will result, by secretly and prudently fomenting dissensions between the great, ruining or augmenting their power. But if we perceive some appearance of reconciliation between them, then we of the Society will treat and act as pacificators; that it shall not be that any others shall anticipate to obtain it.

6. As much to the magnates as to the people, we must persuade them by all possible means, that the Society has not been, but by especial Divine Providence, conforming to the prophecies of the Abbot Joachim, for to return and rise up the Church, humbled by the heretics.

7. Having acquired the favor of the great and of the bishops, it will be an entire necessity, of empowering the curates and prebendaries to more exactly reform the clergy, that in other times lived under certain rule with the bishops, and tending

to perfection; also it will be necessary to inspire the abbeys and prefaces; the which it will not be difficult to obtain; calling attention to the indolence and stupidity of the monks as if they were cattle; because it will be very advantageous for the Church, if all the bishoprics were occupied by members of the Society; and yet, as if it was the same apostolic chair, particularly if the Pope should return as temporal prince of all the properties; for as much as it is very necessary to extend little by little, with much secrecy and skill, the temporalities of the Society; and not having any doubt that the world will enter the golden age, to enjoy a perfect universal peace, for following the divine benediction that will descend upon the Church.

8. But if we do not hope that we can obtain this, supposing that it is necessary that scandals shall come in the world, <u>WE MUST BE CAREFUL TO CHANGE OUR POLITICS, CONFORMING TO THE TIMES, AND EXCITE THE PRINCES, FRIENDS OF OURS TO mutually make terrible wars THAT EVERYWHERE THE MEDIATION OF THE SOCIETY WILL BE IMPLORED; that we may be employed in the public reconciliation, for it will be the cause of the common good; and we shall be recompensed by the PRINCIPAL ECCLESIASTICAL DIGNITIES; and the BETTER BENEFICIARIES.</u>

9. <u>Finally, the Society must endeavor to effect this at least, that having got the favor and authority of the princes, THOSE WHO DO NOT LOVE US SHALL FEAR US.</u>

RECOMMENDED READING

Disclaimer: mentioning the following sources does not constitute endorsement, since some of the authors, even though they recognize Rome as a power of evil, observe some of its traditions, and teach some of the doctrines of Babylon.

50 years in The Church of Rome by Father Charles Chiniquy
A woman Rides the Beast by Dave Hunt
Babylon, Religious Mystery by Ralph Woodrow
Confidence Amid Chaos by Mark Finley
Christ Our Refuge by Norman Gulley
Daniel Verse by Verse by Henry Feyerabend
Day Of The Dragon by Clifford Goldstein
Eleventh Hour By Celeste perrino Walker & Eric Stoffle
Evangelism by E.G.White
Even At The Door by G. Edward Reid
Foxe's Book of Martyrs
Fundamentals of Christian Education by E.G.White
God Cares, volume 2 by C. Mervyn Maxwell
Here I come, Ready Or Not by Morris L. Venden
History of Protestantism by D'Aubigne
Hitler And His Secret Partners: Contributions, Loot and Rewards, 1933-1945. By James Pool
   Last day Events by E.G.White
Maranatha, The Lord is Coming by E.G.White
Marked by Bob Spangler
One nation Under God? by Clifford Goldstein
Preparation for the Final Crisis by Fernando Chaij
Revelation by R. J. Wieland

Steps to Christ By E.G.White

Sunday's Coming by G. Edward Reid

Testimonies for the Church Volume One

The Antichrist- 666 Compiled by The Repairers of the Breach

The Antichrist And The New Word Order by Marvin Moore

The Coming Great Calamity by Marvin Moore

The Crisis Of The End Time by Marvin Moore

The Early And Latter Rain of The Holy Spirit by Gordon W. Collier, Sr.

The Great Controversy by E.G.White

The Keys of This Blood by Malachi Martin

The Law and the Sabbath by Allen Walker

The Secret History of the Jesuits by Edmond Paris

The Two Babylons by Alexander Hislop

The Vatican Billions by Avro Manhattan

The Wine of Babylon by Mary Walsh

Unfolding the Revelation by Roy Alan Anderson

Unholy Trinity: The Vatican, The nazis an Soviet Intelligence by Mark Aarons and John Loftus

Washington in the lap of Rome by Justin D. Fulton;

Recommended websites (Provided typed for those that get the electronic version of this study and don't have Word 97 or access to the Internet):

www.sundaylaw.org www.sundaylaw.org

http://www.iiw.org/ Http://www.iiw.org

http://www.andrews.edu/homes/Staff/aim/shared/www/aim.org/index.html http://www... andrews.edu/homes/Staff/aim/shared/www/aim.org/index.html

http://www.tagnet.org/freebies/Homepage.htm Http://www.tagnet.org/freebies/Homepage.htm

http:/www.sdanet.org/

http://www.egwestate.andrews.edu/ Http://www.egwestate.andrews.edu

http://www.amazingfacts.org/ Http://www.amazingfacts.org

http://www.ssnet.org/ Http://www.ssnet.org

http://www.biblestudy.org/bibleref/main.html Http://www.biblestudy.org/bibleref/main.html

ricefile@foothills.net ricefile@foothills.net
www.thebibletruth.org www.thebibletruth.org
http://www.aloha.net/~mikesch/ http://www.aloha.net/~mikesch/ this
   is one of the best websites)

A good place to contact:
The Bible Sabbath Association
HC 60 Box 8
Fairview, Oklahoma 73737

Where to find most of the books recommended in this study:
1) LAYMEN MINISTRIES
   LMN Publishing International, Inc.
   HC04 Box 94-C
   St. Maries, Idaho 83861
   Phone: (208)-245-5388
   Fax: (208)-245-3280
   Order line: 1-800-245-1844 from 8:00 AM – 4:30 PM
   Monday –Thursday, 9:00 AM- 12 Noon
   To order by e-mail: lmnpubint@nidlink.com lmnpubint@
   nidlink.com
   To check the on-line catalog, www.lmn.com www.lmn.com

2) ABC stores (several in the USA) 1-800- URMYABC
3) www.barnesandnoble.com www.barnesandnoble.com 1-800-242-
   6657 or 1-800-843-2665
4) www.amazon.com www.amazon.com
5) www.hamiltonbook.com www.hamiltonbook.com
6) http://suc.suc.org/~kosta/tar/knjige http://suc.suc.org/~kosta/tar/
   knjige

INDEX

W

Waldenses 151, 152, 160
war criminals 63, 64
Washed in the blood 8
wealth 1, 50, 115, 220, 247
weapons warehouse 165
WE ARE A SOUL 84
werewolves 148
Who is Michael 102
WIDOWS AND METHODS OF
  DISPOSING OF THEIR
  PROPERTY 227
wine of her fornication 13

with- holding the arm of her Son 100
wolf on sheep's clothes 20
wolf shepherding sheep 59
wolves ravening the prey 60
World Council of Churches 74, 77,
  79, 196
world government 53
worship images 19
worship of images and relics 138
worship of the beast 24
wound was healed 20

Y

year 27 AD 10

Printed in the United States
By Bookmasters